*William Miller, PhD, MLS*
*Rita M. Pellen, MLS*
*Editors*

# Improving Internet Reference Services to Distance Learners

*Improving Internet Reference Services to Distance Learners*
has been co-published simultaneously as *Internet Reference
Services Quarterly*, Volume 9, Numbers 1/2 2004.

*Pre-publication
REVIEWS,
COMMENTARIES,
EVALUATIONS . . .*

"ENJOYABLE AND ILLUMINAT-
ING. . . . Provides an excellent
overview of services that were created with distance learners in mind
but that have much to offer all patrons. Several of the contributions left
me thinking that I need to get this to
my administrators!"

**Beth A. Reiten, MLS**
*Assistant Professor and Digital Library
Services Librarian
Oklahoma State University*

*More pre-publication*
*REVIEWS, COMMENTARIES, EVALUATIONS . . .*

"**A** GREAT RESOURCE FOR DIS-
TANCE LIBRARIANS. . . .
Discusses new trends in serving
the distance student. The sections
on embedding and 'lurking' librarians in Web courses are most valuable. In the future we will be seeing
more of this trend. Several contributions mention how librarians
marketed and gained access to Web
courses. It is great to hear how librarians and faculty are working
together to provide exceptional service to our hard-to-reach patrons."

**Lani Draper, MLIS**
*Web Content Specialist*
*Steen Library*
*Stephen F. Austin State University*

"**T**his wonderful collection is
PACKED WITH INFORMA-
TION about recent trends in electronic reference services, and it is
especially useful when it highlights
the variety of pedagogical methods used in teaching and providing
library instruction online. Distance
learning librarians will no doubt
find this A MOST VALUABLE RE-
SOURCE, and many will be able to
transfer ideas from this collection to
their own working environments.
Miller and Pellen are to be con-
gratulated for their editorial work
in compiling such a nice collection of material on such an important and timely topic."

**Stephen H. Dew, PhD**
*Coordinator*
*Library Services for Distance Education*
*University of Iowa*

*More pre-publication*
*REVIEWS, COMMENTARIES, EVALUATIONS . . .*

"**A** PROVOCATIVE AND TIMELY DISCUSSION of distance library service. REFRESHING AND ENGAGING, the articles address themes around the creative use of technology, innovative solutions, the necessity for the 'human touch,' and the importance of communication and collaboration with faculty and students. Particularly interesting are the chapters discussing marketing of library services, service delivery in a joint-use environment, a 'lurking librarian' model, library service for distance library school students, and a university-wide referral service established in the library. Highly readable, this will be A VERY USEFUL RESOURCE for those new to the profession as well as for more experienced librarians."

**Nancy E. Black, MLS**
*Distance and Document Delivery*
*Librarian*
*Geoffrey R. Weller Library*
*University of Northern British Columbia*
*Prince George*

"**T**he editors went to the experts– the actual practitioners–to collect chapters addressing various aspects of service support and delivery. These chapters can serve as a foundation for a library planning to implement or improve services. They provide a range of experiences and examples from different institutions with different populations and concerns. The material in this text can offer guidance to help the beginner avoid certain pitfalls and can suggest alternate approaches that may lead to new directions and added success at institutions with established programs in need of stimulation. The chapters on embedded librarians and marketing library services to remote users resonate with ongoing discussions at conferences and gatherings right now."

**Jack Fritts, MEd, MALIS**
*Director of Library Services*
*Benedictine Library*
*Benedictine University*

The Haworth Information Press®
An Imprint of The Haworth Press, Inc.

# Improving
# Internet Reference Services
# to Distance Learners

*Improving Internet Reference Services to Distance Learners* has been co-published simultaneously as *Internet Reference Services Quarterly*, Volume 9, Numbers 1/2 2004.

## Monographic Separates from *Internet Reference Services Quarterly*™

For additional information on these and other Haworth Press titles, including descriptions, tables of contents, reviews, and prices, use the QuickSearch catalog at http://www.HaworthPress.com.

*Improving Internet Reference Services to Distance Learners,* edited by William Miller, PhD, MLS, and Rita M. Pellen, MLS (Vol. 9, No. 1/2, 2004). *A look at the cooperative activities between librarians and those working outside the library to provide quality services to distance users.*

*Virtual Reference Services: Issues and Trends,* edited by Stacey Kimmel, MLS, and Jennifer Heise, MLS (Vol. 8, No. 1/2, 2003). *Offers practical advice and suggestions for product selection, policy setting, technical support, collaborative efforts, staffing, training, marketing, budgeting, evaluation, and administration.*

*Database-Driven Web Sites,* edited by Kristin Antelman, MS (Vol. 7, No. 1/2, 2002). *Profiles numerous successful uses of database-driven content to deliver common library services on the Internet.*

*Bioterrorism and Political Violence: Web Resources,* edited by M. Sandra Wood, MLS, MBA (Vol. 6, No. 3/4, 2002). *Describes how to find reliable information on bioterrorism via the Internet.*

*The Challenge of Internet Literacy: The Instruction-Web Convergence,* edited by Lyn Elizabeth M. Martin, BA, MLS (Vol. 2, No. 2/3, 1997). *"A source of valuable advice. . . . Recommended for institutions that collect library science materials on a comprehensive level." (Library & Information Science Annual 1999)*

# Improving Internet Reference Services to Distance Learners

William Miller
Rita M. Pellen
Editors

*Improving Internet Reference Services to Distance Learners* has been co-published simultaneously as *Internet Reference Services Quarterly*, Volume 9, Numbers 1/2 2004.

The Haworth Information Press®
An Imprint of The Haworth Press, Inc.

New York • London • Victoria (AU)
**www.HaworthPress.com**

Published by

The Haworth Information Press®, 10 Alice Street, Binghamton, NY 13904-1580 USA

The Haworth Information Press® is an imprint of The Haworth Press, Inc., 10 Alice Street, Binghamton, NY 13904-1580 USA.

*Improving Internet Reference Services to Distance Learners* has been co-published simultaneously as *Internet Reference Services Quarterly*™, Volume 9, Numbers 1/2 2004.

The development, preparation, and publication of this work has been undertaken with great care. However, the publisher, employees, editors, and agents of The Haworth Press and all imprints of The Haworth Press, Inc., including The Haworth Medical Press® and Pharmaceutical Products Press®, are not responsible for any errors contained herein or for consequences that may ensue from use of materials or information contained in this work. Opinions expressed by the author(s) are not necessarily those of The Haworth Press, Inc. With regard to case studies, identities and circumstances of individuals discussed herein have been changed to protect confidentiality. Any resemblance to actual persons, living or dead, is entirely coincidental.

Cover design by Kerry E. Mack.

### Library of Congress Cataloging-in-Publication Data

Improving Internet reference services to distance learners / William Miller, Rita M. Pellen, editors.
    p. cm.
    "Improving Internet reference services to distance learners has been co-published simultaneously as Internet reference services quarterly, volume 9, numbers 1/2 2004."
    Includes bibliographical references and index.
    ISBN-13: 978-0-7890-2717-7 (hc. : alk. paper)
    ISBN-10: 0-7890-2717-8 (hc. : alk. paper)
    ISBN-13: 978-0-7890-2718-4 (pbk. : alk. paper)
    ISBN-10: 0-7890-2718-6 (pbk. : alk. paper)
    1. Internet in library reference services–United States. 2. Electronic reference services (Libraries)–United States. 3. Libraries and distance education–United States. I. Miller, William, 1947- II. Pellen, Rita M. III. Internet reference services quarterly.

Z711.47 .I47 2005

2005003165

# Indexing, Abstracting & Website/Internet Coverage

This section provides you with a list of major indexing & abstracting services and other tools for bibliographic access. That is to say, each service began covering this periodical during the year noted in the right column. Most Websites which are listed below have indicated that they will either post, disseminate, compile, archive, cite or alert their own Website users with research-based content from this work. (This list is as current as the copyright date of this publication.)

Abstracting, Website/Indexing Coverage . . . . . . . . Year When Coverage Began

- *Annual Bibliography of English Language & Literature "Abstracts Section" (in print, CD-ROM, and online)* . . . . . . . . . . . . . . . . . . . . . . . . . . . . . . . . 1996

- *Applied Social Sciences Index & Abstracts (ASSIA) (Online: ASSI via Data-Star) (CDRom: ASSIA Plus) <http://www.csa.com>* . . . . . . . . . . . . . . 1996

- *CINAHL (Cumulative Index to Nursing & Allied Health Literature), in print, EBSCO, and SilverPlatter, Data-Star, and PaperChase. (Support materials include Subject Heading List, Database Search Guide, and instructional video) <http://www.cinahl.com>* . . . . . . . . . . . . . . . . . . . . . 1996

- *Computer and Information Systems Abstracts <http://www.csa.com>* . . . . . . . . . . . . . . 2004

- *Computer Science Index (CSI) (formerly Computer Literature Index) (EBSCO) <http://www.epnet.com>* . . . . . . . . . . . . . . . . . . . . . . . . . . . . . . . . . . . . . . . . . . . 1997

- *Computing Reviews <http://www.reviews.com>* . . . . . . . . . . . . . . . . . . . . . . . . 1996

- *Current Cites [Digital Libraries] [Electronic Publishing] [Multimedia & Hypermedia] [Networks & Networking] [General] <http://sunsite.berkeley.edu/CurrentCites/>* . . . . . . . . . . . . . . . . . . . . . . . . . . . . . 2004

- *EBSCOhost Electronic Journals Service (EJS) <http://ejournals.ebsco.com>* . . . . . . . . 2001

- *ERIC: Processing & Reference Facility* . . . . . . . . . . . . . . . . . . . . . . . . . . . . . . . . . . 1998

(continued)

(continued)

*Special Bibliographic Notes related to special journal issues (separates) and indexing/abstracting:*

- indexing/abstracting services in this list will also cover material in any "separate" that is co-published simultaneously with Haworth's special thematic journal issue or DocuSerial. Indexing/abstracting usually covers material at the article/chapter level.
- monographic co-editions are intended for either non-subscribers or libraries which intend to purchase a second copy for their circulating collections.
- monographic co-editions are reported to all jobbers/wholesalers/approval plans. The source journal is listed as the "series" to assist the prevention of duplicate purchasing in the same manner utilized for books-in-series.
- to facilitate user/access services all indexing/abstracting services are encouraged to utilize the co-indexing entry note indicated at the bottom of the first page of each article/chapter/contribution.
- this is intended to assist a library user of any reference tool (whether print, electronic, online, or CD-ROM) to locate the monographic version if the library has purchased this version but not a subscription to the source journal.
- individual articles/chapters in any Haworth publication are also available through the Haworth Document Delivery Service (HDDS).

# Improving
# Internet Reference Services
# to Distance Learners

## CONTENTS

# ABOUT THE EDITORS

**William Miller, PhD, MLS,** is Director of Libraries at Florida Atlantic University in Boca Raton. He formerly served as Head of Reference at Michigan State University in East Lansing, and as Associate Dean of Libraries at Bowling Green State University in Ohio. Dr. Miller is past President of the Association of College and Research Libraries, has served as Chair of the *Choice* magazine editorial board, and is a contributing editor of *Library Issues*. He was named Instruction Librarian of the Year in 2004 by the Association of College and Research Libraries Instruction Section.

**Rita M. Pellen, MLS,** is Associate Director of Libraries at Florida Atlantic University in Boca Raton. She was formerly Assistant Director of Public Services and Head of the Reference Department at Florida Atlantic. In 1993, Ms. Pellen received the Gabor Exemplary Employee Award in recognition for outstanding service to FAU, and in 1997, the "Literati Club Award for Excellence" for the outstanding paper presented in *The Bottom Line*. She has served on committees in LAMA, ACRL, and ALCTS, as well as the Southeast Florida Library Information Network, SEFLIN, a multi-type library cooperative in South Florida. Honor society memberships include Beta Phi Mu and Phi Kappa Phi.

# Introduction:
# Improving Reference Services
# to Distance Learners
# Through Cooperative Activities

In their efforts to improve reference services to distance learners, librarians are becoming increasingly involved with entities outside the immediate library. This volume highlights such efforts, and our recognition that we cannot exist in a vacuum as we attempt to improve our services to those working at a distance.

Many of the articles here highlight the notion of participation in course management systems, primarily Blackboard and WebCT, in cooperation with the faculty or colleges maintaining such systems, or otherwise "embedding" activities into the online course structure. For instance, Jill Markgraf, in her article "Librarian Participation in the Online Classroom," discusses collaboration with faculty at the University of Wisconsin by "lurking" in Blackboard and Desire2Learn classrooms and monitoring discussion threads to better learn where students need assistance. She remarks that "to be able to observe and participate from within the course management system provides an ideal vantage point."

In their article "Information Literacy and the Distant Student: One University's Experience Developing, Delivering, and Maintaining an Online, Required Information Literacy Course," Elizabeth Mulherrin, Kimberly Kelley, Diane Fishman, and Gloria Orr describe their creation of a "required, credit bearing online information literacy course at the

[Haworth co-indexing entry note]: "Introduction: Improving Reference Services to Distance Learners Through Cooperative Activities." Miller, William. Co-published simultaneously in *Internet Reference Services Quarterly* (The Haworth Information Press, an imprint of The Haworth Press, Inc.) Vol. 9, No. 1/2, 2004, pp. 1-4; and: *Improving Internet Reference Services to Distance Learners* (ed: William Miller, and Rita M. Pellen) The Haworth Information Press, an imprint of The Haworth Press, Inc., 2004, pp. 1-4. Single or multiple copies of this article are available for a fee from The Haworth Document Delivery Service [1-800-HAWORTH, 9:00 a.m. - 5:00 p.m. (EST). E-mail address: docdelivery@haworthpress.com].

University of Maryland University College," a degree-granting part of the University which focuses on adults and part-time students. This course addresses the requirement of the Middle States accrediting agency that instruction be integrated into the curriculum. Librarians were able to work with the UMUC's School of Undergraduate Studies to create the library skills course as a required component of the degree. In a broader vein, Rachel Viggiano, in "Online Tutorials as Instruction for Distance Students," surveys 34 such tutorials at different institutions and describes common practices (such as interactive games and quizzes) which help to conceptualize best practices.

In "Beyond Instruction: Integrating Library Service in Support of Information Literacy," Barbara D'Angelo and Barry Maid describe a collaboration between the library and the Multimedia Writing and Technical Communication Program at Arizona State University East, involving "revision of current courses, development of new courses, and rewriting of Program Outcomes to incorporate information literacy standards." This collaboration has resulted in two special topics courses now offered in the program, "InfoGlut" and "Information Architecture."

Jamie Kearley and Lori Phillips, in "Embedding Library Reference Services in Online Courses," discuss their efforts with the Outreach School at the University of Wyoming. They have worked to simplify access for the distance learners and in addition to their interactive tutorial, offer a variety of chat, ILL, reserves, and guides from within the structure of the School's online courses. Information literacy has become a core component of the School's program. Kearley and Phillips have also worked with the University of Wyoming's Nursing School, which has adopted both the tutorial and several research-related courses for distance students.

James Fisk and Terri Summey describe their marketing efforts in "Got Distance Services? Marketing Remote Library Services to Distance Learners." They describe the adaptation of marketing techniques from the business world to reach distance learners who may not even be aware that services are there for them to use, and describe a survey they undertook to discover the state of distance learners' awareness of such services. This survey was a collaborative endeavor of the School of Library and Information Management at Emporia State University and the University Libraries and Archives, to assess the needs of distance students enrolled in the school.

Two articles in this volume discuss the organizational workings of institutions which are primarily distance educators. Rita Barsun, in

"The Walden University Library: Reaching Out and Touching Students," describes the partnership between Walden and the University of Indiana-Bloomington Libraries. Walden's library operation works out of the IUB Libraries, of which it is a unit, and is far-removed from the rest of Walden's offices. Walden also merges two cultures, corporate and academic. Within this complex framework, Walden serves its many distance learning students with a full panoply of reference and instructional services. A complimentary piece is "Providing Reference in a Joint-Use Library," by Nora Quinlan and Johanna Tuñón, of Nova University, which also caters primarily to distance learning students, but has a growing cadre of on-campus students as well. Quinlan and Tuñón describe the challenges of serving their students in an unusual joint-use arrangement with the Broward County, Florida public library; this library serves not only on-campus students and the general public, but distance learners as well, and librarians have had to adapt to a wide variety of situations and maintain maximum flexibility and openness.

In "Centralizing Information About Library Services and Resources: Delivering the Library to Users at Any Distance," Mary Feeney describes a collaboration between the School of Information Resources and Library Science at the University of Arizona and the overall University Library. Their goal was to provide enhanced resources to distance students in the Library and Information Science program. She notes that the study of provision of services to such students is particularly interesting in view of the "obvious connection between provision of library services and the education of future information providers," and that "it would be especially ironic and vexing if students enrolled in LIS distance education programs were receiving limited and/or inferior services."

Two other articles describe distance services to specialized student populations. Lian Ruan, in "Designing and Developing Internet Reference Services to Support Firefighter Distance Learners in Illinois," describes the development of Internet reference services in support of distance learners in the University of Illinois' Fire Service Institute. In working with the Institute's network of 350 adjunct instructors, as well as with the online course and information technology teams, Ruan has developed a comprehensive suite of services. Similarly, Ulrike Dieterle and Gerri Wanserski, in "Distance Library Services for Doctor of Pharmacy Students: A Case Study," describe their efforts to support Doctor of Pharmacy students at the University of Wisconsin-Madison in their final year of study, as they scatter across the state for internships and no longer have physical contact with the Madison campus.

The final article in this collection, "The Buck Stops *Where*? Establishing a University Information and Referral Service," by Doris Brown and Kara Malenfant, describes a wider role for the library at DePaul University, and a potentially wider role for other academic libraries, as the central provider of information and referral services for the entire university. The librarians at DePaul capitalized on their skills to create a centralized service to meet all outside inquiries from every category of student–adult, distance learner, or traditional–including needs for information not traditionally thought of as being in the library's purview. The establishment of this centralized information and retrieval service, under the library's aegis, has raised its profile while enhancing students services.

Taken together, the articles in this volume show that librarians naturally look for opportunities to cooperate with other entities as they seek to provide and improve services for distance learners. The service orientation of the profession shows itself in their outreach, not only to the users themselves, but also to other entities both within and beyond their own organizations. We can all be proud of such efforts.

*William Miller*
*Director of Libraries*
*Florida Atlantic University*

# Librarian Participation in the Online Classroom

## Jill S. Markgraf

**SUMMARY.** As distance education courses increasingly move to the online environment, librarians are discovering new challenges and opportunities for reaching distant students. Collaboration with faculty is essential in reaching students who may never enter the library building. One such method of collaboration is librarian participation in online courses through "lurking" in Blackboard and Desire2Learn classrooms and monitoring discussion threads devoted to library research. Advantages such as improved access to students, course content, and assessment data are discussed, as are disadvantages, such as time commitment, varying expectations, and privacy issues. Considerations for librarians interested in "lurking" are outlined. *[Article copies available for a fee from The Haworth Document Delivery Service: 1-800-HAWORTH. E-mail address: <docdelivery@haworthpress.com> Website: <http://www.HaworthPress.com> © 2004 by The Haworth Press, Inc. All rights reserved.]*

**KEYWORDS.** Distance education, library services, collaboration, course management software, online courses, Blackboard, Desire2Learn

---

Jill S. Markgraf (markgrjs@uwec.edu) is Distance Education and Reference Librarian, McIntyre Library, University of Wisconsin-Eau Claire, Eau Claire, WI 54702-4004.

[Haworth co-indexing entry note]: "Librarian Participation in the Online Classroom." Markgraf, Jill S. Co-published simultaneously in *Internet Reference Services Quarterly* (The Haworth Information Press, an imprint of The Haworth Press, Inc.) Vol. 9, No. 1/2, 2004, pp. 5-19; and: *Improving Internet Reference Services to Distance Learners* (ed: William Miller, and Rita M. Pellen) The Haworth Information Press, an imprint of The Haworth Press, Inc., 2004, pp. 5-19. Single or multiple copies of this article are available for a fee from The Haworth Document Delivery Service [1-800-HAWORTH. 9:00 a.m. - 5:00 p.m. (EST). E-mail address: docdelivery@haworthpress.com].

Digital Object Identifier: 10.1300/J136v09n01_02

She hangs out in the shadows, waiting for her opportunity to strike. And then she spots it, a sign of confusion, an information need, a desperate plea for help. She makes her move. The lurking librarian posts a message in the online course's library research discussion thread, providing reference assistance or information literacy instruction for the student at the point of need.

How did she come to be a lurking librarian? What activities led to her insidious involvement in an online course? Let me tell you her story.

Librarians have long recognized that collaboration with faculty is the key to reaching students and teaching them to use the library. Wade Kotter writes, "Students use library services only when they are encouraged or required to do so by their instructors" (1999, 295). In reaching online students who may never set foot inside the library, it is arguably even more imperative that librarians work closely with faculty. "The most effective way for librarians to reach distance learners," argue Raspa and Ward, "is through cooperation (at least) and collaboration (at best) with teaching faculty" (2000, 150).

The University of Wisconsin-Eau Claire, home to roughly 10,000 students, currently participates in about 90 distance education (DE) courses a year, two-thirds of which are offered online. Some of these courses originate at UW-Eau Claire and some are delivered from other University of Wisconsin campuses. In spring 2004, distance education courses showed enrollment of 2,436 students. When our lurking librarian came on board in 1998, as the library's first distance education librarian, she worked with colleagues to establish core DE library services, including online and toll-free telephone reference service, remote access to library resources, and document delivery services.

Following the ACRL Guidelines for Library Service to Distance Education (2003), which recommend that the librarian "promote library support services to the distance learning community," she set out to identify and meet distance education faculty and get the word out about library support for distance education. This was no easy task at a university without a centralized DE office. In addition to developing a Web site for DE library services (http://www.uwec.edu/library/distance), the librarian contributed articles promoting the services to the library newsletter and other campus publications. She sent e-mails to DE faculty and distributed brochures outlining the services. She presented campus workshops with varying titles and foci, such as, "Distance education library services," "Teaching and supporting students at a distance," "Library services for remote users," "We're all in this together: How the library can support your teaching," "Off-campus library access for faculty abroad," and "Distance education and copyright: Introduction to the TEACH Act."

As the focus of the university's distance education initiatives shifted from technologies such as teleconferencing and interactive television to the online environment, the librarian joined forces with the instructional technology staff, who were essential in moving courses online and therefore in very close contact with faculty wishing to do so. Instructional technology staff proved to be effective allies of and advocates for the library, referring faculty to the DE librarian as one of the integral steps in developing an online course. Instruction technology staff and the DE librarian collaborated in presenting campus workshops such as "Online teaching faculty workshop," "Supporting online courses: Resources for you and your students," and "Introduction to Desire2Learn," a training session for the new course management system supported on campus.

The librarian's penchant for lurking was first apparent when she hit upon the idea of not only offering campus workshops, but also attending campus workshops where she expected to encounter distance education faculty. Workshops on topics such as facilitating online discussions, developing and teaching online courses, streaming media, and using course management systems were particularly attractive. And because the campus switched course management systems with some regularity (LearningSpace, Blackboard, WebCt, and Desire2Learn had all been used within a five-year period), such workshops were plentiful.

In 2000, UW-Eau Claire offered its first fully online courses, including a graduate course, Marketing Analysis Foundation. Librarians were familiar with this course, as students in the traditional on-campus course relied heavily on library resources and librarian assistance. To provide a comparable level of library support in an online environment would pose a challenge. The DE librarian developed an online guide to library resources that mirrored the structure of the course research project (http://www.uwec.edu/library/guides/sit_anal2.html), and the course professor promoted the guide, as well as the e-mail address and phone number of the distance education librarian, among his students. While these efforts were appreciated and used by students, they did not adequately replace the access that on-campus students had to librarians, the library, and especially, in-class library instruction.

In some cases, instruction was offered on an ad hoc basis as questions arose. Responses to questions often resembled mini-lectures.

What could easily be demonstrated or explained in a face-to-face setting required more time, effort, and wordsmithing to explain via phone or e-mail. While this personalized, point-of-need instruction may have been a boon to those students who recognized a need or faced a problem that compelled them to ask a question, it didn't replace traditional library instruction for all students. (Markgraf and Erffmeyer 2002, 109)

Experience with this course led to several observations:

1. Students preferred to direct their library questions to a specific person (i.e., the DE librarian) rather than to the library reference desk, even though the reference desk offered a toll-free number and hours of availability, via phone and e-mail, that far exceeded those of the DE librarian.
2. Not surprisingly, students experienced similar problems, had similar questions, and needed assistance at roughly the same times during the semester.
3. If the librarian had information or suggestions that would be of use to all students in the course, it was very difficult to disseminate that information.

The following year, the course moved to the Blackboard courseware environment, and the librarian–while lurking in a campus workshop on using Blackboard–learned about the discussion thread feature. Discussion threads on specific topics could be set up within a course. Anyone in the course could post a question, respond to a question, and read all postings. In this feature, she saw an opportunity to address some of the issues she had encountered in communicating with online students. By establishing a library research discussion thread, which she could monitor and to which she could contribute, perhaps she could provide individual attention, address similar problems, and easily disseminate pertinent information, if she was able to gain access to the online classroom. The faculty member was amenable to the idea.

A semester later, the Collaborative Nursing Program, a consortium of six University of Wisconsin campuses, decided to launch a pilot program adding a course librarian to its online Blackboard courses. Our lurking librarian was pleased to participate. After lurking in Nursing and Business courses for five semesters, the librarian has identified some of the advantages and disadvantages of lurking.

## ADVANTAGES

*Opportunity to Introduce Yourself.* We know that libraries and librarians evoke fear in many people. Radford and Radford argue that "fear is the fundamental organizing principle, or code, through which representations of libraries and librarians are manifest in modern popular cultural forms" (2001, 300). Course management systems typically provide a place for students and faculty to introduce themselves. This feature can be used to the librarian's advantage to present a friendly, approachable image, highlight the kinds of assistance the library can provide, and encourage the students to contact the library. When considering the content of her profile, the librarian took her cues from the professor. If the professor provided personal information and a photo, the librarian did too. If the faculty member included simply contact information, the librarian followed suit, cognizant that she was very much a guest in someone else's course and didn't want overstep the boundaries of this new role.

*Broadcast Messages.* Through the framework of the course management software, the librarian was suddenly able to broadcast messages to all members of the course at once. She used the discussion thread feature to post messages likely to be of use to all students in the class. Messages—such as announcements of new databases pertinent to the research assignment, troubleshooting tips for common technical problems, or search strategies for finding information required in class—were easily broadcast to all students in a single posting on the library discussion thread.

*Benefit from Others' Questions.* Just as students were able to benefit from messages broadcast from the librarian, they were also able to benefit from questions, and responses, posted by their classmates. For students hesitant to ask questions themselves, access to these discussions had the potential to provide valuable information they might never otherwise have received. In response to a course evaluation question asking about the usefulness of the library discussion thread, one Nursing student wrote, "Questions I had were asked by fellow students, so I learned the answers that way."

*Point-of-Need Instruction.* Instruction librarians know that the most effective library instruction is integrated into a course at the time when the students most need it. Questions that arise at the reference desk are essentially requests for point-of-need instruction. The lurking librarian had access not only to the library discussion thread in the online course, but to the entire online course. Through the syllabus she could see when various assignments were given and when they were due. She could lurk in other discussion threads. She could view course content and announcements posted by the professor. With all of this information about a course, she could target and time her postings in the library discussion thread to ensure that they were what the students needed, precisely when they needed it. For example, on the day the students were told to find a scholarly article on their topic, she could remind them of how to connect to library databases and provide a link to the online library guide on identifying scholarly articles. When students were asked to research a professional organization, she could suggest they take a look at the *Associations Unlimited* database.

*Access to Class and Student.* Every reference librarian knows that some of the best answers to reference questions emerge *after* the student has left the premises. The librarian is left with the frustration of finally having a good answer but unable to reach the student. In the online course, the librarian has contact information for students and can easily e-mail them pertinent information whenever it comes along.

Every reference librarian also knows that on occasion the details of a student's research assignment can get lost in translation at the reference desk. Sometimes the student is unclear about or doesn't remember the requirements of the assignment, and the librarian is in the difficult position of assisting the student reach a vague goal. When participating in the online course, however, the librarian has access not only to the assignment but also to the discussion surrounding the assignment, and is in a much better position to assist the students.

Access to the other course discussions also enables the librarian to respond to "library" questions that are posted outside of the library discussion area. It became quite clear after a couple of semesters lurking that many students don't interpret "library questions" in the same way that a librarian might. All courses in which the lurking librarian participated included a generic discussion area, usually called something like "Raise your hand." It was here that she encountered several questions that might be considered library reference questions, such as inquiries about citing sources or finding historical information on companies.

*Enhanced Collaboration with Faculty.* When a librarian participates in an online course, both librarian and professor have the opportunity to observe the other in his or her native environment, so to speak. The librarian is not the only one lurking and finding out what's going on in the course. The professor also monitors the discussion on the library thread, learning firsthand about research-related questions the students have and learning more about the library in the process. Increased collaboration leads to increased recognition of the other's area of expertise. It became common for the professor to refer students to the course librarian and to acknowledge areas of librarian expertise, thus increasing her level of legitimacy and relevancy in the eyes of the students. "The collaborative relationship of instructor and librarian can also carry over into the relationship with students, leading to productive online communication between librarian and students" (Dewald et al. 2000, 37).

Because the librarian's role was part of the course, faculty members were willing to include questions about the library service in course evaluations. The comments proved to be useful. Asked if the library discussion thread was helpful, 16 of 18 Nursing students in one class responded that it was. One respondent wrote that it was "nice to know someone was available for assistance in this area." Another wrote that it "gave me information on where to look and how to get into the [UW-Eau Claire] library that I didn't even know I had access to." When asked for reasons why students chose not to take advantage of the library resources available to them, 6 of the 18 respondents indicated that they didn't know how to use them. This apparent need for increased library instruction was underscored by some of the comments. One student requested step-by-step instructions on how to use CINAHL, the Nursing database. Another suggested that "each student should spend a day with the librarian to figure out how to access the online materials." (Interestingly, the Nursing students had been offered optional on-campus instruction with a librarian, but no one had opted to attend!)

*Rich Source of Data*: Course management systems provide varying levels of access to course data, depending on one's role in the course. Cox (2002) describes varying degrees of privileges for instructors, teaching assistants, course builders, and graders in Blackboard courses. He recommends that librarians work to obtain instructor privileges, which offer the greatest degree of access to the course. During the first semester of the project, the librarian was added to the Blackboard course as a student, which was adequate in allowing her to monitor the discussion threads and view the course, as would any other student. Her personal profile, however, was intermixed with those of the students in the class and therefore not very prominent. The subsequent semester, a new instructional technology support person assigned to the online courses added the librarian to the course as an instructor. As such, her profile appeared under Faculty Information, alongside the professor's, making her presence in the course more prominent. In addition, the librarian also had access to a wealth of course statistics, which was–for a lurking librarian–nirvana.

Blackboard offered usage statistics enabling our lurking librarian to learn much about distance education students that could be useful in developing services for them. She was able to see how many times a posting in a discussion thread had been read. She was privy to statistics, at both the individual and aggregate levels, showing total number of times students accessed the course management course and the total number of accesses by hour of the day and by day of the week. She learned, for example, that contrary to her assumption that distance education students did most of their studying on weekends and evenings, students were most active in the online classroom on Tuesday, followed by other midweek days. Four o'clock in the afternoon showed the most student activity, followed by 11:00 a.m. to noon and 7:00 to 9:00 p.m.

In 2003 some UW-Eau Claire online courses migrated from Blackboard to Desire2Learn. While some of the course statistics readily available in Blackboard were not available in Desire2Learn, one could see in Desire2Learn how many postings each student accessed in a given discussion thread. From this data, the librarian observed that Business students accessed approximately 70 percent of library postings, as compared to roughly 33 percent accessed by Nursing students. Differences in faculty behavior, student access to information, and interpersonal communication practices provide some possible explanations for this discrepancy. For example, the influence of the professor seemed to play a role. One Business professor was much more proactive in promoting the library and referring students to the library discussion thread than were other professors, and students in his course rated the highest in percentage of library postings accessed.

Also, in the course evaluation 16 of 18 Nursing students reported having access to library resources elsewhere and may have been less reliant on library services provided through the university. Finally, Nursing students were much more likely to post and respond to questions on the library discussion thread than were Business students, and several of the postings were pleasantries such as greetings to the librarian or thanks for assistance. It is possible that other students were less likely to access these types of postings. Access to such data can assist the librarian in determining the most effective means of communicating information. Should she choose, for example, to use the Desire2Learn chat feature to provide real time interactive reference assistance or "office hours," data showing the most popular times for students to log on could suggest optimal days and times to offer the service.

*Assessment Opportunities.* Access to course statistics and increased collaboration with faculty led to an opportunity for the librarian to assess student outcomes in a way that had heretofore not been possible. By having access to a record of student communication, via the course management system, e-mail, and even telephone calls (if the students identified themselves), the librarian had a somewhat better picture of which students contacted the library for assistance. Was there any correlation between known student interaction with the library and student performance? In order to find out, the lurking librarian requested, and was granted, an opportunity to view the students' final graded research projects for the MBA course.

While the sample was small (15 students), and too many variables made it impossible to draw any sweeping conclusions, the librarian made some interesting observations nonetheless. She found that five of the top seven grades earned on the project were by students who had known contact with the course librarian. Only one of the remaining eight students had known contact with the librarian. She also perused the bibliographies of the projects for evidence of use of library resources. She found that the students used an average of 66 percent library resources, as opposed to about 33 percent "free" Internet resources. Interestingly, she found that the lowest three grades in the class showed the highest *and* lowest percentage of library materials use (100%, 98%, and 3%). One might hypothesize, as Valentine observed in a study comparing student and professor expectations in research papers, "Professors looked for evidence of commitment to the assignment, which took into consideration time and effort expended" (2001, 110). The lack of diversity in resources could indicate a lack of effort in researching and reliance instead on the results of a single database search or a single Google search.

Most encouraging among the librarian's observations was that, in evaluating each of the projects, the professor assessed and commented on the quality of the research and resources cited, giving a very clear and undeniable message that effort spent on finding and selecting reliable information was rewarded. Such a message can be a strong incentive for students to use library resources. Findings of studies described by Robinson and Schegl suggest that "instruction and encouragement has a very limited effect on the quality of student research, but instruction-and-penalty does have significant effects" (2004, 280). These limited observations of student outcomes suggest an area for further research in looking at correlations between library use and student achievement for distance education students.

## DISADVANTAGES

*Privacy Concerns.* While access to course statistics provided the lurking librarian with a wealth of useful data, it also posed an ethical dilemma. As a member of a profession uneasy with certain provisions of the PATRIOT Act, she was uncomfortable with the amount of access she had, not only to student information and identities, but–depending on the courseware–also to data on what they have read and when they read it. Under the USA PATRIOT Act (2001), librarians can be compelled to turn over electronic and other records to FBI agents and are prohibited from informing anyone that they have done so. Of equal concern is that students are not necessarily aware of the nature of the data to which faculty have access in the course management software. Mark Mullen (2002), who shares concern over the lack of notification to students that this usage data is, or can be, collected, criticizes what he calls "surveillance features" of course management systems as encouraging the "pedagogy of suspicion." He argues that statistics gathered by course management systems create "a dangerously decontextualized, essentialized image of your course in which levels of 'participation' stand in for evidence of learning having taken place" (2002, 16). Librarians, longtime defenders of privacy rights, can take an advocacy role on campus urging the development of policies informing students of the data that can be collected in course management systems and how it might be used.

*Changing Technology.* As aforementioned, UW-Eau Claire supported four different course management systems in five years (Lotus LearningSpace, WebCT, Blackboard, and Desire2Learn). In some semesters up to three packages were supported simultaneously. For a librarian working with several faculty members in different departments, this meant learning to use several different interfaces. Also, because each courseware package was different in its ability to gather course statistics, assessing and comparing course activity from semester to semester was difficult.

*Another Communication Tool to Monitor.* Reference librarians are inundated with communication from a number of different sources, such as telephones, cell phones, voicemail, face-to-face reference encounters, virtual reference services, and e-mail. Participation in online courses requires logging into the system and checking yet another communication tool. Depending on the number of courses in which the librarian participates, the number of discussion threads in each course she has decided to monitor, and the frequency with which she monitors them, such involvement can quickly become overwhelming.

*Time Consuming.* Not only is the process of monitoring online courses time-consuming, but librarian participation in online courses generates more interaction between students and the librarian. While this can be considered a success for the library, it poses a challenge as well for libraries with limited budgets and personnel. Statistics on known interaction between DE students and the DE librarian over a five-year period at UW-Eau Claire indicate that the average interaction lasted .56 hours. In the spring 2004 semester, students in the online courses monitored by the librarian made up about two percent of the total number of students enrolled in distance education courses. Yet they accounted for approximately 70 percent of known DE student-librarian interactions. While participating in online courses allows the librarian to reach many students with one message, a potential time-saving advantage, it also appears to encourage students to engage in more one-on-one contact with the librarian. Online faculty experience a similar phenomenon, often "spending an inordinate amount of time communicating by e-mail" (Smith, Ferguson, and Caris 2001, 22).

*Too Many Cooks?* Unlike the traditional on-campus course, which is often under the sole control of the professor, the online course often requires the collaboration and contribution of a team of individuals. The professor remains responsible for content, but may be assisted by a teaching assistant or grader. Course design and development may require the assistance of instructional designers and information technology staff, who may also be responsible for ongoing student and faculty technical support. At UW-Eau Claire, online courses were often taught by different professors in different semesters. Technology support came from department, campus, and state university system levels, meaning that many individuals could be involved with a single course. While a strong system of support is desirable, sometimes the number of people involved in a single course can lead to miscommunication and confusion over respective roles.

For example, when an online Nursing course in which the librarian lurked during fall semester was to be taught by a different professor spring semester, the entire structure and content of the course was copied and posted by a new instructional technology support staff member. The second offering of this online course included the lurking librarian profile and a library discussion thread from the previous semester. Unfortunately, no one had told the librarian that the course was being offered again, or that she was participating in it, until it was discovered two weeks into the semester! The instructor had assumed that instructional technology staff had contacted the librarian, and instructional technology staff had assumed the same of the instructor.

*Volume of Reading in Online Classroom.* Academic librarians view information literacy instruction as a key component of the service they provide. Providing such instruction in the online environment can be particularly challenging. Whereas on-campus students can come into the library for instruction or face-to-face interaction, in the online environment this type of instruction is offered primarily through the written word. Course content and communication that in a traditional classroom takes the form of lectures, discussions, labs, office hours, etc., is for the most part transformed into the written word in the online classroom. Faced with all of this reading, in addition to assigned outside readings, the student in the online course can become overwhelmed by the amount of reading required. Readings that are, therefore, not required may not be read at all. The librarian may want to use caution in adding too much written instruction to the student's load. Instead she may want to experiment with other media, such as audio or visual streaming, to present an instructional message or demonstration.

*Unrealistic Expectations.* Librarians are familiar with the increasing expectation among students that everything is online and instantaneously available. This expectation may be exacerbated by fact that all or most of the course is already online and always available. As a participant in an online course, a lurking librarian faces and possibly engenders increased expectations among students and faculty regarding her availability. Online faculty have faced expectations of availability and taken varying approaches in dealing with the issue. Jeffrey Young writes of several institutions with differing policies regarding availability and response time of online faculty. He reports that some institutions require faculty to respond to a student e-mail within a set period of time because "quick responses are key to making students feel part of a virtual class" (Young, 2004). Other institutions, he reports, recommend that online instructors set limits or online office hours not exceeding those one would establish on campus. Because students in online courses are apt to do some of their research during the wee hours of the morning and on weekends, they may expect a librarian to be available when they need assistance. Clearly communicating when one is available, how often one will be logging into the course, what kind of turn-around time students can expect, and alternatives for getting assistance (such as using online instructional resources or contacting the reference desk), are important for the librarian in ensuring realistic expectations.

Students may bring with them varying expectations based on previous experience. Many students in the online MBA courses were returning students who were or had been in a corporate environment. In such an environment, library assistance often includes doing the research and delivering information rather than assisting patrons in conducting their own research, as is generally the philosophy at an academic library. These conflicting missions between corporate and academic libraries can lead to a gap between student expectations and library service deemed appropriate in an academic setting.

## *CONCLUSION*

In best managing expectations, as well as addressing other disadvantages of lurking in online classrooms, it is important for the librarian and the faculty member to establish guidelines and limits. Questions that the librarian and faculty member should address in advance may include:

- How much of the class will the librarian monitor? Will she read just the library discussion thread, or all discussion threads? Will she be reading course content, such as lectures, on a regular basis? What can she reasonably manage given her existing workload?
- How often will the librarian log on? Every day? Twice a week? On weekends? At a specific time?
- How proactive will the librarian be? Will she simply respond to questions as they arise? Will she offer tips along the way? Will she contribute to other discussions or other areas of the course?

These questions can be sensitive, getting into areas of course control and ownership, many of which are still unclear in the relatively new area of online teaching. Being cognizant of potential turf issues is important for the lurking librarian, and answers to these questions will depend largely on the librarian's working relationship with the professor. "Librarians will need to work with diplomacy and aplomb," say Shank and DeWald, in order to establish "a relationship of mutual trust in which the faculty member feels comfortable sharing editorial control of the courseware content" (2003, 42).

The concept of "lurking librarian," used here to suggest caution and courtesy in establishing a presence in an online course, is not unique to this author. Jacqueline Corinth, Robert Morris University, developed a Web page titled "The Lurking Librarian Project," in which she outlines her similar activities participating in online courses (http://www.geocities. com/lurkinglibrarian/). Patricia Presti, in a posting to the Off-camp discussion list on May 13, 2004, described her activities in equally subversive language. In what she calls "collaboration by infiltration" she describes how as a co-administrator for Blackboard at Lynn University, she was able to get into online classes and look for opportunities to interject information literacy lessons. She offered suggestions to faculty members and "It worked gangbusters. Not only did the professor have an enhanced class . . . but the library was able to expand its [information literacy] presence on a targeted, course by course basis" (http://listserv.utk.edu/cgi-bin/wa?A2=ind0405&L=offcamp&T=0&F=&S=&P=2355).

While playful use of terms like "lurking" and "infiltration" may carry with it negative connotations, the real message is that in this new and changing landscape of online education, the librarian is wise to look, listen, and learn so that she can best determine how the library can support online faculty and students. To be able to observe and participate from within the course management system provides an ideal vantage point.

## REFERENCES

"ACRL Guidelines for Distance Learning Library Services." 2003. American Library Association. <http://www.ala.org/acrl/resjune02.html>. (accessed May 13, 2004).

Cox, C. 2002. Becoming part of the course: Using Blackboard to extend one-shot library instruction. *College & Research Libraries News* 63 (1): 11-39.

Dewald, N., A. Scholz-Crane, A. Booth and C. Levine. 2000. Information literacy at a distance: Instructional design issues. *Journal of Academic Librarianship* 26 (1): 33-44.

Kotter, W. 1999. Bridging the great divide: Improving relations between librarians and classroom faculty. *Journal of Academic Librarianship* 25 (4): 294-303.

Markgraf, J. S., and R. Erffmeyer. 2002. Providing library service to off-campus business students: Access, resources and instruction. *Journal of Business & Finance Librarianship* 7 (2/3): 99-114.

Mullen, M. 2002. "If you're not Mark Mullen, click here": Web-based courseware and the pedagogy of suspicion. Radical Teacher 63 (Spring): 14-20. Education Full Text <http://vnweb.hwwilsonweb.com>.

Radford, G. P., and M. L. Radford. 2001. Libraries, librarians, and the discourse of fear. *Library Quarterly* 71 (3):299-329. <http://web2.epnet.com>.

Raspa, D., and D. Ward. 2000. *The Collaborative imperative: Librarians and faculty working together in the information universe.* Chicago: American Library Association.

Robinson, A. M., and K. Schlegl. 2004. Student bibliographies improve when professors provide enforceable guidelines for citations. *portal: Libraries and the Academy* 4 (2): 275-290.

Shank, J. D., and N. H. Dewald. 2003. Establishing our presence in courseware: Adding library services to the virtual classroom. *Information Technology and Libraries* 22 (1): 38-43.

Smith, G. G., D. Ferguson and M. Caris. 2001. Teaching college courses online vs. face-to-face. *T.H.E. Journal* 28 (9): 18-26.

Uniting and Strengthening America by Providing Appropriate Tools Required to Intercept and Obstruct Terrorism (USA PATRIOT ACT) Act of 2001, Pub. Law 107-56, U.S. Statutes at Large 115 (2001): 272.

Valentine, B. 2001. The Legitimate effort in research papers: Student commitment versus faculty expectations. *Journal of Academic Librarianship* 27 (2): 107-115.

Young, J. R. 2002. The 24-hour professor: Online teaching redefines faculty members' schedules, duties, and relationships with students. *Chronicle of Higher Education*, May 31. <http://web.lexis-nexis.com/universe>.

# Information Literacy and the Distant Student: One University's Experience Developing, Delivering, and Maintaining an Online, Required Information Literacy Course

Elizabeth Mulherrin
Kimberly B. Kelley
Diane Fishman
Gloria J. Orr

**SUMMARY.** This article discusses the development and implementation of a required, credit bearing online information literacy course at the University of Maryland University College. Key factors in its success include administrative support, student and faculty interaction in the online classroom, and outcomes assessment. Student persistence in the course is high, and grade distributions indicate that students are being challenged. *[Article copies available for a fee from The Haworth Document Delivery Service: 1-800-HAWORTH. E-mail address: <docdelivery@haworthpress.com> Website: <http://www.HaworthPress.com> © 2004 by The Haworth Press, Inc. All rights reserved.]*

Elizabeth Mulherrin (emulherrin@umuc.edu) is Instructional Services Librarian; Kimberly B. Kelley (kkelley@umuc.edu) is Associate Provost; Diane Fishman (dfishman@umuc.edu) is Assistant Director, Public Services; and Gloria J. Orr (gorr@umuc.edu) is Director, Information and Library Services, all at the University of Maryland University College, Adelphi, MD 20783.

[Haworth co-indexing entry note]: "Information Literacy and the Distant Student: One University's Experience Developing, Delivering, and Maintaining an Online, Required Information Literacy Course." Mulherrin, Elizabeth et al. Co-published simultaneously in *Internet Reference Services Quarterly* (The Haworth Information Press, an imprint of The Haworth Press, Inc.) Vol. 9, No. 1/2, 2004, pp. 21-36; and: *Improving Internet Reference Services to Distance Learners* (ed: William Miller, and Rita M. Pellen) The Haworth Information Press, an imprint of The Haworth Press, Inc., 2004, pp. 21-36. Single or multiple copies of this article are available for a fee from The Haworth Document Delivery Service [1-800-HAWORTH, 9:00 a.m. - 5:00 p.m. (EST). E-mail address: docdelivery@haworthpress.com].

http://www.haworthpress.com/web/IRSQ
© 2004 by The Haworth Press, Inc. All rights reserved.
Digital Object Identifier: 10.1300/J136v09n01_03

**KEYWORDS.** Information literacy, distance education, outcomes assessment

## INTRODUCTION

The University of Maryland University College (UMUC) is one of 11 degree-granting institutions of the University System of Maryland. Founded in 1947, UMUC continues to serve primarily the adult, part-time learner and military members worldwide. Currently the university has more than 100,000 students from approximately 70 countries, including all 50 U.S. states.

Over the years, UMUC has offered a basic one-credit, elective library skills course, LIBS 100, and an increasing number of bibliographic instruction (BI) sessions to students located at teaching sites throughout Maryland and the Washington DC Metropolitan area. In the early 1990s, UMUC's Middle States accreditation agency began to emphasize the importance of integrating information literacy into the curriculum. In response, the content of LIBS 100 was upgraded and with the advent of UMUC's own proprietary distance education delivery software called WebTycho, the course and individual online BI sessions were made accessible in 1999 to our distant students via WebTycho.

Although the library was actively providing library instruction, there was no systematic means to ensure that students received instruction, especially students who were taking their courses online. At the same time, UMUC's students were flocking to online instruction in significant numbers; by 2002, online course delivery almost equaled our delivery of face-to-face offerings and the trend was growing exponentially. We were also aware that in previous online information literacy course delivery efforts, many students "stopped completing assignments or did them in a haphazard manner once they had attained enough points to receive a Satisfactory grade" (O'Hanlon, 2001) because the courses were not required. We also knew that adult learners returning to college may not have received systematic instruction in using a library in their previous college or high school experience or their education was so long ago that their skills are no longer current for an online research environment. Further, previous studies have suggested that adult learners are not adequately prepared to use library resources and need assistance to become information literate (Caravello, 2000).

In 2000, UMUC's School of Undergraduate Studies (SUS) moved from offering a general studies degree with specializations to majors with general education requirements (GER). In view of our experience with non-credit library instruction and an institutional recognition of the importance of ensuring systematic library instruction, one of the GER's would be a library research and skills course. An information literacy study group (led by the Associate Provost for Information and Library Services) was formed and one of several charges was to recommend an appropriate way to provide a structured, focused experience for all undergraduates. The study group identified a need for a systematic information literacy education that is accessible to all and provides the ability to evaluate and assess learning outcomes. The group reviewed the ALA national standards for information literacy and adapted them to UMUC, developing the following six SUS information literacy objectives that would be used to measure learning outcomes. The information literate student:

- determines the nature and extent of the information needed,
- accesses needed information effectively and efficiently,
- evaluates information and its sources critically,
- incorporates selected information into his or her knowledge base,
- individually or as a member of a group, uses information effectively to accomplish a specific purpose,
- understands many of the economic, legal, and social issues surrounding the use of information and access and uses information ethically and legally.

The study group recommended a two-tiered approach to achieve all six standards. First, it was recommended that LIBS 100 be retired and a new course, designated LIBS 150, be developed as a required one-credit, online course that would provide a solid foundation of basic library information skills needed for all higher level information literacy initiatives. Although the literature is rife with examples of information literacy courses available online (Hansen, 1997; O'Hanlon, 2001; Reynolds, 2001), these previous efforts to provide information literacy instruction were not required and it was difficult to ensure consistent participation from students. Therefore, we decided the course would be required for undergraduate students before they completed 15 credit hours of course work. The course would be taught exclusively online for stateside students and a combination of online and face-to-face classes at overseas locations. The online delivery format was essential to ensure all students could fulfill the requirement without undue hardship (e.g., traveling long distances, attending another course during the week). To ensure all six standards would be achieved, a second tier of activities was recommended whereby information literacy would be infused into the curriculum. This recommendation included incorporating an information literacy assignment into selective major and capstone courses. Based on the study group's recommendation, LIBS 150–Information Literacy and Research Methods–a new more comprehensive, interactive, and assessment-based course was developed, and information literacy was infused into courses across the curriculum.

## DEVELOPING THE COURSE

In Spring 2001 a course development team, consisting of librarians, an instructional designer, and programmers from SUS, was formed to develop the new LIBS 150. The team also worked closely with Information Technology staff. The team's goal was to create an interactive, visually attractive course in which one faculty member (with a grader's support) could provide a meaningful learning environment while working with 100 students per section as mandated by SUS.

## ORGANIZATION

The course begins with a pre-test and is organized into four modules:

1. Beginning the research process (a discussion of how to approach research and develop a thesis statement)
2. Electronic resources (an overview of the Internet and basic search techniques for database searching)
3. Evaluating and documenting your sources and the basics of copyright and plagiarism (an introduction to strategies for identifying unbiased, relevant material; a review of APA citation style; and a discussion of how to identify plagiarism and the associated ethical issues)
4. Libraries and Information and Library Services (ILS) (an introduction to types and organization of libraries in general and to the specific resources and services offered by UMUC).

The main deliverable for the course is a step-by-step research log, which is not visible to the instructor until it is submitted for grading. Learning activities embedded within the course help students practice skills they will need to complete the log. To keep the course manageable, students must pick one of three topics: communication in the workplace, global warming, or computer security (step 1). They next create a thesis statement (step 2), and a search statement with Boolean operators (step 3). In step 4 they choose an article, Web source, and book on their topic, and indicate using radio buttons whether they feel the source was authoritative, current, etc. In the final step (5), students cite and annotate the sources they selected. Students are able to save and revise their work before submitting it. Once submitted, the log is stored on a server to be graded.

The course also includes self-assessments to allow further learning without direct faculty feedback. These generally consist of multiple-choice questions (e.g., What is a search statement?). In addition to the research log, all students complete an open book final exam in which key questions are mapped to the pre-test for analysis. Students randomly receive one of three versions of the exam to encourage them to work independently on their responses.

## THE ROLE OF PROGRAMMING

To teach such high enrollments effectively, Web programming was vital. UMUC's SUS Course Development Team's programmers on the team worked closely with the librarian team members to create course self-assessments, learning activities, and pre- and post-tests that could be scored automatically so students would receive immediate feedback. Previous studies have indicated that immediate feedback is an important and effective means to motivate the learner to achieve and increases students' perceptions that the course is interactive more than assessments where feedback is slower and less consistent (Hansen, 1997; O'Hanlon, 2001). The course team wanted to ensure that when possible, feedback was immediate and meaningful. The development of automated mechanisms to ensure that feedback was consistent and immediate was important to the course designers to maximize learning when the number of students per section made giving consistent, immediate feedback more challenging.

In addition, programmers were able to add touches to make the course more inviting and learning more fun with extensive use of pop-ups and mouse-overs. Whimsical "CD-people" (see Figure 1) introduce each module engagingly and serve as gender/race free substitutes for both librarians and students in illustrations. Animations of

FIGURE 1. Overview of LIBS 150 Course Topics/Modules

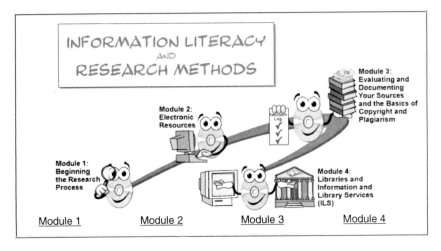

concepts in appropriate areas (URL segments; Boolean operators) increase student interest and provide pedagogical reinforcement.

## *DESCRIPTION OF COURSE*

### *Mechanics*

All interaction in the classroom, other than chat, is asynchronous. This functionality allows students to track unread postings and to only view postings they have not yet seen. Also, students and instructors can view discussion threads by author, topic, or date. Instructors can track individual student postings within a conference or for all conferences by viewing a student's portfolio.

### *Interaction*

The opportunities for interaction in the online classroom among students and with the instructor have increased as instructors became more comfortable handling the load of 100 students per section. Some of the LIBS 150 instructors host online "office hours" and chat sessions, which are optional for students because of time zone issues. Techniques for enhancing interaction in the online classroom include assigning discussion questions posted in an asynchronous conference and requiring that students respond to student postings relating to specific activities (e.g., thesis statement drafts, APA citations).

Instructors are given some flexibility in weighting the grade for student participation as long as they assign the required learning activities and the pre-test; any remaining points they assign must be included in the 20 percent participation grade. Popular activities devised by instructors include a scavenger hunt of the UMUC Information and Library Services Web page, comparing search results from Web search tools, and bibliographic citation practice. Instructors are encouraged to give all students individual feedback on the activities submitted via e-mail, although some instructors also use the conferences to enhance feedback on the concepts introduced by the learning activities to include the other students in the class.

The online gradebook in WebTycho was introduced to LIBS 150 instructors in January 2003. Previously, instructors tracked all submitted work and calculated grades using an Excel spreadsheet. The introduction of the gradebook enabled students to see their progress in the course through their WebTycho portfolio, which significantly decreased the number of questions for faculty from students wondering about the status of their graded work in the course. However, the instructor must track activities manually. The gradebook setup (point distribution and weight), as well as the conference discussion topics and reserve readings from previous classes, can be imported into new classes to help streamline setting up to teach a class.

### Course Revisions and Maintenance

The required library course is on a two- to three-year revision cycle. Minor changes to the course content (correcting URLs or other errors in the content) are possible by submitting the edits to course development staff and then republishing the course at the beginning of a term, but major revisions are determined by the instructional designers' schedules.

In the spring of 2003, major revisions were made to the course to accommodate the removal of the required textbook, the migration to a new library catalog system, and changes in library database access. Ordering and receiving a print textbook within the timeframe of a seven-week online class proved problematic for some students so the decision was made to only require readings available online. Once the course had run for several terms, we realized that the order of some of the earlier activities (Boolean searching and thesis statement) could be revised, with some additional content added, to help improve the flow of the course. Also, a pre-test was added to the course at that time.

## SUPPORTING THE FACULTY

Since SUS expected high enrollments for this required online course, adjunct faculty were needed to staff the multiple sections that would be necessary each term. The academic director for the course and library staff agreed to the hiring criteria (MLS and teaching experience required, and bibliographic instruction or online teaching experience preferred) and also collaborated on writing the ad, posting the ad to the appropriate listservs, reviewing the submitted resumes, and making a recommendation to hire.

All UMUC faculty members who are hired to teach online are required to take a five-week online training class to become familiar with the WebTycho platform and to discuss issues related to working with adult students in an online environment. The online training introduces instructors to UMUC resources to support their teaching, including library resources; however, due to the unique nature of LIBS 150, a supplemental online forum (LIBS 900) was created for ongoing support of LIBS instructors.

Graders, when they are available, are assigned to sections to assist with grading the final research log project. New instructors are encouraged to be graders in a LIBS section before teaching a class, and a few graders have graduated to being LIBS instructors once they have earned their MLS degrees. Future plans for new hires include having them shadow a LIBS class taught by a seasoned instructor while taking the online training for new faculty.

### LIBS 900

The online LIBS 900 forum is set up and maintained by the course chair, a library staff member, with support for administrative issues from the SUS academic director for the course. All adjunct faculty members and graders are enrolled in the online forum. The conference topics include teaching strategies and tips, difficult students, and aspects of course logistics such as grading and scheduling issues. The online forum is also a bulletin board, where information can be shared about university holidays, technical issues, policy changes, and course content changes. Many topics introduced by adjunct faculty, who were alerted to an issue by their students, have resulted in changes to the course. Also, proposed policy and course content changes can be reviewed in the forum for feedback and consensus. Since there are many policy and procedural questions that come up repeatedly, library staff reviewed the conferences and developed an online primer of frequently asked questions. The primer is reviewed by library staff before the beginning of each term and revised with updated information as necessary.

## *STANDARDIZATION*

A sample course schedule is posted in LIBS 900 to help instructors plan the seven-week course and faculty members are provided with a standard syllabus and grading scale. Because the course is a general education requirement, both the library and SUS staff were concerned that assessment of the research log project be as consistent as possible across the many sections. To help the LIBS faculty to be more consistent when grading, a rubric was developed for each step of the research log assignment with criteria provided for evaluating the steps. The rubric is designed both as a grading tool for the faculty member and as an evaluative measure that instructors can share with students.

## *COURSE AND FACULTY EVALUATIONS*

As the course content has been revised and the instructors have become more adept at handling the large class size, negative student comments about the course have decreased. There has also been an overall decline in the number of negative comments about course content and navigation, as well as technical issues and the online format. Some students comment that they would prefer a face-to-face class, but the majority of the students appreciate the flexibility of the online format.

Most of the feedback on faculty members is positive, and many students comment on how responsive instructors are to their questions, especially considering the number of students in the class. Over three terms of student course evaluations, from Summer 2002 to Spring 2003, 83 percent of students commented positively about faculty/student interaction in the course.

## EVALUATION MEASURES, STUDENT PERSISTENCE, AND OUTCOMES ASSESSMENT

The development and implementation of LIBS 150 was unique because of (1) the number of students per section (i.e., 100 students), (2) the use of an online delivery format, (3) the development of an electronic research log as a developmental tool for assessing student learning, and (4) the design team's efforts to create a course that had both course outcomes *and* evaluation of the students' attainment of the SUS information literacy (IL) objectives. In our view, it was not enough to simply ensure students learned the objectives of the course. Instead, our goal was to ensure that students achieved both mastery of the course content and further, achieved at least two of the basic IL standards as set forth by SUS.

### The Pre- and Post-Test

In order to evaluate *both* course goal attainment and IL objectives, we used several evaluation measures in concert to have multiple methods of evaluating what students learned. One important measure was the post-test we developed for the course where we mapped the questions on the exam to the course material and to the SUS IL objectives. The post-test was designed to evaluate student mastery of course content and in addition, we created questions that measured student mastery of SUS IL objectives. When we examined performance on the post-test, we were looking for both the level of learning of course material and achievement of IL goals. When developing the post-test, we determined that of the six SUS IL objectives, LIBS 150 could reliably measure four of them: (1) objective 1, "determines the nature and extent of the information needed," (2) objective 2, "accesses needed information effectively and efficiently," (3) objective 3, "evaluates information and its sources critically," and (4) objective 6, "understands many of the economic, legal, and social issues surrounding the use of information and access and uses information ethically and legally." The other two objectives, "incorporates selected information into his or her knowledge base" and "individually or as a member of a group, uses information effectively to accomplish a specific purpose" we considered to be "higher order" and therefore, more difficult to achieve in an entry level course. However, the research log requirement for LIBS 150, which is one means of using information to accomplish a specific purpose, does represent a project that is a meaningful contribution to "using information effectively to accomplish a specific purpose."

The large number of students per course section meant that we had to deliver the post-test in a highly efficient manner. To achieve this, we compromised and used a multiple choice-type online exam that provides a grade both to the student and instructor via an e-mail message when the student presses the "Submit" button. To discourage cheating, we created multiple versions of the examination; students receive one of the versions randomly when they select the final exam option in the online classroom. The problems with delivering online examinations are well documented (Olt, 2002). As Olt suggests, one important means to combat potential cheating is to have multiple versions of the examination so that sharing answers on the test is extremely difficult. Further, to combat the problem of students "illegally" using course materials while taking the exam, we simply made the examination open book. Interestingly, student achievement on the research log and their performance on the final exam were highly consistent. So, in our view, the open book exam design does not seem to have lessened the exam's ability to accurately evaluate the extent of student achievement of the learning outcomes. The professor for the course section determines their policy on the length of time the exam will be available and students are on an honor system to comply with whatever limitations are set by their instructor.

Since a multiple choice exam may miss subtle learning that takes place and may not be the most informative method of evaluating learning, we made the final exam less than 50 percent of the grade, emphasized student success on the research log, and included course participation as the primary elements of the course grade.

We quickly learned that a post-test, while informative when examined in conjunction with the research log and course participation, did not provide any data on how much students learned by taking LIBS 150. We felt it was important to learn more about the actual course impact on student learning. As a result, after the first year of offering the course, we developed a pre-test, which we mapped both to the SUS IL objectives and to the course objectives, *and* made a concerted effort to ensure the pre-test questions mirrored the post-test questions so we would be able to examine where students showed improvement. In order to ensure the reliability and validity of the course questions, we coordinated the development of both the pre- and post-test with our Institute for Research and Assessment in Higher Education (IRAHE). After several evaluative measures to ensure reliability and validity, we unveiled the pre-test in Spring 2003.

## The Initial Pre- and Post-Test Results

A statistical analysis of the LIBS 150 pre- and post-tests was performed for the spring, summer, and first term of the Fall 2003 semester (N = 3,828 students). In the initial analysis of the pre- and post-test data we found that student performance improved significantly. The improvement was one standard deviation, or approximately 17-18 percent improvement overall. Second, we found that although students did significantly better on the post-test questions in most areas, there were three questions where students consistently showed a decline rather than improvement. Two of the questions were very similar and both were designed to evaluate student understanding of how to develop a search statement and use Boolean logic. The third question dealt with how to choose the most appropriate source for a database search. All three questions related to student knowledge of licensed databases and the use of the more sophisticated search techniques required to successfully search in UMUC's licensed databases. However, the techniques needed for searching these databases are rarely used in a typical Web-based search tool such as Google.com. We learned from our analysis that students did not gain enough of an improved understanding of the difference between database searching and searching on the "free" Web. One of the SUS IL objectives, objective 2, "accesses needed information effectively and efficiently," is directly tied to student understanding of which resource is most appropriate (i.e., database or "free" Web?) and we must revise the course, and work with the teaching faculty, to ensure that students leave LIBS 150 with a better understanding of searching strategies and techniques in order to increase their information literacy and ensure their attainment of the SUS IL objectives by their graduation from UMUC.

## STUDENT EVALUATIONS OF THE COURSE

We did a qualitative analysis of student comments from the standard course evaluation for LIBS 150. We were interested in examining student attitudes about the course to determine student perspectives on the course content, delivery format, and student-faculty interaction. We were aware that student-faculty interaction might pose a serious challenge, with 100 students in the course, so we were particularly concerned with students' perspectives on the quality of student-faculty interaction in the course. Student responses were combined into a total score for each area we examined.

In examining the students' responses, we found the following trends in student comments from January 2003 through the Fall 2003 semester:

- Initially, students gave a high number of negative responses concerning the student/faculty ratio ($N = 70$). However, over the three semesters and on the most recent examination of their comments, the number of students giving a negative response decreased by 24 percent. Consistently, every semester, fewer students are concerned about the 100/1 student/faculty ratio. This finding suggests that as the faculty becomes more sophisticated, and we automate the course to a greater extent, faculty may have more time for interaction thereby offsetting student concerns about student/faculty ratio.
- Students consistently rate three aspects of the course most highly across the three semesters when analysis was performed: The quality of student/faculty interaction, the course delivery format, and the quality of the course content. These findings suggest that a majority of the students think the online format and the course materials themselves are helpful and the course offers good interactivity as well.
- The students provided negative comments about the course being a requirement and about the amount of work required to complete the course. These findings are not particularly unexpected. Previous studies using an online format to deliver a research skills course found that students expected the workload to be less and objected to the amount of work they were required to complete (Manuel, 2001). Further, students prefer complete flexibility and having to complete a course within the first 15 credit hours presents a loss of flexibility, not a positive thing in their view. We did not interpret these comments as a reflection on the course *per se* but instead, a typical response when presented with a required course that must be completed early in the student's academic career.

## STUDENT PERSISTENCE AND GRADE DISTRIBUTIONS

Student persistence in LIBS 150 is, in a word, remarkable. Consistently, student withdrawal rates in online stateside classes are low and remain at or below 7 percent per semester. We were concerned that requiring students to take an online course early in their academic career might cause withdrawal rates to be higher either because of students' lack of experience with an online course format or their lack of the necessary time to complete a one-credit course successfully. Based on the analysis of the withdrawal rates, we are not seeing a problem with student persistence, and this is a very positive outcome for the LIBS 150 model. If student persistence remains high, we are reaching more students consistently, early in their academic careers, and this helps ensure a consistent level of knowledge upon completion of LIBS 150. Further, this finding suggests that the course is not overwhelming and students are able to persist and complete the course successfully.

Additionally, the grade distributions indicate that students are being challenged. Overall, the number of "A" grades assigned was 40 percent or less and the number of students getting either a "B" or "C" was equal to the students receiving a letter grade of "A" (approximately 39 percent). Few students receive a grade of "D" (less than 3 percent). Therefore, we can extrapolate from these numbers that students are being challenged and additionally that they persist *in spite* of this and complete the course with a "C" or better.

## CONCLUSIONS

LIBS 150 was a "grand experiment" in delivering a required, online course to teach students basic research skills and additionally, ensure they attain a basic level of information literacy before they move forward to higher level courses in the curriculum. There is no doubt that as the faculty became more experienced and the course content was systematically revised and improved based on faculty feedback, the course experience for the students also improved. Unlike previous studies that found "underlying tension between distance education and information literacy" (Manuel, 2001), we learned that delivering an online course for teaching information literacy skills *is* a very successful method for teaching students. It is important to point out, however, that in achieving a successful course, we learned the following lessons:

- If the course is to thrive with a large number of students, much of the course content must be automated to ease the faculty burden and permit the faculty member to focus on student interaction rather than grading endless assignments.

- Systematic assessment tools must be developed which require little faculty intervention to administer. Although a pre- and post-test assessment may not be ideal, it does offer a systematic means to assess student learning *and* it is least burdensome for the faculty. Therefore, this assessment method was best suited for our situation and needs.
- The course *may* be the student's first introduction to online learning. As a result, having a systematic introduction to online learning *prior* to the student's involvement in the course is essential. A required orientation was added to WebTycho in Fall 2003. This enhancement lessens students' worry about their ability to handle an online course and helps to focus students' attention on the course content, not the delivery format.
- Using the assessment findings (and faculty feedback) to improve the course is imperative. Just having findings, without actually using them to improve the course, hampers the faculty's ability to teach and students' ability to learn.
- The course requires constant, systematic revision to ensure currency and relevancy. We knew that the information environment changes rapidly. Therefore, we tried to minimize the aspects of the course that could become dated rapidly. However, even with this precaution, we have learned that the key to the course's success is systematic updating and changes as resources, Web sites, and the library's delivery of resources change.
- Having an online seminar dedicated to faculty discussions and interactions is important to ensure faculty are supported and have ample means to discuss issues that arise in teaching the course. Faculty need information and because they are teaching online, staff dedicated to helping them navigate the many logistical issues involved in the delivery of the course is an important support mechanism. Further, the online seminar for faculty is a repository for faculty teaching methods that they share and use to improve course content and delivery.

The LIBS 150 course meets UMUC's students' needs very well. Students tell us they appreciate an online course that gives them flexibility in deciding when to participate and complete the course. Further, the students indicate that they prefer the course to be credit-bearing so they receive credit for the course work towards their degree. Previous online information literacy courses have been less successful (O'Hanlon, 2001; Manuel, 2001). However, in both cases the courses were not required and in one case, the course was non-credit. In our view, making the course a requirement *and* for-credit is an essential piece in ensuring the success of any information literacy offering, especially one offered on-line.

Further, we have learned that having faculty intervention in the course, no matter the extent to which parts of the course are automated, contributes to student satisfaction and eventual learning in the course. Faculty involvement also ensures the course content remains up-to-date and helps improve the delivering of the course content considerably.

Although required, online information literacy courses are still less common than non-credit online seminars or face-to-face offerings (Manuel, 2001; Parang, 2001). We believe our experience offers one example of a successful large, online course that colleges and universities might consider as they decide how to approach (or revise) information literacy instruction at their institution. In April 2002, the LIBS 150 course was awarded the Best Distance Learning Course Award for 2001-2002 by the Maryland Distance Education Association (MDLA). The receipt of the award offers confirmation of the success of this complex, yet rewarding online course development, delivery, and maintenance effort that is achieving its goal of fostering information literacy among a diverse, non-traditional undergraduate student population.

## REFERENCES

Caravello, P. S. "Library Instruction and Information Literacy for the Adult Learner: A Course and Its Lessons for Reference Work." *The Reference Librarian* 69/70 (2000): 259-69.

Dewald, N., Scholz-Crane, A., Booth, A., & Levine, C. "Information at a Distance: Instructional Design Issues." *The Journal of Academic Librarianship* 26, no. 1 (2000 January): 33-44.

Hansen, C. & Lombardo, N. "Toward the Virtual University: Collaborative Development of a Web-Based Course." *Research Strategies* 15, no. 2 (1997): 68-79.

Manuel, K. "Teaching an Online Information Literacy Course." *Reference Services Review* 29, no. 3 (2001): 219-28.

O'Hanlon, N. "Development, Delivery, and Outcomes of a Distance Course for New College Students." *Library Trends* 50, no. 1 (2001): 8-27.

Parang, E., Raine, M., & Stevenson, T. "Redesigning Freshman Seminar Library Instruction Based on Information Competencies." *Research Strategies* 17 (2001): 269-80.

# Online Tutorials
# as Instruction for Distance Students

## Rachel G. Viggiano

**SUMMARY.** Many academic libraries offer an array of library services to their off-campus and distance students, but library instruction for these populations is still a challenge. Librarians and teaching faculty struggle with how to effectively reach students that are truly distant, offering them the same library instruction and information literacy training that is possible in the classroom. The online tutorial has gained popularity in recent years and this article will address Web-based interactive tutorials as a means of providing library instruction to distance learners. Examples of tutorials aimed at distance students are examined, along with studies assessing the effectiveness of online tutorials. *[Article copies available for a fee from The Haworth Document Delivery Service: 1-800-HAWORTH. E-mail address: <docdelivery@haworthpress.com> Website: <http://www.HaworthPress.com> © 2004 by The Haworth Press, Inc. All rights reserved.]*

**KEYWORDS.** Distance learners, library instruction, tutorials

Rachel G. Viggiano (rviggian@mail.ucf.edu) is Reference Librarian and Distance Learning Liaison, University of Central Florida Libraries, PO Box 162666, Orlando, FL 32816-2666.

[Haworth co-indexing entry note]: "Online Tutorials as Instruction for Distance Students." Viggiano, Rachel G. Co-published simultaneously in *Internet Reference Services Quarterly* (The Haworth Information Press, an imprint of The Haworth Press, Inc.) Vol. 9, No. 1/2, 2004, pp. 37-54; and: *Improving Internet Reference Services to Distance Learners* (ed: William Miller, and Rita M. Pellen) The Haworth Information Press, an imprint of The Haworth Press, Inc., 2004, pp. 37-54. Single or multiple copies of this article are available for a fee from The Haworth Document Delivery Service [1-800-HAWORTH, 9:00 a.m. - 5:00 p.m. (EST). E-mail address: docdelivery@haworthpress.com].

The rapid growth of distance learning is probably apparent to most academic librarians, as more than half of all 2- and 4-year colleges and universities offered distance education courses in the 2000-2001 academic year. Fewer than one-third of the schools surveyed by the National Center for Education Statistics had no plans to offer distance courses in the following three years.[1]

Extended campus and distance learning library services have been a formal topic of discussion in the library community since the 1980s with the formation of ACRL's Extended Campus Library Services discussion group, and informally much further back. The literature concerning library services for distance learners is diverse and plentiful. Reference services, remote access, document delivery, library instruction, and electronic reserves have long been hot topics among librarians interested in serving distant populations. Many of these services, solutions intended for meeting the needs of distance patrons, have benefited local and even on-campus students as well. Extended reference hours, toll-free telephone numbers, and remote access to library resources can be of assistance to all students who live off campus or occasionally travel out of the area.

## BLUR BETWEEN DISTANCE LEARNER AND TRADITIONAL STUDENT

At many institutions there is difficulty defining the distance learner, whether the classification is based on course enrollment or place of residence. "Distance" students could be living within a mile of campus and taking online courses, while at the same time "traditional" students could be living in a neighboring state and commuting to campus for class. Hansen notes that "at WSU and many other similar campuses, 'on campus' students engage in the library experience as if they were distance learners, and the line between distance and not distance students becomes very blurred."[2] The long-held notion of the dichotomy between conventional and non-conventional students has fallen by the wayside and is being replaced by the new contemporary student, who balances work, family, and educational responsibilities, and is not defined by course delivery method or location.[3]

With these blurring lines between types of students, on campus or online, there emerges a new class of library patron–the "hidden user."[4] Since library services developed for distance students are increasingly used by all students, perhaps there should be a resulting shift away from specialized services for the distance student population and towards good service for all students, both hidden and apparent. In the 2003 article "Distance Learners: Not Necessarily Distant," the author proposes "that libraries begin to consider blending distance library services with traditional services."[5] Unfortunately this cannot be wholly accomplished, as there are still some specialized services that truly distance students are entitled to if they are to have access to equitable library services as outlined in the ACRL Guidelines for Distance Learning Library Services. The Guidelines state: "effective and appropriate services for distance learning communities may differ from, but must be equivalent to, those services offered on a traditional campus."[6]

## DISTANCE LIBRARY INSTRUCTION AS CHALLENGE

Library Instruction is one example of a service that cannot be denied to distance learners, but which cannot be provided in the traditional manner. It is not reasonable to expect distance students to physically visit the library in order to attend an instruction session or information literacy training. The Information Literacy Competency Standards for Higher Education support this by stating: "information literacy competencies for distance learning students should be comparable to those for 'on campus' students."[7]

In their article concerning the transfer of a library instruction class component from in-class to online, Markgraf and Erffmeyer state that "improving library instruction for DE students poses perhaps the greatest challenge but also the greatest potential for innovation."[8] This is borne out in the literature as librarians document the various ways they've undertaken this challenge.

Methods for delivering library instruction range from in-person visits at off-site locations to teleconferencing and videoconferencing, from paper workbooks to online chat. Delivery methods may be high- or low-tech, synchronous or asynchronous, one-on-one or broadcast to hundreds of students on multiple campuses. Librarians supporting distance students have shown their creativity in attempting to overcome this obstacle, and they've also shown their frustration.

Often by necessity, the method of delivering library instruction will parallel that of the course itself. Some institutions offer courses in so many different formats that, according to Pival and Tunon, "it has been a major challenge for the library to deliver consistent bibliographic instruction to students in programs where classes are delivered in such a variety of modalities.'"[9] It makes sense to use the technology the students are used to, although it may not be technology the librarians are used to.

While teaching faculty have months to perfect their teaching style via videoconferencing or broadcast television, this is a particular challenge to librarians who may instruct a class only once via that technology. In "Watch for the Little Red Light," Dunlap describes his frustrating initial experience with a closed circuit television broadcast of his library instruction session. With time and practice, his subsequent broadcast classes were better.[10] Shannon and Henner point out that it is to the students' learning advantage when we teach "on their turf" (when possible).[11]

In-person, off-site instruction is probably the librarian-preferred method, the most familiar, and the closest to traditional library instruction. The principal concerns are access to technology in the off-site location, and the ability of staff to travel to remote locations. It is also only feasible if classes regularly meet off-site. With the growth in online course offerings, off-site courses may diminish in popularity, and library budgets may not permit travel to any and all places that courses are offered.[12]

For those who feel that students respond to the visual or audio "presence" of the librarian, broadcast and videoconferencing allow for the recognition of the librarian as a person. Students literally see that there is help available and when they seek help, it will be from a familiar person or place. Broadcast, video-, audio-, and tele-conferencing all rely on the ability of the institution to provide the necessary infrastructure. Many schools have compressed conferencing abilities or software to allow online collaboration, but this also relies on the ability of the students to receive the communication on their end. Instruction via conferencing is often limited to regional campuses and sites where classes meet remotely or where the institution has a physical presence. Desktop conferencing is also limiting in that it requires librarians and students to have access to and mastery of specific software. Using some conferencing software can be technologically challenging, for both the librarian and patron.

As online instruction becomes more popular, students are less likely to be located together, in one place at one time. Early attempts at online library instruction often involved transporting library instruction workbooks into the online environment, transferring handouts to the Web, or even capturing video of search examples with voice-over. In recent years more and more librarians are finding their way into Web-based classes that are offered using course management software such as WebCT or Blackboard. Collaboration with faculty is essential in this environment, and librarians can often participate more in class, including follow-up discussions of library research methods.[13] Streaming audio and video offer the representation of the librarian as expert, but standing alone do not allow interaction with the librarian. Streaming video has become a popular way to deliver a more traditional library instruction session–perhaps from the library instruction classroom itself. It is not without technological restraints, and can be time consuming and costly to update when changes occur within databases, for example.

Within courseware or via freestanding chat rooms, librarians have even offered library instruction via chat. This method is necessarily synchronous, while many online classes are not. Online text-based instruction can be time-consuming and technologically frustrating as well. If interaction is to occur student-to-student or student-to-librarian, manageable class size is critical.[14] Each of the above-mentioned methods of delivering library instruction to distance students presents a distinct set of obstacles to overcome, and librarians are continually adapting to find innovative ways to meet the needs of distance, distributed, or "hidden" students.

## TUTORIAL AS INSTRUCTION

The online, interactive tutorial is a relative newcomer in the field of Library Instruction. One notable effort is from the University of Texas at Austin, whose tutorial (the Texas Information Literacy Tutorial, or TILT) garnered so much attention, the library has begun sharing it with others via an Open Publication License.[15] While TILT and many other tutorials were designed to supplement in-person instruction, they may also serve as a replacement if traditional library instruction is not feasible, as is sometimes the case with distance education.[16]

Some articles describing the development and creation of online tutorials mention distance students in passing, or almost as an afterthought. There are many tutorials designed specifically for online or Web-based students, since their library instruction often needs to be asynchronous in nature, but many of these tutorials still assume that the student is not at a great distance from the college or university. Most of the tutorials reviewed for this article (see page 44ff.) included specific instructions for finding books within the physical library, and no mention of how students can obtain books if they are not on campus. Notable exceptions include tutorials with separate modules directed at distance students, and one tutorial that incorporated information for distance students throughout.

Much of the literature on distance library instruction focuses on synchronous means of delivery. Perhaps one reason is the feeling that interaction is necessary and that personalization, a human touch, counts. Whether in-person at a remote location, via tele-, video-, or desktop conferencing, synchronous instruction allows patrons to form some sort of relationship with the librarian, and often their fellow classmates. The interaction is with other human beings, which can be comforting to students and allows for question and answer and clarification of anything that was not fully grasped when initially presented. While it has been posited that real-time interaction cannot fully occur in asynchronous instruction, there are other types of interaction besides instructor-to-student or student-to-student. Student-computer interaction can occur in "real time," regardless of when a tutorial is used.[17] Not all students need immediate person-to-person interaction or clarification, and a hyperlink to contact a reference librarian can lead students to get help when and how they prefer.

There is no shortage of literature concerning the benefits of active learning, including literature specifically focusing on library instruction and information literacy training. Whether face-to-face in a library classroom or via one of the many methods discussed above, involved students who experience active learning are more likely to retain what they learn. Online tutorials, because of their asynchronous nature, have challenged librarians to incorporate active learning opportunities, often in the form of interactive games or exercises. Dewald, Scholz-Crane, and Booth provide a review of the literature on active learning in distance education and distance information literacy instruction, concluding, "interactivity of Web tutorials is the key to active learning and reinforcement."[18]

Dewald's 1999 article, "Transporting Good Library Instruction Practices into the Web Environment," first identifies the elements of good library instruction and then outlines how these characteristics can be applied to Web-based instruction.[19] The article then examines 19 tutorials, only seven of which included some form of active learning exercises. Since then, online tutorials have come a long way and there are many more examples of tutorials that are interactive and provide the active learning experience that librarians hope to offer all students.

## EFFECTIVENESS OF TUTORIALS AS INSTRUCTION

The question still remains whether tutorials are an effective means of instruction, as compared with traditional face-to-face library instruction. Only a few studies have been undertaken specifically testing interactive Web-based tutorials, but most of the results suggest that tutorials are as effective as librarian-led training at teaching basic library skills. A 2000 study of first-year students at the University of Albany found the same level of effectiveness of instruction for two groups of students who had either an in-person instruction session with hands-on practice or a Web-based tutorial.[20] A study of first-year English students at the University of North Carolina at Chapel Hill had similar findings, indicating that "the tutorial group's post-test scores were not significantly different from those of the class group."[21]

Beile and Boote found that graduate education students scored equally well on a quiz after participating in a traditional instruction session or completing a tutorial, and suggest that "Web-based tutorials appear to support students as well as traditional instruction, meeting the need for off-campus instruction to information resources."[22] In a study of the TILT Web-based tutorial, Orme found that it was "at least as effective as face-to-face instruction for teaching first-year students fundamental information research skills." However, the author then goes on to point out that there has not been enough research in this area to draw definitive conclusions.[23]

In a study of first-year sociology students at a university in Australia, Churkovich and Oughtred did find a significant difference in the improvement between pre- and post-test scores of three groups of students, those who had in-class instruction, those who completed the tutorial with the assistance of a librarian in the classroom, and those who completed the tutorial in a computer lab with no librarian present. While students' "posttest scores improved significantly as a result of library instruction, regardless of method," the students who had traditional face-to-face instruction improved the most. This was the only study to find such a difference, and the authors suggest that it was due to "flexible instruction, variety in presentation styles and reinforcement of concepts by a librarian."[24]

Whether librarians view tutorials as effective is another question. In a 2003 study, 78% of surveyed librarians felt that online tutorials were effective at teaching library skills online, although many of these librarians qualified their answers with statements regarding the quality of the tutorial. Of the surveyed librarians, 32% noted the convenience of the tutorials, particularly for access around the clock and by distance students. To summarize, Hollister and Coe state: "librarians generally regard online tutorials as effective in a limited sense, and as supplemental to other methods of instruction."[25]

## REVIEW OF TUTORIALS

For this article, 34 currently available online library instruction or information literacy tutorials were reviewed. The tutorials were located using the PRIMO database (Peer-Reviewed Instructional Materials Online, formerly known as the Internet Education Project), a project of the ACRL Instruction Section's Emerging Technologies in Instruction Committee.[26] This sample of 34 tutorials was derived from the 92 entries in the PRIMO database. Only general library orientations and information literacy tutorials were considered.[27]

For the purposes of this article, the author chooses not to differentiate between information literacy and library instruction tutorials, believing that a combination of the two is what distance students need. Information literacy skills are very important, as truly distance students may be using local libraries, and possibly many different libraries. Equipped with an understanding of the cycle of information and the theory behind information seeking, they can put their knowledge into practice in a variety of settings, including local public or academic libraries.

Step-by-step library instruction is also important as users learn the idiosyncrasies of their own library and the services offered to distance learners. Often there is a very specific manner in which distance students must request materials or seek help in order to receive the services they are entitled to. Straightforward instruction of required steps is often necessary.

This informal survey of online tutorials shows that many have now incorporated some form of interaction between the student and the computer. All but three of the 34 tutorials had interactive games and quizzes that provided an immediate response to the student, live or simulated searches of the library catalog or databases, or fill-in-the-blanks or mouse-over activities that gave immediate feedback on the users' answers. Of the 34 tutorials, 10 had some sort of student login to courseware, presumably so that tests and quizzes could be scored and reported to the instructor, and many more had completion certificates that could be printed out.

Of the 34 tutorials examined, only three had content specifically aimed at the distant student. These three were: the Naval Postgraduate

School's "Dudley Knox Library Orientation," Georgia's "Online Library Learning Center," and "InfoTrekk" from the Curtin University of Technology. The Naval Postgraduate School has a large percentage of distance students, and they address this issue by having two student guides who lead the tutorial user through the modules. One of the guides is an on-campus student, and the other is a distant student. In this way, needs of both user groups can be addressed.

The "Dudley Knox Library Orientation" is comprised of four sections, each containing a set of modules. Most topics have a corresponding interactive exercise, which is graded. Students can log in to the tutorial via Blackboard course management software, or access it as a guest with no login via the Web. The advantage to logging in via Blackboard is access to contact information that is restricted and cannot be posted on the open Web.

The tutorial from Georgia offers instruction to students from the many institutions of the University System of Georgia, and is made up of ten units, the tenth being "For Distance Education Students." By separating the information for distance learners, traditional or on-campus students do not need to complete the distance unit. However, students must self-identify as distance students and select the module in order to learn about the resources and services available to them. This can be a problem if students aren't familiar with the terminology or, for whatever reason, do not consider themselves "distant." The "Online Library Learning Center" has mouse-over activities, but does not offer any feedback to facilitate true active learning. There are pages of exercises for users to print, fill-in, and turn in to their instructor.

Curtin University of Technology in Australia has a long tradition of distance education, and its "InfoTrekk" tutorial reflects this. "InfoTrekk" is made up of 10 "treks," or modules, and the 10th trek addresses "Using library services from home." This section makes reference to distance students, but also addresses users with disabilities and those taking classes on campus who wish to do their research from the comfort of their home. There is no true interaction within the treks, but there is a graded quiz at the end of each, which provides feedback for each answer given.

"Safari," from the Open University in the United Kingdom, does a great job of introducing library catalogs and databases as concepts, explaining that students may need to use different catalogs in different libraries. While this tutorial does not specify that it is aimed at distance students, Open University is an open and distance institution, so most of its users are online students, and most are distant from the physical library. "Safari" has users fill in answers, complete interactive exercises, and do live database searches using browser frames.

Besides these tutorials, the author searched to see if more tutorials aimed at distance students could be located on the Web. Many Web pages and guides are available, but few true tutorials. There may be more examples than those mentioned below, but this sample should represent what was available at the time of this writing.

The University of New Brunswick has the "Research Tutorial for Off Campus Students," which does include quizzes. The quizzes are scored and provide the user with correct answers once they are completed. There are nine units in the tutorial, and four quizzes.

The University of Leicester has an "Electronic Journals Tutorial for Distance Learners," and the "Information Retrieval Skills for Distance Learners" tutorial, both with online exercises. The "Information Retrieval Skills" tutorial contains six substantive sections and four quizzes, while the "Electronic Journals Tutorial" has five sections, four quizzes, and one online searching exercise to be performed in another browser window.

Washington State University has an "Online Library Tour for DDP (Distance Degree Program) Students," with exercises and quizzes. This online tour consists of three sections, one in which the student learns about the library's resources and services, one in which the student practices using the resources available (using browser frames), and one in which the student's knowledge is tested using a quiz that is graded and provides immediate feedback on the student's responses.

Nova Southeastern University, a leader in the distance education field, has a list of subject-specific tutorials on its Distance and Instructional Library Services (DILS) Web page. After viewing several different tutorials, it appears that there are no interactive exercises that accompany them. One nice feature of the Nova Southeastern tutorials is that there are modules that repeat from tutorial to tutorial, which must save librarians time and energy. When making a new subject-based tutorial, only the portions specific to that subject would need to be created from scratch, while general modules that had already been created could be incorporated easily.

The Rochester Institute of Technology has a "Scavenger Hunt for Online Learners" which functions as an interactive exercise. For each of the 24 questions, there is a hint that the students can use to help them answer, but there is no tutorial to accompany the quiz itself. It is difficult to tell from the Web page if the scavenger hunt is meant to be used following library instruction, or stand on its own.

The Council of Prairie and Pacific University Libraries (COPPUL) has the online guide "Doing Research from a Distance: A Guide for Western Canadian Students." This is really not a tutorial in the truest sense, but is a guide for distance students with no interactivity or exercises to accompany it. This guide is adapted from the Memorial University of Newfoundland's "Doing Research" guide, and is intended for use by students at 22 university libraries located in Manitoba, Saskatchewan, Alberta, and British Columbia.

"Library and Research Services Tutorial for the Distance Learner" is located on the Dallas TeleCollege Library Web page. This tutorial contains five modules but no exercises or activities and no interaction. The University of Tennessee has an "ILLiad Tutorial for Distance Education Students," but this covers just one aspect of distance library services, interlibrary loan. This tutorial is really only one module and has no interactive components to facilitate active learning. The University of Wisconsin-Eau Claire has a "Research Tutorial" that is intended for off-campus students. There are seven modules in this tutorial, but no interaction.

This review of tutorials aimed specifically at distance students shows that the advances made in general online library tutorials have not necessarily been adopted for use in specialized tutorials aimed at distance students. This could be because librarians do not want to duplicate efforts by creating tutorials for special populations, or it could be because the instructional needs of distance students are being met in different ways. There may be countless reasons why tutorials have not been adopted as the instruction method of choice for this population. Some libraries find a middle ground by adding a module or unit on distance services so that their general tutorials accommodate all students, regardless of how they use the library.

## IMPLICATIONS AND PRACTICE AT UCF

The University of Central Florida (UCF) is a very large metropolitan research university located in Orlando, Florida. It is one of the state's 11 public universities. UCF began offering classes in October of 1968, although at the time it was known as Florida Technological University. In recent years, UCF has grown rapidly in both size and character, overcoming a reputation as a "commuter school" and becoming much more residential. UCF has also expanded to include 14 regional campuses in the surrounding counties, in a sense courting the non-traditional student who is not willing or able to relocate to attend a university. Fall 2003 enrollment at UCF was a staggering 41,685 with 1,158 full-time faculty.[28]

The University of Central Florida delivers distributed learning courses in many modalities, including entirely Web-based, mixed-mode (reduced-seat time), two-way interactive television, video, online streaming video, and radio (although no radio or video classes have been offered since Spring 2003). In the Spring 2004 semester, there were 10,324 enrollments in 558 courses that could be considered "distance" (i.e., no class attendance required).[29] There are seven undergraduate degree programs, eight graduate degree programs, and seven graduate certificate programs that can be completed entirely via the World Wide Web. These numbers do not include the FEEDS (Florida Engineering Education Delivery System) courses via the College of Engineering and Computer Science or courses offered at regional locations where there is no library onsite.

Of the many regional campuses and centers where UCF offers classes in-person, only three are full-service campuses with joint-use libraries and UCF Librarians. Another nine locations are centers, usually located on the campus of a community college, where the library is limited in nature and lacking a UCF librarian to assist students. There are at least three other sites that lack any adequate library resources. It is the author's opinion that students taking classes at these sites are indeed distance students, at least from the perspective of the library.

The Libraries at UCF are comprised of the main library on the Orlando campus and six branch, special, and joint-use libraries at various campuses. The library holds over 1.5 million print volumes, over 11,000 periodical subscriptions, and conducted library instruction sessions for over 11,000 students in 2003.[30]

The UCF Libraries have been providing library services for distance learners for years, including telephone, e-mail, and chat reference, a toll-free telephone number, document delivery (articles and books delivered to distance students residing in Florida), remote access to library databases, and an arrangement for students to get a library ID number without coming to campus. Library instruction for distance students has not been an issue until recently. Very few professors have inquired about instruction for distance and online classes. Several years ago, at least one library instruction session was broadcast to a remote site via ITV (two-way Interactive Television), and librarians occasionally travel to regional campuses and centers within reason (generally the Daytona Beach and South Lake campuses–both within 55 miles of UCF).

A UCF professor recently inquired about instruction for the students in her Web-based class, and every effort was made to accommodate them one-on-one, via chat or telephone or e-mail. As stated in ACRL's Guidelines for Distance Learning Library Services, "because students and faculty in distance learning programs frequently do not have direct access to a full range of library services and materials, equitable distance learning library services are more personalized than might be expected on campus."[31] Since the UCF Libraries have not established an efficient method of delivering library instruction to a group of online students, currently we must do what we can to instruct students on an individual basis.

UCF Reference Librarian Donna Goda created a streaming video tutorial in 2002 with the help of a UCF In-House grant. The two video modules are also available in CD-ROM format and distributed in the library. This project was completed on campus with the assistance of UCF's Office of Instructional Resources, and a faculty member provided a Spanish translation. One lesson learned while working on this project was that it would be beneficial to have the ability to update the tutorial in-house as things change in the library. Since the completion of the video, UCF has upgraded from EBSCO's Academic Search Elite to Academic Search Premier, and the search interface has been revised. Because these videos were produced by a third party outside of the library, and paid for with grant funds, it has not been feasible to create an updated version.

There have been several online tutorials developed by UCF librarians, including the "WebLUIS Tutorial" (which is no longer available),[32] the "ENC 1102 Tutorial," which includes a graded quiz with scores reported to faculty via WebCT, the Education Tutorial (available only to students in particular classes via WebCT) and the Education Library Skills Tutorial. Of these, only the Education Library Skills Tutorial includes active learning exercises within the tutorial, with quizzes that test the students' skills and provide immediate feedback.

While some schools have an institutional mandate regarding Information Literacy, and some have credit courses in library or information skills, UCF relies on faculty to determine when students need library instruction. It is suspected that a generic library tutorial would not get much use without the teaching faculty requiring it. In 2003, 2,173 students completed the "ENC 1102 tutorial." The average quiz score was 85.5%.

A group of UCF Librarians is currently working on a project to replace the "ENC 1102 Tutorial" with a more general library skills tutorial that could benefit all students. The reference librarian designated as the Distance Learning Liaison is part of this project and the team hopes to address the needs of distance students while also realizing that the majority of UCF students do take classes on campus. As at other institutions, the tutorial will be used in conjunction with in-class instruction for most students, but may serve to replace instruction for those hard-to-reach distance learners.

## CONCLUSION

There is no simple solution for providing library instruction to distance and online students. Librarians in the field are continually working to improve the instruction methods they currently use, and to develop new methods that will better serve the growing class of "hidden users." Online tutorials seem to work well for introductory library instruction and information literacy training, provided they incorporate active learning components. Further research into the effectiveness of tutorials would be helpful for librarians serving distant and online users. Rather than reinventing the tutorial for a specialized population, generalized tutorials can be used to instruct distance students. In this case, it is most helpful if the tutorial also addresses the special needs of distant students and the services that are available to them.

## NOTES

1. Tiffany Waits and Laurie Lewis, "Distance Education at Degree-Granting Postsecondary Institutions: 2000-2001." (Washington, DC: National Center for Education Statistics, 2003), <http://nces.ed.gov/pubs2003/2003017.pdf>.

2. Carol Hansen, "The Internet Navigator: An Online Internet Course for Distance Learners." *Library Trends* 50, no. 1 (2001): 58-72.

3. Rick Powell, Sharon McGuire, and Gail Crawford, "Convergence of Student Types: Issues for Distance Education." In *The Convergence of Distance and Conventional Education: Patterns of Flexibility for the Individual Learner*, edited by Alan Tait and Roger Mills, 86-99 (New York: Routledge, 1999).

4. Shelda Debowski, "The Hidden User: Providing an Effective Service to the Users of Electronic Information Sources." *OCLC Systems & Services* 16, no. 4 (2000): 175-80.

5. Rachel G. Viggiano, "Distance Learners: Not Necessarily Distant." *The Southeastern Librarian* 51, no. 3 (2003): 31-34.

6. American Library Association, "Guidelines for Distance Learning Library Services" (2004), http://www.ala.org/ala/acrl/acrlstandards/guidelinesdistancelearning.htm.

7. American Library Association, "Information Literacy Competency Standards for Higher Education" (2000), <http://www.ala.org/ala/acrl/acrlstandards/informationliteracycompetency.htm>.

8. Jill S. Markgraf and Robert C. Erffmeyer, "Providing Library Service to Off-Campus Business Students: Access, Resources and Instruction." *Journal of Business & Finance Librarianship* 7, no. 2/3 (2002): 99-114.

9. Paul R. Pival and Johanna Tuñón, "Innovative Methods for Providing Instruction to Distance Students Using Technology." *Journal of Library Administration* 32, no. 1/2 (2001): 347-60.

10. Steven Dunlap. "Watch for the Little Red Light: Delivery of Bibliographic Instruction by Unconventional Means." *Journal of Library Administration* 37, no. 1/2 (2002): 279-85.

11. Amy W. Shannon and Terry A. Henner, "Providing Library Instruction to Remote Users." In *Attracting, Educating and Serving Remote Users Through the Web*, edited by Donnelyn Curtis, 149-70 (New York: Neal-Schuman, 2002).

12. Paul R. Pival and Johanna Tuñón, "Innovative Methods for Providing Instruction to Distance Students Using Technology." *Journal of Library Administration* 32, no. 1/2 (2001): 347-60.

13. John D. Shank and Nancy H. Dewald, "Establishing Our Presence in Courseware: Adding Library Services to the Virtual Classroom." *Information Technology and Libraries* 22, no. 1 (2003): 38-43; Nancy K. Getty, Barbara Burd, and Sarah K. Burns. "Using Courseware to Deliver Library Instruction Via the Web: Four Examples." *Reference Services Review* 28, no. 4 (2000): 349-59.

14. Rachel G. Viggiano and Meredith Ault, "Online Library Instruction for Online Students." *Information Technology and Libraries* 20, no. 3 (2001): 135-38.

15. Elizabeth A. Dupuis, "Automating Instruction." *Library Journal* 126, no. 7 (2001): 21-22.

16. Clara S. Fowler and Elizabeth A. Dupuis, "What Have We Done? TILT's Impact on Our Instruction Program." *Reference Services Review* 28, no. 4 (2000): 343-48.

17. Nancy H. Dewald, Ann Scholz-Crane, and Austin Booth, "Information Literacy at a Distance: Instructional Design Issues." *The Journal of Academic Librarianship* 26, no. 1 (2000): 33-44.

18. Dewald, Scholz-Crane, and Booth, "Information Literacy at a Distance."

19. Nancy H. Dewald, "Transporting Good Library Instruction Practices into the Web Environment: An Analysis of Online Tutorials." *The Journal of Academic Librarianship* 25, no. 1 (1999): 26-31.

20. Carol Anne Germain, Trudi E. Jacobson, and Sue A. Kaczor, "A Comparison of the Effectiveness of Presentation Formats for Instruction: Teaching First-Year Students." *College & Research Libraries* 61, no. 1 (2000): 65-72.

21. Lucy Holman, "A Comparison of Computer-Assisted Instruction and Classroom Bibliographic Instruction." *Reference & User Services Quarterly* 40, no. 1 (2000): 53-60.

22. Penny M. Beile and David N. Boote, "Library Instruction and Graduate Professional Development: Exploring the Effect of Learning Environments on Self-Efficacy and Learning Outcomes." *Alberta Journal of Educational Research* 48, no. 4 (2002): 364-67.

23. William A. Orme, "A Study of the Residual Impact of the Texas Information Literacy Tutorial on the Information-Seeking Ability of First Year College Students." *College & Research Libraries* 65, no. 3 (2004): 205-15.

24. Marion Churkovich and Christine Oughtred, "Can an Online Tutorial Pass the Test for Library Instruction? An Evaluation and Comparison of Library Skills Instruction Methods for First Year Students at Deakin University." *Australian Academic & Research Libraries* 33, no. 1 (2002): 25-38.

25. Christopher V. Hollister and Jonathan Coe, "Current Trends vs. Traditional Models: Librarians' Views on the Methods of Library Instruction." *College & Undergraduate Libraries* 10, no. 2 (2003): 49-63.

26. ACRL Instruction Section, Emerging Technologies in Instruction Committee, "PRIMO: Peer-Reviewed Instructional Materials Online," http://cooley.colgate.edu/etech/primo/index.htm.

27. Of the 92 entries, 22 were eliminated on the basis of currency because they were submitted to the database prior to 2000. Also ruled out were the subject-based tutorials and materials aimed at teaching only one resource (such as a single library catalog or online database, or tutorials covering only computer usage or Internet searching). Two entries were eliminated because they were the product of a public library and as such would not concern themselves with distance students. One tutorial no longer existed, and seven entries were eliminated because they were streaming videos, an interesting means of delivering library instruction, but not appropriate for this article.

28. University of Central Florida, "Current Facts about UCF," <http://www.iroffice.ucf.edu/character/current.html>; The UCF student population is 83% undergraduate, 69% full-time, and has an average age of 24.

29. The Center for Distributed Learning at the University of Central Florida, "Trends: UCF Enrollment by Modality,"<http://distrib.ucf.edu/dlucf/rstenroll.htm>; The Center for Distributed Learning at the University of Central Florida, "Trends: UCF Course Sections by Modality," <http://distrib.ucf.edu/dlucf/rstsect.htm>.

30. University of Central Florida Libraries, "Quick Facts about the UCF Library," <http://library.ucf.edu/Ask/facts.htm>.

31. American Library Association, "Guidelines for Distance Learning Library Services" (2004), <http://www.ala.org/ala/acrl/acrlstandards/guidelinesdistancelearning.htm>.

32. Stefanie Dennis, Sallie Harlan, and Athena Hoeppner, "All About Web Tutorials." In *Library User Education in the New Millennium: Blending Tradition, Trends, and Innovation*, edited by Julia K. Nims and Ann Andrew, 69-78 (Ann Arbor, Michigan: Pierian Press, 2001).

APPENDIX

Tutorials mentioned in the text of the article can be found online using these URLs.

Naval Postgraduate School "Dudley Knox Library Orientation" <http://library.nps.navy.mil/home/orientlaunch.htm>.

University System of Georgia "Online Library Learning Center" <http://www.usg.edu/galileo/skills/>.

Curtin University of Technology "InfoTrekk" <http://library.curtin.edu.au/infotrekk/index.html>.

Open University "Safari" <http://ltssolweb1.open.ac.uk/safari/signpostframe.htm>.

University of New Brunswick "Research Tutorial for Off Campus Students" <http://dev.hil.unb.ca/disted/tutorials/index.html>.

University of Leicester "Electronic Journals Tutorial for Distance Learners" <http://www.le.ac.uk/li/sources/subject3/ejournals/dltut.html>.

University of Leicester "Information Retrieval Skills for Distance Learners" <http://www.le.ac.uk/li/distance/training/search/index.html>.

Washington State University "WSU Libraries Online Tour: Undergraduate DDP Students" <http://www.wsulibs.wsu.edu/electric/trainingmods/DDP_Student_Online_Tour/trainer.html>.

Nova Southeastern University "Tutorials and Research Modules" <http://www.nova.edu/library/dils/tutorialmodules.htm>.

University of Victoria, Canada "INFOLINE Library Research Tutorial" <http://web.uvic.ca/nurs/cd/nurs/infoline/basics.htm>.

Rochester Institute of Technology "Scavenger Hunt for Online Learners" <http://wally.rit.edu/instruction/DLquestions.html>.

Council of Prairie and Pacific University Libraries "Doing Research from a Distance: A Guide for Western Canadian Students" <http://www.royalroads.ca/coppul/default.htm>.

Memorial University of Newfoundland "Doing Research" <http://www.library.mun.ca/instruction/doingresearch/>.

Dallas TeleCollege "Library and Research Services Tutorial for the Distance Learner" <http://ollie.dcccd.edu/library/Default.htm>.

APPENDIX (continued)

University of Tennessee "ILLiad Tutorial for Distance Education Students" <http://www.lib.utk.edu/offcamp/illiad/>.

University of Wisconsin-Eau Claire "Research Tutorial" <http://www.uwec.edu/library/tutorial/>.

University of Central Florida "ENC1102 Tutorial" <http://library.ucf.edu/Reference/Instruction/ENC1102Tutorial/>.

University of Central Florida "Education Library Skills Tutorial" <http://library.ucf.edu/CMC/edtut/>.

# Beyond Instruction:
# Integrating Library Service in Support
# of Information Literacy

Barbara J. D'Angelo
Barry M. Maid

**SUMMARY.** For several years, librarians have grappled with problems and issues surrounding provision of library services to distance students. The Multimedia Writing and Technical Communication Program at Arizona State University East offers the majority of its courses online. To date, the library and Program collaboration has focused on an information literacy initiative. To support this initiative and other course needs, the program director and a campus librarian have discussed integrating library services in support of coursework. This article focuses on the need for library support from the perspective of the program director and librarian as well as potential methods of delivery. *[Article copies available for a fee from The Haworth Document Delivery Service: 1-800-HAWORTH. E-mail address: <docdelivery@haworthpress.com> Website: <http://www.HaworthPress.com> © 2004 by The Haworth Press, Inc. All rights reserved.]*

---

Barbara J. D'Angelo (bdangelo@asu.edu) is Lecturer in Information Literacy, and Barry M. Maid (barry.maid@asu.edu) is Professor and Head Faculty of Technical Communication, Multimedia Writing and Technical Communication, both at Arizona State University East.

[Haworth co-indexing entry note]: "Beyond Instruction: Integrating Library Service in Support of Information Literacy." D'Angelo, Barbara J., and Barry M. Maid. Co-published simultaneously in *Internet Reference Services Quarterly* (The Haworth Information Press, an imprint of The Haworth Press, Inc.) Vol. 9, No. 1/2, 2004, pp. 55-63; and: *Improving Internet Reference Services to Distance Learners* (ed: William Miller, and Rita M. Pellen) The Haworth Information Press, an imprint of The Haworth Press, Inc., 2004, pp. 55-63. Single or multiple copies of this article are available for a fee from The Haworth Document Delivery Service [1-800-HAWORTH, 9:00 a.m. - 5:00 p.m. (EST). E-mail address: docdelivery@haworthpress.com].

http://www.haworthpress.com/web/IRSQ
© 2004 by The Haworth Press, Inc. All rights reserved.
Digital Object Identifier: 10.1300/J136v09n01_05

**KEYWORDS.** Library services, distance learning, information literacy, collaboration

## INTRODUCTION

Arizona State University (ASU) East is one of four ASU campuses. Located in the east valley of the metropolitan Phoenix area, ASU East opened in 1996 on the grounds of a former U.S. Air Force base. With a focus on applied and professional programs, the campus has experienced enrollment growth of approximately 30% each year. East is evolving into a polytechnic institution as part of an overall university redesign. With new programs and continued rapid enrollment growth, the campus is expected to grow from current enrollment of 3,800 students to 10,000-15,000 within 10 years. Unfortunately, the growth rate in enrollment has not been matched by equivalent growth in resources. Although funding and staffing resources are beginning to increase, one of East's challenges will be to meet the service needs of a rapidly growing student body.

ASU East Library Services is a hybrid library consisting of a small core collection of print materials relevant to programs on campus. The Library shares access to electronic indexes and databases with the other ASU libraries as well as with the libraries of the other public universities through consortial arrangements. A document delivery service provides supplemental access to materials not available in full-text electronically at no charge to East faculty, students, and staff. Reference service is available in-person, by phone, and e-mail as well as through text chat and voice-over-IP.

The Multimedia Writing and Technical Communication Program was created in 2000 as the only technical communication program offered in the state of Arizona. It currently offers a Bachelor of Science Degree and a Post-Baccalaureate Certificate. As in many technical communication programs, the student population in both the undergraduate and certificate programs is primarily comprised of non-traditional students. Some of the students are transferring from community colleges, others are transferring from other programs at any of the other ASU campuses, while still others are returning to school (many only part-time) after spending time in the workplace. It is this group, those who have observed problems with workplace communication first hand, who often help create a "real world" context for the classes.

The nature of the MWTC Program presents some challenges to collaboration and integrating library services. Until the Fall 2004 semester the program had only one full-time faculty member beyond the program head. As a result, most courses are taught by adjunct faculty using a variety of delivery methods. Some are taught on campus in a traditional classroom environment, some are hybrid, and others are taught completely online. Many of the adjuncts teaching the online courses are physically located throughout the country, creating the additional complication of not only students being distant but the faculty member as well. With so many of the faculty having never set foot on the campus, they naturally possess little or no knowledge of campus services–including library services.

## INTEGRATING INFORMATION LITERACY

The partnership between the MWTC Program and the Library at ASU East has primarily been focused on instruction and the infusion of information literacy into the curriculum. Beginning in 2001, the MWTC Program and Library began an instructional collaboration which has resulted in the revision of current courses, development of new courses, and rewriting of Program Outcomes to incorporate information literacy standards.[1] To this point two courses, "InfoGlut" and "Information Architecture," have been delivered as special topics offerings.

InfoGlut focuses on the impacts of technology on the production, dissemination, and use of information. Course topics include copyright, intellectual property, organization and access to information, censorship, privacy, and more. This upper division course emphasizes ACRL Information Literacy Standards 3, 4, and 5 reflecting the critical thinking aspects of incorporating new information with that previously known, selecting information to accomplish a specific purpose, and understanding the economic, legal, social, and ethical issues surrounding information. Information Architecture focuses on the organization of information for effective retrieval with an emphasis on electronic environments. As designers of multimedia documents, students will learn to effectively classify and categorize information as well as to apply metadata and controlled vocabulary.

Both courses are on the program's agenda to move through the university process to become part of the standing program curriculum. Since the Library at ASU does not, itself, serve as the "home" for academic courses, the information literacy courses offered through the

MWTC Program will continue to serve as a test-case for other academic programs to see how information literacy can effectively become part of their curriculum.

## *INTEGRATING SERVICE*

As integration of information literacy into program and campus curricula continues and expands, it is evident that access to library resources and services needs to be addressed. Distance learning has, to some extent, provided programs with the flexibility to overcome resource limitations by hiring faculty located in areas outside of Arizona. It has also provided programs with the opportunity to provide students with more flexibility for taking courses that better suit their schedules. However, it has also exacerbated problems with access to library services. Adjunct faculty who are located remote from campus and teach one or two courses a year are unfamiliar with the services provided by the East campus, including the Library.

Budget and resource limitations restrict the amount of outreach that the Library is able to do and curb its ability to provide service. The lack of resources is compounded in the MWTC program. Until January 2004 when a staff member was hired to serve four programs, all administrative tasks in the program were handled by the program head. Although the MWTC Program is not the only department to offer online courses (an Environmental Technology Management Program offers an online MS program which attracts students internationally), our focus here is on the needs of the MWTC Program and the Library's ability to fulfill those needs.

### *Faculty Services*

Current faculty in the MWTC Program consists of one full and one associate professor. The full professor is also program head and most of his time is consumed with administrative duties. A lecturer joined the Program in the Fall 2004 and two additional tenure line faculty will be on board in Fall 2005. In anticipation of this growth, we have discussed and added print materials to the Library collection that will begin to address the research needs of the faculty. However, the amount of material added to this point has been minimal and will need to be extended. Access to core journals in the discipline is provided through full-text indexes and databases. As new faculty join the Program, additional journal subscriptions will need to be reviewed and evaluated depending on research areas and interests.

The range of material that faculty will need, both for their teaching and research, will increase, as one of the areas the program is looking to hire in will be medical rhetoric and health communication. This is an area that fits nicely with other health-related programs in the college (e.g., Nutrition, Exercise and Wellness, and Human Health) but is not an area that has been supported to this point. Faculty will also continue to have access to the Library's document delivery service which provides desktop delivery of materials not available in full-text through a subscription database. This service is currently provided at no charge to those affiliated with ASU East.

### Student Services

Since inception of the MWTC Program in 2000, use of the library has primarily been confined to reserves. Although one of the distance faculty has taken advantage of the Library's services to provide access to materials for his students through online reserves, the remainder have not. Some may encourage students to use a library on one of the other ASU campuses while others simply do not require students to do research or use the Library. The fact that many of the faculty have no contact with the Library also seems to predispose them to simply provide helpful links on class Web sites rather than refer students to library resources. Students may also take classes at any ASU campus and many are more familiar with the resources and services of the larger libraries of the Tempe or West campuses.

Geography may also play a role here, as students prefer to use a library, whether it be another ASU library or a public library, that is close to their home or workplace. Since they can take program classes without coming to the East Campus, they often look for alternative libraries as well. In part this lack of exposure to the Library and to research in general is due to the applied nature of the program and a lack of understanding of how the library and information literacy fit in program goals. While these issues are being addressed by the librarian working with the Program to infuse information literacy, the concern over lack of service from the library to students remains.

This remains problematic from an academic perspective as well. One of the skills students, including students in applied programs, need to learn is that the information they need is often stored in designated repositories or accessed through databases. Assignments that use library services support these skills. Students often approach information seeking with the attitude that "all" information is available on the Internet for free or that the free information available via the Web is "good enough." Guiding students away from this perception and to the understanding that more relevant and useful information is available in licensed databases is a challenge with all students, but particularly in the case of students who are balancing school and work and family and want very directed and quick research results.

Raising awareness of library services may be one way of alleviating this problem. For example, faculty can be encouraged to link directly to Library services from their course sites (whether in Blackboard or on course Web sites) so that students have ready access to them. Sometimes just informing new faculty who are not physically located on the campus that this possibility exists is a positive act.

As information literacy becomes a core focus of MWTC courses, the need for access to research materials will increase. Many students currently perceive of the Library's resources as inadequate due to its hybrid nature and small print collection. Awareness and understanding of the Library's indexes, databases, and document delivery service should improve this situation. This awareness can be emphasized by coursework that demonstrates that much workplace information is accessed by similar means. Through consortial arrangements with the other ASU campuses and public universities in Arizona, East Library provides access to a wealth of indexes and databases, many of which are full-text. Remote access is provided through a proxy service. Students are generally unaware of this service and lack information on how to establish and use an account. The problem is exacerbated by the fact that many faculty, especially the adjunct faculty, are also unaware of the service. Links to help guides and instructions may be provided so that students are encouraged to use the resources available to them.

Access to books and articles not available physically in the East Library is provided through the Library's document delivery service. Materials are accessed from the larger print collections of the ASU Tempe and West campuses or purchased from commercial vendors when unavailable from another campus. Articles are scanned and made available electronically to the user in pdf format. Turnaround time for requested materials is approximately 24-48 hours and is currently provided at no cost to the student.

Research assistance is available to students via e-mail, text chat, and voice-over-IP. MWTC students have rarely taken advantage of this service; whether due to lack of assignments requiring research or lack of awareness is currently unknown. However, due to the online nature of MWTC courses, it would seem logical that providing direct access to the Library's electronic reference service could potentially increase the likelihood of students using it. The Library uses OCLC's QuestionPoint software. This software allows for a seamless integration of electronic reference services and is the only software that at this time allows for voice-over-IP assistance. A small client program attaches a button onto the user's browser when viewing the Library's Web site to allow for connection to the service. Adding the button to program desktops, and encouraging students to download the client on their home computers may be some strategies to increase student awareness of the Library's presence and ability to assist with research questions. OCLC is also planning an enhancement to the software that would allow it to be embedded into Blackboard course management software. This may be a key improvement and may allow research assistance to be rooted directly into students' course sites so that it is easily accessible when needed.

Even without the ability to integrate the OCLC software into Blackboard, opening up more communication with the distant faculty that ensures that they know of the online reference services that are being offered may allow them to build more research-based assignments into their courses. This would be especially helpful in several of the program's introductory courses.

## WHEN GOOD INTENTIONS ARE NOT ENOUGH

Despite all the good results that have already taken place as well as the potential future benefits from the information literacy collaboration between the Library and the MWTC Program at ASU East, we still have been unable to achieve some very basic goals such as ensuring that all undergraduates in the program are engaging in assignments that use the already existing resources provided by the ASU East Library. The easy answer to this is the usual complaint of inadequate resources. We have already mentioned that the full-time staff for the MWTC Program has been two faculty. The professional staff of the Library consists of a Director and two librarians. However, inadequate resources, especially insufficient professionals–both librarians and faculty, are a reality that is endemic to most institutions. It is also a reality that is unlikely to change.

We hope that by understanding this reality, we will be more able to take steps to work around it. Ironically, the success of the information literacy program exacerbates the resource problems. As information literacy continues to be integrated into program curricula, students (and faculty) will increasingly expect and demand that resources be accessible and that services be provided locally. From the academic program perspective, it seems clear that we must find ways to better educate our adjunct faculty, both local and distant, to the resources already available. The usual ways of making all faculty, including adjuncts, aware of services such as presentations by library staff at meetings, flyers, brochures, and the like, are impossible. While there is an emerging stable pool of adjuncts, such populations, by their very nature, tend to be volatile. It is normal for new adjuncts to be hired almost at the start of the semester. Expecting those hires to automatically know of available library resources is unrealistic. The real challenge is for the program and the library to provide a means that will provide all faculty, continuing and new, adjuncts and full-time, local and distant, the kind of information they need to create information literacy-based assignments.

## CONCLUSION

Increasing the visibility and use of Library research materials and services is essential for building on the success of the planned information literacy program. While logistical solutions can help from the perspective of increasing visibility and usage, the issue of resource limitations cannot be ignored. Though resource limitations are a campus-wide issue as enrollment grows rapidly, the demands on the Library are especially problematic as the need for service rises and the Library's needs often appear invisible. What we have been able to see in the collaboration between the Library and the MWTC Program is that significant positive accomplishments (rewriting outcomes, new courses, integration into program curriculum) only go so far in an environment when resources that do exist may be ignored because they remain invisible. Part of what this means is that it is necessary to change the culture of bad times from one of merely bemoaning our fate. Instead, we need to move to recognize existing realities so we can make the most effective use of all resources–including those that are not readily evident. Our next challenge is to create a means to communicate to all program instructors what resources are available and to give them some suggested ways to integrate information literacy goals into each course's syllabus.

While the resources are limited, we are still off to a good start. We have established a good working relationship. The Library is equipped to work with students whose educational experience may primarily be virtual. The MWTC Program realizes that it is in its students' best interests to integrate information literacy outcomes. What looks like the next step is for the Library, along with the MWTC Program, to more effectively communicate existing resources to all program faculty. Then the MWTC Program, in collaboration with the Library, needs to begin to create sample information literacy-based assignments so program instructors can begin to create new, information literacy-enhanced syllabi.

## NOTE

1. D'Angelo, B. J. & Maid, B. M. (2004). Moving Beyond Definitions: Implementing Information Literacy Across the Curriculum. *Journal of Academic Librarianship*, *30* (3), 212-217.

# Embedding Library Reference Services in Online Courses

Jamie P. Kearley
Lori Phillips

**SUMMARY.** The University of Wyoming has a long tradition of providing library services to distance education students. As technology changed and enhanced the delivery mode of distance education courses, the library altered the ways in which it offered services to distance learners. The institution was an early adopter of Web courses, so offering library support in this new environment was a natural expansion of our services. This expansion supports the goals of the ACRL Guidelines for Distance Learning Library Services and the goals of the University. This article will describe the integration of library reference services into online courses. *[Article copies available for a fee from The Haworth Document Delivery Service: 1-800-HAWORTH. E-mail address: <docdelivery@haworthpress.com> Website: <http://www.HaworthPress.com> © 2004 by The Haworth Press, Inc. All rights reserved.]*

**KEYWORDS.** Distance education, online courses, reference services, bibliographic instruction, Internet, college and university libraries

---

Jamie P. Kearley (jkearley@uwyo.edu) is Outreach Librarian, and Lori Phillips (lphil@uwyo.edu) is Associate Dean, both at the University of Wyoming, 1000 East University, Department 3334, Laramie, WY 82071.

[Haworth co-indexing entry note]: "Embedding Library Reference Services in Online Courses." Kearley, Jamie P., and Lori Phillips. Co-published simultaneously in *Internet Reference Services Quarterly* (The Haworth Information Press, an imprint of The Haworth Press, Inc.) Vol. 9, No. 1/2, 2004, pp. 65-76; and in: *Improving Internet Reference Services to Distance Learners* (ed: William Miller, and Rita M. Pellen) The Haworth Information Press, an imprint of The Haworth Press, Inc., 2004, pp. 65-76. Single or multiple copies of this article are available for a fee from The Haworth Document Delivery Service [1-800-HAWORTH. 9:00 a.m. - 5:00 p.m. (EST). E-mail address: docdelivery@haworthpress.com].

http://www.haworthpress.com/web/IRSQ
© 2004 by The Haworth Press, Inc. All rights reserved.
Digital Object Identifier: 10.1300/J136v09n01_06

## INTRODUCTION

The popularity of distance education in recent years has resulted in a dramatic increase in the number of courses and degrees offered by universities and colleges and the number of students taking these courses (Hansen, 2001; U.S. Department of Education, 2002). Traditionally, these courses were taught in a variety of ways, such as correspondence, instructor at a remote site, audio conference, or through video (live interactive or prerecorded).

The advent of the Web lent itself well to a new method for course delivery: online courses. Prior to the emergence of Web courses, constraints of time, distance, and technology restricted the expansion of distance education. In contrast, online courses offer the opportunity for asynchronous instruction and learning, thereby globally expanding the boundaries of the university. Online courses have become quite popular because students appreciate the convenience that enables them to take a course at any time from any location (Tabs, 2003). This national trend of offering online courses and degrees is prospering at the University of Wyoming.

Librarians at the University of Wyoming realize that demand for online instruction is driven by the personal circumstances and preferences of our students. We believe that library services are integral to the academic success of these students. Furthermore, we believe providing instruction and reference services to all students regardless of location will assist them in developing information literacy skills that will enrich them for a lifetime. Consequently, we are continually extending and adopting new services to support academic endeavors. This article discusses recent efforts to serve the needs of online students.

## HISTORY OF DISTANCE EDUCATION AT UNIVERSITY OF WYOMING

The University of Wyoming has a longstanding commitment to distance education, having offered extension courses to the citizens of Wyoming since 1891 (Johnson, 1987). It is the only four-year university in a state of 97,914 square miles and a population under 500,000. The University's land grant mission has combined with factors such as the geographical dispersion of students, sparse population, and a harsh climate to advance the University's commitment to distance education. The first formal extension courses offered by the University were short courses in agriculture conducted in various communities around the state and it was not long before demand for courses in other subject areas arose. Teacher training was a second prominent focus of early outreach education. Efforts to deliver education to Wyoming citizens coalesced in 1983, when the University established the Office of Teleconferencing and began using technology to deliver courses and degree programs in a number of disciplines. The name has changed several times since then and today it is known as the Outreach School; classes are referred to as outreach courses.

The University of Wyoming was an early adopter of Web courses with the introduction of Online UW in the spring of 1999. In just five years, course offerings have expanded from 10 courses with enrollment of 153, to 65 courses with enrollment of 1,466. Currently three bachelor's degrees, three master's degrees and two certificates can be completed through Online UW courses. The most impressive enrollment increases at the University of Wyoming have occurred in the online classes offered through the Outreach School, our distance education unit. While UW's on-campus enrollments have long hovered around 10,000 students, outreach headcounts now contribute almost 3,000 additional students, a growing number of whom are enrolling in online courses. This trend is obvious in the percentage of total enrollments in online courses. In 1999, 10% of UW distance enrollment was in online courses. By fall 2003 the percentage had risen to 41%.

Although the distance education program originally functioned apart from campus programs, in recent years the two have merged. The Outreach School does not have a separate faculty to deliver degree programs. Rather, it depends upon university faculty to deliver instruction. Courses are cross-listed and faculty teaching distance courses are all affiliated with a campus department. This close integration with academic units is a real strength of the outreach effort. Our philosophy is best summarized by University President Philip Dubois' statement, "we are one university with one student body."

## *LIBRARY OUTREACH SERVICES FOR DISTANCE LEARNERS*

The Libraries support the University's outreach mission by providing library services to distance education students. This service practice is founded on two assumptions that have guided University of Wyoming library outreach services for twenty years.

- Library priorities should be founded on institutional priorities, and
- Distance learners and faculty are entitled to the same resources and services as the campus population.

This practice reflects the major premise of the ACRL Guidelines for Distance Learning, 2003 that "Access to adequate library services and resources is essential for the attainment of superior academic skills in post-secondary education, regardless of where students, faculty, and programs are located. Members of the distance learning community are entitled to library services and resources equivalent to those provided for students and faculty in traditional campus settings."

Current library services for distance students at the University of Wyoming include:

- Reference assistance via a nationwide toll-free telephone number, e-mail, and online chat,
- Document delivery and interlibrary loan for supplying material not owned by our library,
- Web access to library catalogs, databases, electronic books, journals, and reserves, and
- A librarian to oversee library outreach services.

The cost of services and resources is absorbed by the Libraries' budget and is offered free of charge to distance learners.

The role of the outreach librarian has changed dramatically over the past 20 years. This specialized reference position has always been responsible for managing library services to distance learners and as such has been the primary contact and provider of reference service, mediated searching, document delivery, and instruction. Library outreach services and off-campus students were viewed as "different" at a time when access to resources and librarians was severely restricted by proximity to the campus library.

Advances in technology have directly affected the ways in which distance clientele are served. Technology has eliminated the need for mediated searches and increased the means, speed, and efficiency of document delivery. However, responsibilities for technical advice and system interface have been added to the job (Matson, 1997; Gandhi, 2004). The Web accessible digital library of today requires knowledge of proxy servers, copyright, and monitoring of library Web pages for content, organization, and navigation. Furthermore, the outreach librarian has been proactive in initiatives that resulted in the addition of an online tutorial, e-reserves, and online chat reference service.

The most recent change occurred in the summer of 2003 when we began routing e-mail and toll-free telephone requests to the central reference desk rather than directly to the outreach librarian. All reference librarians began serving distance learners. This decision was made for several reasons. First, the distinctions had blurred between on-campus and off-campus users of the library because anyone using the library from outside the campus network had to do so via the proxy server. Increasingly, our campus students and faculty were using the library remotely so all reference librarians needed to be proficient in serving everyone. Second, was the desire to expand the hours of reference service to evenings and weekends for remote users without adding additional staff. Finally, all reference librarians were assigned times for handling online chat and consequently had to be able to answer questions from remote users.

## *COOPERATIVE RELATIONSHIPS WITH THE OUTREACH SCHOOL*

The extensive array of library services for UW distance learners is feasible because of a close working relationship between the Outreach School and the Libraries. Both units have a strong commitment to the principle that geography ought not make a difference for student learning. Consequently, there is a high degree of synergism in the relationship between the two units. Library services for distance students are integral to the mission and the academic plans of both units. The academic plan of Outreach Credit Programs states "the Division will initiate cooperative efforts to design and implement the enhancement of student-centered support services and efficient administrative systems. These initiatives will involve the academic departments, the Graduate School, [and] the Libraries" (2004). The Libraries academic plan mirrors this sentiment when it states "the Libraries have a strong commitment to providing remote users with equitable access to library services and resources regardless of location. UW students, faculty, and staff can access our online databases, books, and journals from anywhere using a proxy server to authenticate their UW affiliation" (2004).

Ongoing dialogue between librarians; Outreach School administrators, instructional designers, academic advisers; University faculty, information technology staff; and Wyoming community college librarians is essential. The Libraries actively seek ways to engage each of these constituent groups in conversations, both formal and informal, about matters of mutual concern. These relationships have been developed over time and are a testament to the careful planning and vision of Library and Outreach School administrators during the 1980s. Librarians attempt to meet with Outreach School administration and academic designers once a semester to compare notes and make sure our services are visible and appropriate to their needs. Our Outreach librarian is proactive in contacting university faculty who are teaching outreach courses to make them aware of the scope of library services available to their students.

Communication with campus information technology staff is frequent and tends to deal with patron authentication, security, and firewall issues. We have a formal agreement with Casper College, a Wyoming community college, to provide library services to a large cohort group of UW outreach students taking classes and pursuing degrees under the auspices of the UW/CC Center. There are a number of other agreements between UW and Wyoming community colleges that require some level of attention in terms of library support. Since community college libraries host University of Wyoming outreach students in their libraries with regularity, they benefit from having current information about our resources and services, and we need current information about their needs.

## INTEGRATION OF LIBRARY SERVICES
## INTO ONLINE COURSES

Offering library support in the online environment was a natural expansion of our services. Since the UW Libraries already had a robust structure of policies and services relating to distance students and their library needs, moving into a new arena was a logical progression. Prior to the introduction of Online UW in the spring of 1999, the Libraries sat in on initial discussions between the Outreach School and its partner eCollege.com to determine how to serve the library needs of the online population. Embedding the Library and its services into online courses has included two components. The first component involved making library resources accessible within the online courses. The second component involved integrating information literacy/bibliographic instruction into online courses.

Although embedding library reference services and resources into online courses was easily accomplished with links to the library from the Online UW course platform, links alone were insufficient. As is the case in most libraries, access to electronic resources is restricted and accomplished through a proxy server that authenticates and authorizes use of licensed resources. While proxy servers facilitate access to licensed resources, they are not transparent to students who must use them. Instructions for creating a username and password and using the proxy server were needed. In addition, questions about requesting materials, document delivery, assistance from a librarian, and cost of service had to be addressed.

In the past five years, we have refined the links and information based on student problems and confusion. Currently, the basic links are:

- Getting started: doing research from a distance
- UW Libraries–Search for books, articles, subject resources, and more
- Ask Us–Chat online, e-mail, or speak with a librarian
- Interlibrary loan form–Request materials be sent free of charge
- Reserves
- Style guides and writing resources
- *TIP–Tutorial for Info Power*

Each link opens a new window so students can move easily between their course and the library. "Getting started: doing research from a distance" describes as succinctly as possible obtaining a username and password, finding books, finding articles, accessing e-reserves, requesting materials, and getting help from a librarian.

Instruction has also evolved over time and been more challenging and time consuming than making resources accessible. Initially it was done one on one via e-mail exchanges or through telephone conversations. These options continue to be available but two other instructional methods that are more proactive are also used. First, the distance-learning librarian, in conjunction with reference librarians, was instrumental in developing *TIP*, an interactive Web tutorial that has been in use since fall 2001. *TIP* was designed as an introduction to information literacy skills and is currently used primarily by first-year undergraduates, although it is also used in some upper division and graduate courses. In approximately 45 minutes, *TIP* provides a foundation for thinking strategically about information and research. (For a thorough discussion of

*TIP* see Kearley, 2002 and Phillips, 2003.) Five modules teach students how to:

- Investigate a topic
- Search for information
- Locate information in the library
- Evaluate the quality of information
- Utilize the information in papers, speeches, or projects

While *TIP* provides a basis for our campus-wide information literacy initiative, it is not completed in isolation. Information literacy is a core component of our first-year University Studies Program. Courses for this program are rooted in an academic discipline. Faculty members incorporate information literacy into course objectives, teaching methods, assignments, and assessment criteria. Completing *TIP* and passing the quiz is only a piece of the campus initiative. Typically a face-to-face class with a subject librarian complements *TIP*. The librarian focuses on bridging the gap between the theoretical and the reality of the electronic and physical library environment. Teaching information literacy calls for a partnership between librarians and teaching faculty. At the University of Wyoming, the endorsement of information literacy as a skill needed for graduation has allowed librarians to partner with faculty in a meaningful way to realize this goal. The online Nursing program is a case in point.

## CASE STUDY:
## NURSING INSTRUCTIONAL SUPPORT

Nursing is a discipline that has recognized the need for information literacy. According to Shorten (2001, 86):

> In the new millennium, healthcare environments will increasingly demand nurses to be flexible, innovative and "information literate" professionals, able to solve complex patient problems by utilizing the best available evidence.

> A demand for safe and effective healthcare requires the necessary skills in order to incorporate research findings into practice.

The University of Wyoming Fay W. Whitney School of Nursing has whole-heartedly adopted this position and integrated it into its *mission and philosophy*.

The faculty believe that professional nurses function in the roles of carer/helper/counselor; advocate; consumer of research. . . . Research links the science and practice of nursing. The role of consumer of research is demonstrated by participating in, valuing, and using research findings to improve practice and to modify care based on a changing and expanding body of knowledge. (2004)

Consequently, Nursing faculty members have worked closely with the outreach librarian to ensure that Nursing students learn how to use the library to conduct research. Nursing students are distributed throughout the United States and overseas so it is imperative that they have access to an academic library and the ability to use it.

The Nursing program has taken full advantage of the *TIP* tutorial and requires students in two different research courses to complete it. One course is required for the RN/BSN degree and the other for the Master's in Nursing. While *TIP* provides a foundation for thinking strategically about information, it is supplemented in online Nursing courses with an assignment that focuses on the mechanics of using the digital library. Students in both courses obtain a username and password, find a book in the catalog, locate a research article in a health database and an online journal, and e-mail a full-text article. Graduate students have the additional tasks of using the advanced searching capabilities, creating a list of marked records, and using the linking feature from the article database to the catalog. This assignment is completed very early in the semester so that students are equipped to conduct the research required by the Nursing faculty.

We consider these efforts a strong beginning but believe more instruction for online Nursing students is warranted. We are in the initial stages of developing an additional tutorial for Nursing specific databases. In particular, we want Nursing students to be proficient in searching health databases and Web sites that are free and accessible to the public so that after they graduate and no longer have access to the university's licensed databases they can continue to "incorporate research findings into practice."

We also want to promote more communication between online Nursing students and librarians. All students are e-mailed a reminder about library outreach services two to three weeks into each semester. However, our online chat and evening and weekend reference hours are underused and need to be marketed. Another possibility is to include in the assignment the requirement to consult a librarian about research strategy.

## *CONCLUSION*

Two factors influence future consideration of how to most appropriately provide library reference services to University of Wyoming distance learners. First, the profile of an "average" outreach student will continue to change. To be sure, there will remain a group of people for whom taking classes on the main campus is impossible. The challenge of keeping their learning environment personal and connected will remain with us. We will continue to dedicate a library faculty position to working directly with students and instructors who reside outside the main campus community who are truly distance learners.

At the same time, many campus students are beginning to perceive outreach classes, particularly online classes, as a desirable option. There is no longer a distinct demarcation between regular classes and outreach classes. The shift in enrollment growth to the online sector is indicative that on campus students are taking them in preference to courses relying on synchronous delivery. We anticipate that this group of students may find using the library online a better option than physically coming into the building, despite the fact they are able to do so. Our challenge will be to provide needed services to them in an effective and efficient manner. All librarians must possess strong knowledge and expertise in dealing with issues of remote access to the library, as this becomes the norm rather than the exception.

Second, expectations upon librarians to provide expertise and leadership in teaching and evaluating information literacy will continue to grow. We must seek ways to work in collaboration with faculty and make our expertise more generally available to the online community. The Outreach librarian will continue to seek ways to make faculty aware of the existence of the information literacy tutorial, and its use in meeting graduation requirements. Currently, Wyoming community college transfer students are allowed to fulfill the information literacy requirement of the University Studies Program by taking the tutorial and passing the quiz with a grade of 70% or higher. Information about the tutorial and the availability of a librarian to work with classes will be shared with Wyoming community college academic advisors to enable transfer students to meet this requirement. We will explore the feasibility of developing an online course that will be an option for students seeking to fulfill the University Studies requirement for information literacy.

All of this will require the Outreach librarian to devote more time to online students. If this is done on a student-by-student basis, instruction will be extremely time consuming and labor intensive. Therefore, methods to instruct an entire online class will need to be developed. Two possibilities to be explored are e-mailing a series of library briefings to online students (with permission from the course instructor) and developing subject specific tutorials. In addition, we plan to work cooperatively with the Outreach School to include information about our chat reference service and evening reference hours in the orientation packets sent to every outreach student.

We will continue to adhere to the principle that we seek to meet varied needs by services appropriate to student circumstances. We realize that there can be no one-size-fits-all approach to meeting the reference and instructional needs of online students. Our challenge is to be flexible in response to the ever-changing face of distance education.

## REFERENCES

ACRL Guidelines for Distance Learning Library Services. American Library Association. 2003. Accessed June 11, 2004, http://www.ala.org/ala/acrl/acrlstandards/guidelinesdistancelearning.htm.

Giles, Kara L. "Reflections on a privilege." *C&RL News*, 65:5 (2004): 261-263.

Gandhi, Smiti. "Academic librarians and distance education." *Reference & User Services Quarterly*, 43:2 (2004): 138-154.

Hansen, Brian. "Distance Learning." *The CQ Researcher Online* 11, no. 42 (December 7, 2001): 993-1016. http://library.cqpress.com/cqresearcher.

Hardy, Deborah. *Wyoming University: The first 100 years 1886-1986*. Laramie, WY: University of Wyoming, 1986.

Johnson, Jean. "Two models for providing library services to off-campus students in Wyoming." In *The Off-campus Services Conference Proceedings* (ed. B. M. Lessin). Mount Pleasant, MI: Central Michigan University Press, 1987: 135-142.

Kearley, Jamie, and Lori Phillips. "Distilling the Information Literacy Standards: Less Is More." Co-published simultaneously in *Journal of Library Administration* 37 (2002): 411-424, and *Distance Learning Library Services: The Tenth Off-Campus Library Services Conference* (ed. Patrick B. Mahoney) (2002): 411-424.

Matson, Lisa Dallape and David J. Bonski, "Do Digital Libraries Need Librarians? An Experiential Dialogue." *Online*, 21:6 (1997). Accessed June 17, 2004, http://www.onlinemag.net/NovOL97/matson11.html.

Phillips, Lori, and Jamie Kearley. "TIP: Tutorial for Information Power and Campus-Wide Information Literacy." *Reference Services Review*, 31 (2003).

Schloman, Barbara F. "Information literacy: The benefits of partnership." *Online Journal of Issues in Nursing*, (2001). Accessed June 2, 2004, http://www.nursingworld.org/ojin/infocol/info_5.htm.

Shorten, Allison, Margaret C. Wallace, and Patrick A. Crookes. "Developing information literacy: A key to evidence-based nursing." *International Nursing Review*, 48 (2001): 86-92.

U.S. Department of Education, National Center for Educational Statistics. *The Condition of Education 2002*, NCES 2002-025 (Washington DC: U.S. Government Printing Office, 2002) 102.

University of Wyoming Fay W. Whitney School of Nursing. *Mission and Philosophy*. Accessed June 17, 2004, http://uwadmnweb.uwyo.edu/nursing/aboutschool/missionphilosophy.asp.

University of Wyoming Libraries. *Academic Plan*. Accessed July 20, 2004, http://www-lib.uwyo.edu/movingforward/LibrariesAcademicPlan.pdf.

University of Wyoming Outreach Credit Programs. *Academic Plan*. Accessed July 20, 2004, http://outreach.uwyo.edu/academicplan/ocp.htm.

Waits, T., and L. Lewis, "Distance Education at Degree Granting Postsecondary Institutions: 2000-2001," NCES 2003-017. Washington, DC: Government Printing Office, 2003. Accessed June 21, 2004, http://nces.ed.gov/pubsearch/pubsinfo.asp?pubid=2003017.

# Got Distance Services?
# Marketing Remote Library Services
# to Distance Learners

James Fisk
Terri Pedersen Summey

**SUMMARY.** Distance learning students may not think of the "campus" library as the first place to fulfill their information needs and may not even be aware of the services available to them. One way to reach these students is to adopt and adapt marketing techniques from the business world. This article examines the findings of a survey conducted at Emporia State University concerning the awareness of distance learning services. It will also examine marketing techniques and illustrate how they can be applied to increase awareness of reference support services for distance learners. *[Article copies available for a fee from The Haworth Document Delivery Service: 1-800-HAWORTH. E-mail address: <docdelivery@haworthpress.com> Website: <http://www.HaworthPress.com> © 2004 by The Haworth Press, Inc. All rights reserved.]*

**KEYWORDS.** Off-campus library services, distance education, distant learners, marketing, academic library

James Fisk (fisk@morningside.edu) is Reference/Bibliographic Librarian, Morningside College, Hickman-Johnson-Furrow Library, 1601 Morningside Avenue, Sioux City, IA 51106. Terri Pedersen Summey (summeyte@emporia.edu) is Head of Distance and Access Services, Emporia State University Libraries and Archives, 1200 Commercial–Box 4051, Emporia, KS 66801.

[Haworth co-indexing entry note]: "Got Distance Services? Marketing Remote Library Services to Distance Learners." Fisk, James, and Terri Pedersen Summey. Co-published simultaneously in *Internet Reference Services Quarterly* (The Haworth Information Press, an imprint of The Haworth Press, Inc.) Vol. 9, No. 1/2, 2004, pp. 77-91; and: *Improving Internet Reference Services to Distance Learners* (ed: William Miller, and Rita M. Pellen) The Haworth Information Press, an imprint of The Haworth Press, Inc., 2004, pp. 77-91. Single or multiple copies of this article are available for a fee from The Haworth Document Delivery Service [1-800-HAWORTH, 9:00 a.m. - 5:00 p.m. (EST). E-mail address: docdelivery@haworthpress.com].

## INTRODUCTION

Distance learning programs continue to proliferate at academic institutions. The faculty and students involved in these programs also continue to grow in numbers. These remote learning communities present both opportunities and challenges for the academic library. In response, libraries are not only adapting traditional services to meet the needs of these learners, but are also offering specifically tailored new services. However, for these programs to be successful, the students being served must also be aware of the support and services available to them through the library. Without such awareness, the services will go unused. Through a survey conducted with students at the School of Library and Information Management, the librarians at Emporia State University learned that making distance students aware of services is a key to the success of distance learning library service programming.

## THE SURVEY

During the spring and summer of 2000, a student at the School of Library and Information Management (SLIM) at Emporia State University collaborated with librarians of the University Libraries and Archives to assess the library needs of students enrolled at SLIM. The assessment came in the form of a 30-question survey sent to over 400 SLIM students with only a few of these students residing in or near the Emporia campus. He solicited information in regard to student demographics, their access to information, and their attitudes and beliefs as relating to library services available to them as tuition-paying students of Emporia State.

A major finding of the study indicated that for most students, the William Allen White Library at Emporia State played only a small role in their academic lives. In addition, many of these students generally had little or no knowledge of the library services to which they were entitled. For example, full access to FirstSearch, a staple of online databases, was available to all students of SLIM. Yet, 53% of those students responding to the survey were either unaware of its availability or rarely made use of it.

In response to the findings of the survey, the following recommendation was made to the administration of the William Allen White Library:

Aggressively market remote library services! These services have no value if they are not used. One student's bulleted recommendation is brief but insightful. "Better advertisement of the library services than now provided to distance students, I had not a clue!" (Fisk 2000, 8)

The School of Library and Information Management is not the only division to offer distance education programs at Emporia State. The Office of Lifelong Learning coordinates a number of other programs. Students of the Teachers College may complete any number of different master degrees either exclusively online or by enrolling in classroom courses taught at sites other than in Emporia and through the Internet. These students may also add endorsements to their teacher licensures through an online curriculum. Programs extend to undergraduates as well. They may earn a Bachelor's of Integrated Studies on the Internet or complete a Bachelor's of Science Degree in either Business or Education at several sites throughout the state of Kansas.

The students enrolled in the online or Internet enhanced programs are by virtue of technology and/or their place of residence, distance students. As such, they likely do not have convenient access to the campus-based William Allen White Library. Nevertheless, the Library can play an important role in their academic lives.

To be able to reach these distance students, the library has worked hard to develop new services and provide resources. William Allen White Library purchases both e-books and databases with full-text content to be able to provide resources in electronic formats. Access to materials and databases is available off-campus through e-reserves, document delivery, and a proxy server. Library staff may be contacted for assistance through a variety of methods including a toll free number and chat reference. But in order for students to use these valuable services and resources, they need to know that they are available.

## WHY MARKET DISTANCE REFERENCE SERVICES?

These survey results highlighted a severe need for some kind of marketing to occur and prompted the library administration and staff to look at developing a marketing campaign in order to promote library services and e-resources to its distance learning community. Since a university library is considered to be central to the educational mission of an institution, one may not understand the need to market such a visible resource. Although the library may have a large physical presence on the "brick and mortar" campus, it may not be so obvious to those at a distance from the campus. In the past, when it came to the provision of information, the academic library enjoyed a monopoly. This is no longer true, because even "traditional" college students physically at a university may look to other sources to meet their information and research needs.

Several reasons may be cited as justification for the expenditure of efforts associated with marketing library services to the students of distance education. According to the Guidelines for Distance Learning Library Services, institutions of higher learning and their libraries "must meet the needs of all their faculty, students, and academic support staff, wherever these individuals are located." As delineated in the "Guidelines," it is the responsibility of the librarian-administrator in charge of distance library services to discover the needs of the community being served, provide equitable services and resources, and "promote library support services to the distance learning community" (ACRL DLS, 2000). Thus, the "Guidelines" specifically mandate promotion of the resources and services available to those involved in distance learning at academic institutions. McDonald and Keegan, in their book *Marketing Plans That Work*, echo the call from the ACRL by observing that "the central idea of marketing is to match the capabilities of a company with the needs and wants of customers to achieve a mutually beneficial relationship" (1997, 1). Operating a customer oriented library requires using business marketing techniques to not only market services, but to also identify the needs of customers and to tailor services to meet those needs.

But the reasons for promoting what is available go beyond adhering to the "Guidelines." Similar to that of many other academic libraries, the stated *Mission* of the William Allen White Library in part, is to provide "access to resources in print, multi-media, and electronic formats" (University Libraries and Archives, 2001). If students remain unaware of these resources, there is no access. This may be particularly true in the case of distance education as there is no "physical proximity" to a library in this learning environment (Ghandi, 2003).

Marketing may also pay for itself in the form of funding during the institutional budgeting process as a library as a cost center within a university competes for scarce resources. Edinger (1980) touches upon these points when she advocates for library marketing in this way:

> If the library is seen by its clientele and onlookers as vital to the university or to the community, it will be less in the position of

having to justify the existence of its program and policies. . . . By actively marketing the library's services, the library can reach more potential users, encourage use of the library's resources, and work towards becoming an indispensable source of information for the community. (p. 328-329)

A marketing effort may also overcome what often faces libraries, a need for "brand identity." This is a marketing concept that refers to what consumers envision when they think of a product, service, or institution. It includes the look and feel of a library, its slogan and logo. A "brand identity" may also point to what a library does well or to the kinds of services it provides. Unfortunately, librarians are not very good at publicizing what they do or how well they do it. People are not aware of the amount of work that transpires in libraries and thus take information professionals and the work they do for granted. In this electronic age, to be able to sustain old customers and gain new ones, libraries must take a proactive approach to marketing their resources and services.

Many authors write about marketing principles and strategies in the context of libraries with four walls. Wolpert addresses issues associated with, and unique to, library services delivered at a distance when she writes "libraries should approach support to distance education as a new business opportunity, utilizing techniques of market evaluation and analysis" (1998, 21). She also discusses the need for a "brand identity" to create a unique look and feel for the library that becomes clearly recognizable by distance learning students.

Perhaps the greatest challenge academic libraries face in distance education is the potential loss of "brand identity." When students and faculty must visit the library to find what they need, the value of the library's products and services is immediately obvious. . . . One emerging threat to libraries' brand identity is the visibility and credit for the services and products they provide to distance learners. Where the physical library world provides constant reinforcement to the relationship between the library and the material and information a patron needs, the virtual library permits a patron to bookmark a site within the library's electronic connections and never again be reminded of how that product or service is made possible. . . . Unless a library has created a recognizable "look and feel" that clearly identifies its work, the work may not be attributed to the Library. (Wolpert 1998, 10)

Gandhi makes a strong case in recommending that planned marketing efforts also be extended to both faculty teaching distance courses and administrators. By collaborating with course instructors, librarians can recommend assignments that require library work. In addition, the product that we sell may not be known to adjuncts who so often teach in a distance environment. According to Gandhi, administrators may also not be aware of all of the issues, such as accreditation requirements and the indirect costs associated with course offerings delivered in a distance setting. "The increased visibility will ensure that librarians have a seat at the table when important technology and fiscal decisions related to distance education are made" (2003).

## HOW TO CONDUCT A MARKETING CAMPAIGN

The literature offers a number of suggested strategies to library administrators and planners contemplating the development of a marketing campaign. These strategies are also applicable to distance services. The State Library of Ohio, in *Marketing & Libraries DO Mix: A Handbook for Library and Information Centers*, lists six elements of effective library marketing (1993, 8). *Self-assessment* is a process by which an information agency identifies the services that it provides and the level of quality with which each is delivered. *Market definition* is an activity during which the patron population is identified. During this phase of planning, the authors of the handbook recommend to library professionals that they categorize and segment the existing and future patron population, review their agency's mission statement to ensure that all patron groups are specifically named, and prioritize the needs of these constituent groups.

*Product planning* is a determination of what services are required by the library's patrons and the development of plans to deliver them. This information may be obtained through surveys, individual interviews, and focus groups. *Product creation* is the development of new and enhanced services. The keys to the successful implementation of a new product set are a focus on quality, the use of project management processes, flexibility during the planning process and frequent communications to patrons and management.

*Selling* is an ongoing process. In addition to informing patron groups of what services are available to them, selling also includes the actual delivery of high-quality service and the continuous evaluation and improvement of those services. *Closing the loop* is reference to the fact that all of these named elements form a network. "The objective is to ensure that information flows freely through that network. Each element provides input to all of the others and receives their feedback. Closing the loop means you must keep each information path open and make certain that feedback is not ignored by customers, management, and the library staff" (State Library of Ohio 1993, 35).

Once a library has identified its market and has positioned itself, it is ready to develop strategies and tactics. Walters suggests a fundamental approach to marketing, known as the four 'P's, *product, price, place, and promotion*, terms coined by Philip Kotler (1986). A *product* strategy includes a clear identification of the services being offered, the features of those services, and how they might benefit customers using those services. *Pricing* is an exercise during which library administrators identify the actual costs of services being delivered and determine charges (if any) to the patron. *Place* simply refers to where a patron is to receive service. In the case of distance education students, this may be via the Internet, by mail, on the telephone, or through a local library. *Promotion* is highly visible. It may include such marketing strategies as advertising, direct mail, telemarketing, public relations, and special events.

Suzanne Walters in *Marketing: A How-To-Do-It Manual for Librarians* describes library marketing in terms similar to the steps identified by the authors of *Marketing & Libraries DO Mix*. She emphasizes the need for a mission statement that clearly states "who is to be served" (p. 3). Walters considers *market definition* and *product planning* as aspects of market research. She recommends in her approach, the notion of *positioning*. "The purpose of a positioning strategy is to create distinction in the minds of your customers between your library's product/service and other similar products/services. Unsupported claims to distinction do not work when promoting your service. . . . You should only promote what you can deliver" (Walters 1992, 33).

When looking at customers, the target market refers to not only those individuals that already use the services and resources of the library, but also those who do not. Thus, the needs of potential customers should be considered along with those of current customers. To those faculty and students at a distance who do not already use the services and resources of the library, the question needs to be posed, "Why not?" Do they have their information needs met elsewhere or are they simply not aware of what the library can offer to them? The answer to that question will provide valuable information to complete the marketing plan, to develop potential services, and to guide the acquisition of appropriate resources.

To be successful, the library needs to approach the resources and services from the view of the customer or to "walk in their shoes." The staff, however, needs to be very honest with itself about the quality of service provided to students, especially those at a distance. If it is concluded that services are inadequate, the question, "Why not?" again should be considered. In working with distance learning communities, a library staff also needs to consider geographic factors and lifestyles when determining and marketing services and resources.

Lebowitz (1998) takes a slightly different approach as she defines library marketing strictly in the context of distance services. She recommends six components.

1. *An assessment* of the target audience and environment might include gathering information and data relative to the existing and future users of library services, faculty attitudes about and usage of the library, distance education program offerings, and course requirements.
2. *An analysis of user needs* and an examination of current marketing practices, is an evaluation of the skills and abilities of the target audience and the effectiveness of library promotion activities.
3. *A mission statement* articulates the philosophy of the library and/or department delivering remote services. A mission statement ought to identify specifically who is to be supported by the library.
4. *The development of objectives and goals* follows the formulation of the mission statement. This process might include a review of existing services and/or consideration of new remote offerings.
5. *An evaluation of the marketing mix* considers the 4 P's of marketing. In a remote service environment, the marketing mix may be very different. Product refers to service rather than to tangibles. Position or place may be subjective and reflects the perceived relevance of the library vis-à-vis the library user. Promotion may often require a visual representation of library service.

> If materials are being developed specifically for the off-campus users, there are some questions which might be considered beyond that of informational correctness. For instance, is there a consistency about the materials that will identify them as directed toward distance users? Is the total package effective? Because first impressions are so important, it can be very advantageous to develop a constant visual image and perhaps a logo for off-cam-

pus students. . . . Having an effective package will draw attention to the services and will aid in the overall impression made by the library and the institution. (Lebowitz 1998, 217)

Price may also become an issue if the institution requires the recovery of costs associated with the provision of remote services.

6. *An evaluation* of the marketing plan consists of a review of its effectiveness as indicated by an increased awareness of library services by the user community, and by a determination of whether or not the library meets the needs of its remote-user base.

As mentioned earlier, the marketing plan will vary with the situation. It needs to identify key issues, serve as a way to mobilize resources and use them efficiently, and include methods to measure accomplishments or results. It is a policy document, a strategic planning document, a management tool, and an implementation document. The plan will also serve as an assessment tool with built-in evaluation processes and measures. Although there is not a set formula to follow, there are certain elements that should be included and particular questions that need answers. It is also important to remember that the marketing plan is never really completed as it will require updating and revision. This goes along with the fact that the planning process is just as important as the final plan. The process forces the library to consider its current situation and the future directions that it would like to go. Throughout the process, staff at all levels should be consulted and involved in creating the final product.

## MARKETING AT EMPORIA STATE

Shortly after the survey was conducted, the faculty and staff of William Allen White Library participated in the process of strategic planning. Several of the core values that emerged from the process directly related to customer service and outreach. The strategic planning process allowed the library faculty and staff to evaluate the environment of the library, celebrate what was being done well, and develop goals to guide future improvements. Participants assessed the current services and resources of the library. A mission and vision emerged from the process to guide the library as it moved forward. And library employees determined that customer service or creating a "user-centered" library was a priority. Providing good customer service includes making customers aware of what is available to them to meet their curricular and research needs.

The literature mentions many elements that make up a successful marketing campaign. One of the key pieces is a marketing plan. The final document written during the strategic planning process had elements that could be used by the library's faculty and staff in creating the marketing plan for both the William Allen White Library and more specifically for Distance Services. The first section of the marketing plan includes an assessment of the library and the environment surrounding it. It includes a SWOT analysis, strengths-weaknesses-threats-opportunities, that examines the strengths and weaknesses of the library along with the opportunities and threats that face it. These are the portions available in the Strategic Plan written for the library.

The sections following the Environmental Analysis in a Marketing Plan include a market analysis or information on the market to be reached; the goals and objectives to attain through the marketing campaign; marketing strategies to reach those goals and objectives; implementation details; and a final evaluation or assessment of the process and product. Because of internal changes within the library, the marketing plan for the William Allen White Library is still in the development stages and has not been formally completed. But some changes have taken place as a result of what was learned from the survey.

At the time during which the survey was conducted, services to meet the needs of distant learners had been developed and electronic resources purchased. Both services and resources were up and available, but intensive marketing did not occur.

The segment to be reached in a marketing campaign targeted to distance library services not only includes students, but others associated with distance learning. At Emporia State University, some of the distance learning programs are taught in cohorts, each having its own administrator and national faculty members. In these instances, not only do the cohort students need to know about services and resources available to them, but also those administrators and part-time national faculty members need to be made aware of what may be accessed from off-campus. Other programs are offered either online or through teleconferencing capabilities using faculty that are on the Emporia State University campus. These faculty members also need to be familiar with the services available to their students to assist them not only in the teaching of their courses, but also in their initial design.

Initial goals and objectives of a marketing campaign such as one at Emporia State might include the following:

1. Work with the Office of Lifelong Learning to identify distance learning students and faculty members to target with direct marketing methods to inform them of resources and services available to them.
2. Promote to students, faculty, and administrators currently involved in distance learning the research and curricula support tools and resources through a variety of methods. In this effort, especially target new faculty and those who are in the process of developing new courses to be offered at a distance.
3. Survey those involved with distance learning to discover their library related needs and their awareness of current library resources and services.
4. Identify students and faculty members that do not currently use the Emporia State University Library discovering how to meet their needs to encourage them to use what is available to them.

The next step is for the library to determine what strategies or action steps will be used to achieve the identified goals. Although the library has not completed this portion of the marketing plan at this time, strides have been made towards achieving some of the listed goals.

One of the findings of the Emporia State survey showed that users did not have a clear idea of where help might be found. Emerging from the aforementioned strategic planning process was the conclusion that there was not a clear contact person for distance library services. This was remedied in early 2001 with the appointment of a distance services librarian. She is not only the point of contact for distance students but is also the primary "marketer" of the library services for distance education students. In this role, she has developed press kits and brochures, both in electronic and print formats. The distance services librarian continually updates these, being sure to highlight services and resources specifically available to distance learning community members. This brochure is distributed on a wide basis and is also made available through the library's Web site. The library also set up telephone access to the library and its staff through a toll free number. Although this seems like a very simple or elementary step, the amount of use that the toll free service has received justifies the cost and causes wonder that its acquisition was not made earlier. The number is publicized through the distance services brochure and also listed prominently on the library's Web site.

The library at Emporia has also taken some steps to establish a "brand or graphic identity." Graphic identity refers to such things as a two- or three-dimensional logo, a slogan, typography, or the use of color. Following the survey in 2001, the library at Emporia State University undertook the task of creating such an identity for itself. Library staff worked with a graphic designer to create a logo for the University Libraries and Archives. This logo is present on the library's home Web page and is starting to appear on library publications. The library staff adapted the slogan of the Department of Lifelong Learning, "Students Going the Distance," to reflect the mission of the library. The library now uses the motto "Helping Students Go the Distance" in its brochures. Soon it will also be present on the redesigned library Web site for distance learners.

For distance students, faculty, and support staff, one of the most important points of service is the library's Web site. This may also be the only "view" of the library at Emporia that some students see. As such, it needs to be clear, informative, and easy to use. Using the William Allen White Library Web site as a marketing tool also allows library services to reach beyond its walls to those faculty and staff that are at a distance from the main campus.

When creating a library Web site for distance users, it is not necessary to reinvent the wheel. During the planning stage of a redesign of the main site of the Emporia State University Libraries and Archives, a Web Advisory Team met and looked at different library sites, selecting those elements that appealed to the team. These choices formed the basis for the Web site redesign. The team designed a banner with crucial links to carry throughout the Web site. Frequently used items and answers to often asked questions enjoy top level status on the site. Library faculty and staff are working to continue to create more informative pages along with online tutorials and research guides to assist distance users in finding resources and using the library. A complete redesign of the distance services page is also now underway. A persistent link to this page is on the courseware used by faculty members in teaching distance learning courses. Having an effective Web site and making crucial information available to users through it, allows libraries to take advantage of technological advances to not only promote the library, but also provide the library with the means to reach out and "virtually" pull users into the library.

## CONCLUSION

Although the Emporia State University Libraries and Archives has come a long way since the initial survey completed in 2000, it still has some distance to go before the marketing campaign targeting distance learners is considered a success. The survey results were very informative and provided a foundation that the library continues to build upon. Marketing is not a linear process that has a clear beginning and end. It requires ongoing evaluation and openness to changing circumstances. Such a change might be in the demographics of a distance learning population. At Emporia State, this data is easily gathered by surveying various population groups enrolled in distance learning and by studying statistics gathered by Emporia State's Office of Lifelong Learning.

Needs may also change over time. As such, it would be advisable to inventory and assess services and resources as they are offered. The library should therefore be prepared to offer new services and strategies when it becomes apparent that the present mix is not meeting the ever-changing needs of a distance learning population.

At Emporia State, the librarians work closely with individual faculty, departments, and schools. They work to stay informed relative to distance education offerings within their areas of liaison. By communicating frequently with their client-faculty, they can advise the distance services librarian of opportunities to promote resources and services. The distance services librarian also collaborates with the department that coordinates the technological infrastructure of distance learning. In addition, during various planning cycles, she facilitates "brown bag" workshops for online faculty to encourage them to integrate library services with online courses.

There are other ways in which the library staff at Emporia can become more involved. Orientation sessions for distance learners using various technological methods such as streaming video and either asynchronous or synchronous chat may be developed. The Library will continue to add to its course reserves materials that are available electronically. In the near future, after policies are finalized and approved, staff will work with more faculty members to offer e-reserves as a part of their online or distance learning courses.

In the past, libraries have not taken a very proactive stance with regards to marketing themselves and their services. In our current technological age, when developments such as the World Wide Web compete with the library as providers of information, libraries, to remain competitive, must become more active in making people aware of what they have to offer. This is especially true in a market where distance learners do not necessarily have the "physically proximate" reminder of library resources. It has also been shown at universities such as Emporia State that the expectations of these students are low as they concern library services.

Using and adapting marketing techniques from the business world is one of the keys to remaining competitive in today's technological environment. Technology has not only changed how the library can market its services, but also to whom the marketing can be targeted. The importance of promoting libraries and what we offer is backed up by the recent proliferation of articles concerning marketing. As the Association of College and Research Libraries (ACRL) emphasizes in its literature for "The Campaign for America's Libraries @ your library: Toolkit for Academic and Research Libraries," academic libraries have important messages that need to be publicized widely. ACRL stresses that librarians are the best advocates for libraries and services offered by libraries.

The messages that the Association developed on behalf of its membership may be used by any academic library as a starting point of a marketing campaign. These are as follows:

- College and research libraries are an essential part of the learning community.
- College and research libraries connect you with a world of knowledge.
- College and research libraries are investing in the future, while preserving the past (Association of College and Research Libraries 2003, 4).

As ACRL points out in its campaign materials, academic libraries have a great story to tell regarding their services and resources. Librarians now need to work even harder to get the word out to distance learning communities without proximity to a "bricks and mortar" library about what is available through the presence of a "virtual" library.

## REFERENCES

Association of College and Research Libraries, @ Your Library Task Force. "The Campaign for America's Libraries @ your library: Toolkit for Academic and Research Libraries." American Library Association, 2003.

Association of College and Research Libraries, Standards Committee. "Information Literacy Competency Standards for Higher Education." American Library Association,

2000. <http://www.ala.org/ala/acrl/acrlstandards/informationliteracycompetency. htm> (accessed June 19, 2004).

Association of College and Research Libraries, Distance Learning Section. Guidelines for Distance Learning Library Services. American Library Association, 2000. <http://www.ala.org/ala/acrl/acrlstandards/guidelinesdistance.htm> (accessed June 19, 2004).

Edinger, J. "Marketing and the Academic Library." *College & Research Libraries* 41, no. 4 (1980): 328-29.

Emporia State University. University Libraries and Archives. "Mission." <http:// www.emporia.edu/libsv/menu1/libinfodep/mission.html> (accessed June 19, 2004).

Fisk, Jim. "A Community Analysis and Library Services Needs Assessment of the Students of the School of Library and Information Management of Emporia State University: An Executive Summary." Unpublished research project, School of Library and Information Management, Emporia State University, 2000.

Ghandi, Smiti, "Academic Librarians and Distance Education: Challenges and Opportunities." *Reference and User Services Quarterly* 43, no. 2 (2003): 138-155.

Kotler, Phillip. *Principles of Marketing.* 3rd ed. Englewood Cliffs, NJ: Prentice Hall, 1986.

Lebowitz, Gloria. "Promoting Off-Campus Library Services: Even a Successful Program Needs a Marketing Plan." *The Eighth Off-Campus Library Services Conference Proceedings.* Mount Pleasant, MI: Central Michigan University, 1998.

McDonald, Malcolm H. B. and Warren J. Keegan. *Marketing Plans that Work.* Boston, MA: Butterworth-Heinemann, 1997.

The State Library of Ohio and H. Baird Tenney et al. *Marketing and Libraries DO Mix: A Handbook for Librarians and Information Centers,* Columbus, OH: The State Library of Ohio, 1993.

Walters, Suzanne. *Marketing: A How-To-Do-It Manual for Librarians,* New York: Neal-Schuman Publishers, Inc., 1992.

Wolpert, Ann J. "Services to Remote Users: Marketing the Library's Role." *Library Trends* 47, no. 1 (1998): 21-41.

# The Walden University Library: Reaching Out and Touching Students

Rita Barsun

**SUMMARY.** Although it is a unit of the Indiana University-Bloomington Libraries, the Walden University Library serves only Walden students and faculty. It is a true virtual library, one that has no print collection but only online databases. Because it is located far from Walden students, faculty, staff, and administration, library personnel put forth great efforts to overcome the negative effects of distance. This article will describe how the library fits into the IUB and Walden institutional structures, and how its librarians and staff proactively connect with the people they serve as Walden experiences fast-moving growth and change. *[Article copies available for a fee from The Haworth Document Delivery Service: 1-800-HAWORTH. E-mail address: <docdelivery@haworthpress.com> Website: <http://www.HaworthPress.com> © 2004 by The Haworth Press, Inc. All rights reserved.]*

**KEYWORDS.** Distance learners, distance library services, library anxiety, organizational change

Rita Barsun (rbarsun@waldenu.edu) is Walden University Librarian, Indiana University-Bloomington, Walden Library, IU Main Library E-164, 1320 East Tenth Street, Bloomington, IN 47405-3907.

[Haworth co-indexing entry note]: "The Walden University Library: Reaching Out and Touching Students." Barsun, Rita. Co-published simultaneously in *Internet Reference Services Quarterly* (The Haworth Information Press, an imprint of The Haworth Press, Inc.) Vol. 9, No. 1/2, 2004, pp. 93-109; and: *Improving Internet Reference Services to Distance Learners* (ed: William Miller, and Rita M. Pellen) The Haworth Information Press, an imprint of The Haworth Press, Inc., 2004, pp. 93-109. Single or multiple copies of this article are available for a fee from The Haworth Document Delivery Service [1-800-HAWORTH, 9:00 a.m. - 5:00 p.m. (EST). E-mail address: docdelivery@haworthpress.com].

http://www.haworthpress.com/web/IRSQ
© 2004 by The Haworth Press, Inc. All rights reserved.
Digital Object Identifier: 10.1300/J136v09n01_08

## WALDEN UNIVERSITY:
## THE FIRST 30 YEARS

An essay by Harold Hodgkinson (1969) inspired social activists Bernie and Rita Turner to found Walden University in 1970. The paper described a university where "the basic unit consists of the faculty member working with students in a research mode," (177) which still serves as the model for the University's curriculum. Walden benefited from Hodgkinson's continuing involvement as, 30 years later, it had grown into an academic institution where students worked collaboratively with faculty as scholar-practitioners who would, upon graduation, apply their knowledge and skills to effect positive social change in their local community, in their workplace, or in the world community.

In the beginning, Walden offered only an Ed.D. completion program but gradually the curriculum grew to include full doctoral programs in Administration/Management, Education, Health and Human Services, and Psychology. A summer residency has been an integral part of the University from the beginning, and in the mid eighties Walden began to offer monthly four-day academic residencies in addition to the summer session.

Walden was awarded NCA accreditation in 1990. The nineties also saw the development of the Walden Information Network (WIN) in 1994, the initial step in the creation of an electronic university. An M.S. in Educational Change and Technology Innovation was offered in 1995, followed by a program of Web-based courses for a Ph.D. in Psychology. Additional Master's degree programs and course-based Ph.D. programs were soon developed. Until that time, the curriculum was based solely on KAMs (Knowledge Area Modules), a series of seven scholarly documents averaging 90 pages each in which students examined the theoretical underpinnings and current research of selected thematic areas in their academic discipline and then applied the theory and research to a project related to their profession (Yob 2000).

## WALDEN UNIVERSITY:
## THE 21st CENTURY

In early 2001, Sylvan Learning Systems (now Laureate Education, Inc.) purchased a 41% interest in Walden and, by acquiring an additional 10% in February 2002, gained a controlling interest in the University. At that point, Walden began its transition from a graduate-only university to a comprehensive institution offering bachelor's, master's, and doctoral degrees (Collins 2001). The number of courses and programs increased dramatically, although still within the basic academic framework of Administration/Management, Education, Health and Human Services, and Psychology.

One of the most significant changes was the move of technology support from the Office of Academic Affairs in Minneapolis to Online Higher Education (OHE) in Los Angeles. Another major move was the relocation of Walden's financial and recruiting operations from Florida to Laureate headquarters in Baltimore. Both transfers resulted in the departure of some veteran staffers and the hiring of new employees, who are gradually being integrated into the Walden service ethic.

The merging of two cultures, corporate and academic, has seen some bumps along the way but both are putting forth efforts to ensure that the merger succeeds. It is not unlike a second marriage that blends two families, each of which must yield in some areas and take the lead in other areas, where it is strong. While the corporation is contributing a robust structure to the University, Walden in turn is working to infuse its emphasis on social change into the corporation. To that end, the Academic Council formed a Task Force on Social Change, with faculty and student members, to counter a concern that "the focus on social change has been somewhat diluted by the effort to grow the institution" (Goes 2004).

## THE PLACE OF THE LIBRARY IN THE UNIVERSITY

The Walden Library office is on the eighth floor of the Main Library on the IUB campus. Geographically, the library is far removed from the rest of the Walden/Laureate organization: approximately 600 miles from the Walden academic office in Minneapolis; a similar distance from Laureate corporate headquarters in Baltimore; and about 2,000 miles from Online Higher Education (OHE), the technical support, in Los Angeles.

However, in a virtual environment physical distance need not be equated with isolation. The Walden librarian reports directly to the University's Dean of Student Services. They meet weekly by telephone to discuss matters of concern, share progress reports, and plan a course of action. In addition, they correspond frequently by e-mail. They are currently collaborating on a strategic plan to envision where the library should be in 2007. The librarian serves on the Library Planning Committee, which has a faculty representative from each school and is chaired by the Dean of Student Services. The committee first met in December 2003, at which time it set five goals for 2004, including a process for selecting online databases.

Because the librarian and assistant librarian are on the Walden staff and faculty mailing lists, they are privy to updates to staff as well as debates and discussions among faculty. Frequent telephone conversations and e-mail exchanges keep the librarians in touch with other Walden staff, including the residency team, academic advisors, technical support, and the dissertation editor. There are also opportunities for face-to-face formal and informal meetings with administrators, faculty, and staff at student residencies. Occasional visits by the librarian to the Walden offices in Minneapolis are an important part of the communication process.

Although the Walden Library serves the Walden academic community exclusively and is considered part of the Walden student support team, the two librarians and their staff are actually employees of the IUB Libraries.

## THE PLACE OF THE WALDEN LIBRARY IN THE INDIANA UNIVERSITY-BLOOMINGTON (IUB) LIBRARIES

A Memorandum of Understanding (MOU) between Walden and the IUB Libraries provides monetary support for the library program as well as an overhead amount commensurate with the percentage required for grant projects. When the MOU was signed in 1992, after Walden's first Summer Session at IUB, it provided for a half-time professional position and 20 hours of student assistance (Weaver and Shaffer 1995). The program, which was unique at the time, later served as a pattern for two other academic institutions that support distance learners.

The Walden Library is under the umbrella of the IUB Libraries Customer & Access Services Department (CASD) and the librarian reports directly to the Head of CASD. The Walden Library could not function without the ongoing excellent support of each component of the CASD. The CASD Head meets regularly with the librarian and serves as a confidant, guide, and mentor. The CASD Assistant Head provides invaluable help with financial matters. The department's technical support is quick to respond when there are hardware problems or questions about software. Although the Document Delivery Service unit must respond to 500-1,000 requests a day from all over the world, its employees go out of their way to fill requests from Walden students.

IUB Libraries' circulation personnel must create approximately 500 temporary library cards in less than a week right before the beginning of Summer Session. They also contend cheerfully with the many problems endemic to serving students unfamiliar with the IUB Libraries during the few weeks they are on campus. Last but not least among CASD staff, those responsible for reshelving books make every effort to ensure that Walden students can find the books they need during their stay on campus. The CASD is not alone in supporting the Walden Library and Walden students, as all units of the IUB Libraries put forth exemplary efforts to welcome Summer Session students and make their stay pleasant, enlightening, and academically profitable.

Being part of the IUB Libraries' personnel has multiple advantages for Walden Library staff. They participate in IU's insurance and retirement policies. They have access to IUB's more than 200 online databases, which they can use to respond to Walden student and faculty's reference questions. However, license restrictions forbid sending materials from the IUB databases to Walden students.

## *VIRTUAL LIBRARY, REAL PEOPLE*

Full-time personnel of the Walden Library consist of two "visiting" librarians and a staff level position. Although the normal term for visiting librarians is only two years, the status for the Walden librarians has been extended indefinitely. They are non-tenure track but they enjoy the same privileges as other librarians, including faculty status, remote access to electronic resources, faculty borrowing and interlibrary loan privileges, and professional development opportunities. An MIS/MLS graduate currently holds the full-time staff position. Her excellent skills enable her to function as Web architect, reference librarian, and office manager.

Reference assistants are drawn from a pool of top-notch students in IU's School of Library and Information Science (SLIS). The Walden Library's reputation among SLIS students is such that each job posting results in a plethora of excellent candidates. The relationship between librarians and student workers is mutually beneficial. Students contribute their enthusiasm and formal education and, in turn, they receive excellent training and experience in providing public service both virtually and face to face. The students are not treated as only the "subjects" of training but as "co-learners" with the librarians, colleagues involved in many aspects of the program, from planning to implementation (Wu 2003, 145).

## LIBRARY SERVICES AND RESOURCES

Like reference desk personnel in physical libraries, the Walden librarians and reference assistants respond to reference questions, provide research assistance, help students locate and obtain the materials they need for their courses or KAMs, and guide them around the virtual library. The Walden Library differs from a reference desk in a physical library in that the library houses no print materials and that, with the exception of situations described later in this paper, all communication with students is conducted via telephone or asynchronous e-mail. The toll-free telephone line is a valuable tool, especially at the beginning of a quarter, when calls from new students come almost every hour the library is open. As a service that supports working professionals, the library must be open during the students' free times–evenings, weekends, and holidays, especially holiday weekends (Fidishun 2000). Although the office is closed on holidays, the librarian monitors and replies to e-mail from home at such times.

Interaction with students ranges from a single encounter lasting only a few minutes to a series of transactions that continue over a period of weeks. The most frequent requests for assistance are prompted by trouble accessing the databases or consternation because "All I see is an abstract. Why don't I see the article?" Access problems are often simply a result of using the wrong username and/or password, but sometimes there is a need to help a student troubleshoot a technical problem. Responding to "Why don't I see the article?" is an excellent opportunity to educate students about the limitations of online databases and to introduce them to other options for obtaining the resources they need. It can also serve as a segue to instruction in efficient and effective ways of searching the databases.

One-to-one interaction with students is supplemented by online materials that include a "Help & Tips" Web page to address access problems, general information about the online databases and about options for obtaining materials, and step-by-step instructions for the primary database of each school. Walden Library resources consist of citation and full-text or partially full-text databases that index the scholarly literature of each school, access to digitized Walden dissertations written in 1997 or later, and links to a selection of carefully chosen Web sites.

Students are encouraged not to limit their research to electronic resources, as not everything on reading lists is available online. In addition, the curriculum demands extensive library research. Walden's contract with the IUB Libraries subsidizes the provision of books and copies of journal articles through IU's Document Delivery Service (DDS). Books are mailed to students' homes but the articles are scanned and mounted as PDF files on a password-protected Web site. As librarians at Nova Southeastern University have found, document delivery to students in other countries can offer challenges, including delays by customs officials, difficulties accessing the PDF files online, and the high cost of toner or connection time for printing the documents (Chakraborty and Tuñón 2002). DDS works diligently with the Walden Library and the individual students to overcome such obstacles.

As others have noted, no one library can supply all a student needs, so it is important for students to be able to find nearby libraries that can complement the services and resources of their home library (Moyo and Cahoy 2003). In addition, some students prefer using familiar brick-and-mortar libraries. When the online resources or DDS cannot meet students' needs, the Walden Library helps students identify local libraries that may be able to provide the resources directly or through interlibrary loan. Much care is taken to ensure that students understand and respect the policies of those libraries, especially academic libraries, regarding distance learners enrolled in an out-of-state, for-profit institution. Students are also informed of the limitations of public libraries' collections and the possible costs of interlibrary loan.

## THE LIBRARY TODAY:
### REACHING OUT AND TOUCHING STUDENTS VIRTUALLY

The students and their needs are at the center of all library planning, decisions, policies, and actions. Because students are not standing at the desk, where their body language can speak as loudly as their words, it is important to be alert to nuances in telephone calls and to the real question, concern, or need in an e-mail message. Equally important is to be sensitive to indications that a student needs more than library-related assistance and that he or she may be experiencing some measure of anxiety, especially if the student is new to the University or just beginning a new quarter. Starting a new online course may fill even experienced students with fear, anxiety, and apprehension (Conrad 2002). Such emotions can be compounded as students contemplate the need to use an unfamiliar online library for their research and may begin to experience library anxiety.

Library anxiety has been recognized in the library literature as a psychological hindrance to effective use of library resources and a deterrent to asking librarians for help. The concept was introduced almost 20 years ago, the result of a two-year study of 6,000 undergraduate students (Mellon 1986). The study found that 75-85% of the students used terms such as "scary, overpowering, lost, helpless, confused" when describing their initial forays into the library. Some went so far as to use the word "phobia," while another said she felt like a lost child (162). Studies by Jiao and Onwuegbuzie, in the Works Cited section, confirm Mellon's findings.

Until a study of distance learners initially reported in 2002, the subjects of empirical research on library anxiety were students taking courses on campus and with convenient location to a physical library (Veal 2002). Veal used the Library Anxiety Scale (Bostick 1992) to measure five variables:

1. Barriers with staff–The perception that librarians or library staffs are intimidating.
2. Affective barriers–A student's feelings that only he/she has inadequate library skills.
3. Comfort with the library–Students' perceptions of how safe and welcoming the library is.
4. Knowledge of the library–How familiar students feel that they are with the library.
5. Mechanical barriers–An inability to operate equipment in the library; e.g., copy machines and printers [by extension, computers and databases].

Findings reported later indicate that affective and mechanical barriers were statistically significantly higher than the others (Collins and Veal 2004). As Collins and Veal note, the results are consistent with what other studies have shown, that the reliance on technology and the need to learn to use a variety of database interfaces simultaneously result in a heightened degree of library anxiety.

The above study and the experience of distance librarians argue against the assumption held by those unfamiliar with online graduate education, who judge that graduate students, in contrast to undergraduates, want or need little assistance in using a library, whether physical or virtual. They fail to understand that adult learners as graduate students in online course face unique challenges. Few move directly from a research-based undergraduate or even graduate course into their current program. In addition, there is often a gap of several years–even 20 years–between present and former schooling. As a result, their research and study skills may be sorely out of date (Garten 2001).

Even "physiological changes wrought by the aging process" or the anxiety about such changes has an impact on students' attitudes (Niemi and Ehrhard 1998, 67). The need to adjust to new technologies, the pressures of job and family responsibilities, a fear of failure and losing face, and a sense of isolation add to their anxious feelings (Black 2001). It is obvious from interactions with Walden students, especially doctoral students, that "I'm the only one who doesn't know this" is a common misperception. Moreover, students who are competent professionals in leadership roles often find it difficult to admit a lack of knowledge about the virtual library, a lack they view as incompetence and ignorance.

What many students need is the personal touch, which Tait sees as important also in promoting retention (2000). The key is to exhibit patience, flexibility, and compassion when interacting with students, especially in the earliest encounters (Harrell 2002). Even something as simple as acknowledging that libraries have changed, not just from the time a student was last in school but also very recently, can put him or her at ease (Veal 2000). It is also important to acknowledge that a student's anxiety is legitimate and to provide positive experiences to counteract the negative feelings (Mellon 1986).

As a fellow distance librarian explains, "We put people first" is not just a motto but a basic tenet of service (Meyer 2003, 67), a philosophy shared by the Walden Library. Furthermore, we believe that it is possible to "put your arm around a student on the Internet" (Brunt 1996, 115). E-mail messages are carefully crafted to make students feel welcome and to put them at ease. If it is obvious that a student just needs to talk, we listen, even if it takes 45 minutes or more. Phone calls are usually followed within a few hours by an e-mail message to tell the student that we were pleased to hear from him or her and to invite the student to contact us again if there are still unanswered questions or unresolved issues.

In addition, our routine is to send a follow-up e-mail message one week after the latest contact with a student. The practice is in accord with the RUSA reference guideline that "The reference transaction does not end when the librarian walks away from the patron. The librarian is responsible for determining whether the patron is satisfied . . . " (RUSA 1996, 5.0). Students are often pleasantly surprised at hearing from us again, and the message may encourage them to enter into a deeper discussion about their research topic. Informal feedback from students confirms the value of the follow-up messages. Like librarians at St. Edward's University, we make "a concerted effort" to establish relationships with students (Brownlee and Ekkers 2001, 72). Thus, it is not unusual for students to feel comfortable enough with us to share personal triumphs and concerns. Interaction continuing over a period of years may move the relationship with some students to a deeper level, even if they do not meet us in person. Occasionally we see them for the first and last time at graduation, the culmination of each Summer Session, where we share in their jubilation.

Besides supporting students individually, we can contribute to building community. Unlike faculty, who are familiar with students in only one school or academic discipline, we are acquainted with hundreds or even thousands of students across all schools. We can introduce students who live in the same geographic area, who have similar research interests, or whose work environments are similar. For example, we expedited a virtual meeting of students, police officers who were living in several states and different academic programs, and who shared concerns about the stress and suicide rates of their fellow officers. The Dean of Student Services, who played a major role in developing a Virtual Peer Network in his previous position at Excelsior College (Brigham 2001), has expressed interest in seeking support for technology to expedite such contacts on a larger scale.

The librarian sometimes participates in courses as a "guest lecturer." An example is a more than five-year role in PSYC8000, the online orientation course for doctoral students in Psychology (Barsun 2000). The librarian developed an information literacy site with emphasis on psychology resources and assisted individual students with their literature searches, but an underlying goal was to provide them with a positive introduction to the people, services, and resources of the Walden Library, a goal not unlike that of other librarians privileged to interact with students in courses (Duesterhoeff and Cunningham 1995). Subsequent interaction in other courses has fostered both the formal aspect, assistance with library research, and the informal, that of helping students feel comfortable with the Walden Library. Participation has ranged from the entire quarter, as in PSYC8000, to only one or two weeks out of the quarter.

# THE LIBRARY TODAY:
## REACHING OUT AND TOUCHING STUDENTS
## IN PERSON

Although students often appreciate the anonymity of the virtual academic environment, they may benefit from at least some in-person time with a school's faculty and staff. Two guidance workers in Great Britain who served distance learners assumed that face-to-face contact was not a priority because of the positive feedback they had received regarding their virtual interactions. When tasked with obtaining qualitative data from students, they arranged focus groups throughout their service region. Upon meeting the students in person, they were surprised at how many expressed a need for more face-to-face contact and the desire to put a face with a name. As one student commented, "We only came along to see what you looked like" (Stenning and Hensworth 2001).

A face-to-face component is an important part of the Walden doctoral program, as it has a 32-unit residency requirement. At least 13 units must be earned by attending two weeks of the three-week Summer Session on the IU-Bloomington campus. Options for the remaining units include another two or three weeks at Summer Session or four-unit increments gained by attending Continuing-4 (C-4) residencies, which convene for four days at hotels or conference centers. C-4s are offered ten times a year, and locations vary from year to year in an effort to make it easier for students and faculty from different geographic areas to attend.

The residencies provide an opportunity to present group library instruction as well as one-to-one consultations, especially during Summer Session. Until 2003, the University rented a high-speed printer and upwards of 30 computers to emulate the local area network of IUB databases in the dormitory where most students stay. The dormitory library was open 8:00 a.m. to midnight every day, including July 4. The convenient central location enabled us to sit beside students and guide them through literature searches but we also made it into a social center by providing snacks and national and local newspapers.

As of 2003, the University discontinued the Summer Session library in the dormitory and action moved to the Main Library. We now do our best to identify and assist Walden students there. The IUB Libraries have graciously let us use the staff instruction room, right off the lobby of the Main Library, as our library "concierge," which we advertise heavily to students as their first stop. In addition, we circulate among the computer clusters in both the graduate Reference Commons and the undergraduate Information Commons to assist Walden students who choose to work in those areas. A library advising station in the Walden office in the dormitory was tested during Summer Session 2004 and proved highly successful as a supplement to the library "concierge."

As in serving students virtually, our focus is in meeting their immediate need, making them feel at ease, and then helping them develop skills that will result in informed, competent, and confident seekers of information. Interaction is not limited to formal group sessions or individual consultation; we often join them for meals or on excursions into the nearby community.

## THE LIBRARY TOMORROW: EMBRACING CHANGE

So far we have been able to maintain the personal touch, even as the University has become part of a larger corporation and as the student body has grown from 1,800 in January 2002 to 11,500 in May 2004. Will we be able to do so when the student population reaches 20,000, predicted for January 2005? The key word is *scalability*. How can current practices be improved and/or adapted to respond to and serve students within an acceptable time frame? Some steps have already been taken. For example, the librarian no longer participates in PSYC8000, as there are now too many sections to monitor. Interaction in other courses has also been limited.

At the time of this writing, only one service has been discontinued. We no longer go into the stacks for one last check when informed by DDS that a requested item is not on the shelf. We still offer to help students explore options for materials not available online or through DDS, and we will continue doing so until sheer numbers make it no longer feasible.

On the advice of an earlier administration, we kept paper files of student transactions, discarding and shredding them at the end of the five years. The assistant librarian created an Access database to track student transactions, but much information was still maintained in hard copy. The database proved cumbersome as the number of students continued to increase. When Walden's e-mail moved from Outlook Express to Lotus Notes in the spring of 2003, electronic folders replaced the Access database and the paper files were abandoned. As the increase in traffic is rendering this system inefficient, we are looking into commercial reference tracking systems or the possibility of hiring an MIS or IST student to develop an in-house system.

A Web-based tour of the library's people, services, and online resources saves us from time-consuming explanations by telephone or e-mail and it spares students the embarrassment of asking the most basic questions. Each member of the Walden Library team is contributing to a file of templates, generic messages that address the most frequently asked questions or requests for assistance but which can also be adapted to other questions or requests.

The library Web site is slowly undergoing a total revision, to become more instructional in nature as well as informational. There are already detailed instructions for "mimic searches" and a guide to IUCAT, IU's online catalog. A FAQ page will be an important part of the new look. In addition, during the summer of 2004 the librarian participated in three sections of a pilot online orientation course for doctoral students, in which writing skills and library research play a prominent role. Her observations, coupled with feedback from students in the course, will permit refinement of a recently developed Library Orientation/Information Literacy Web site.

Once the pilot online orientation courses end, there will be no personal library presence in them but only the Web site and the hope that faculty will inform us when students post questions about the library or will encourage students to contact us directly. The pilot Web site targets students in the KAM programs but a version for students in the course-based Psychology program was planned for the fall of 2004, to be followed by further program-specific iterations.

Technology works well in addressing generic issues and questions and in introducing students to the basics of database searching, which can then be used as a springboard to advanced techniques. Without having to spend time responding to questions that a Web page can address, we hope to gain freedom to work with students on challenging searches or to help them ferret out hard-to-find information or resources. However, students who contact us will not simply be given a URL. We will continue to greet them warmly, explain where they can find the information, and invite them to contact us again once they have read and thought about the information. The follow-up messages will continue, although they too may in some cases use a template.

Students are customers of a university, especially of a for-profit institution, and consequently of its library. As customers, they have a right to expect "good customer service and a satisfying learning experience" (Sausner 2003, 54). Knowing their needs and whether their needs are being met is essential, especially during efforts to scale services to match the University's growth. An online survey and a focus group at a C-4 in the spring of 2004 were the first steps. Additional in-person sessions and online surveys are a major part of the library's strategic plan.

## *CONCLUSION:*
## *FACING AND EMBRACING CHANGE*

Earlier in this paper, the merger of Walden University and Laureate Education, Inc., was likened to a second marriage, in which compromises had to be made by both parties. A similar situation exists as the Walden Library contemplates compromises it may have to make in the future. We will use technology to streamline tasks, deliver services in a convenient and timely fashion, provide access to the online resources, and enhance the quality of library instruction, but it cannot replace, and is not intended to replace, personal interaction (Black 2001). The "package alone" is not enough; students need help and support from "the human element" (Rowntree 1992, 73). Otherwise, they have no one to turn to when they encounter problems. The personal touch is one of our greatest strengths. Although we will endeavor to offer it as long and as often as reasonably possible, we will accept the limitations imposed by having to serve ever-increasing numbers of students. A Hewlett-Packard advertisement claims that it will help companies "face, manage, and love change." As we face change, we are looking to both human resources and technology to manage it. We have not yet reached the point of loving the changes, but we are making every attempt to embrace change.

## REFERENCES

Barsun, Rita. 2001. Computer mediated conferencing, e-mail, telephone: A holistic approach to meeting students' needs. *Journal of Library Administration* 31 (3/4): 31-44. Also published in *Off-Campus Library Services*, ed. Anne Marie Casey (Binghamton, NY: The Haworth Information Press, 2001): 31-44.

Black, Nancy E. 2001. Emerging technologies: Tools for distance education and library services. *Journal of Library Administration* 31 (3/4): 45-59. Also published in *Off-Campus Library Services*, ed. Anne Marie Casey (Binghamton, NY: The Haworth Information Press, 2001): 45-59.

Blair, Amy. 2001. And a free 800 line! Managing technical and information support for distance education. (2001). *Journal of Library Administration* 31 (3/4): 61-65. Also published in *Off-Campus Library Services*, ed. Anne Marie Casey (Binghamton, NY: The Haworth Information Press, 2001): 61-65.

Bostick, Sharon Lee. 1992. The development and validation of the library anxiety scale. Ph.D. Diss., Wayne State University.

Brigham, David. Converting student support services to online delivery. (2001). *International Review of Research in Open and Distance Learning* 1 (2): 1-15.

Brownlee, Dianne, and Frances Ebbers. 2001. Extending library boundaries without losing the personal touch. *Journal of Library Administration* 31 (3/4): 67-73. Also published in *Off-Campus Library Services*, ed. Anne Marie Casey (Binghamton, NY: The Haworth Information Press, 2001): 67-73.

Brunt, Jill Mannion. 1996. Can you put your arm around a student on the Internet? *Adults Learning* 7 (5): 115-116.

Chakraborty, Mou, and Johanna Tuñón. 2002. Taking the distance out of library services offered to international graduate students: Considerations, challenges, and concerns. *Journal of Library Administration* 37 (1/2): 163-176. Also published in *The Tenth Off-Campus Library Services Conference*, ed. Patrick B. Mahoney (Binghamton, NY: The Haworth Information Press, 2002):163-176.

Collins, Kathleen M. T., and Robin E. Veal. 2004. Off-campus adult learners' levels of library anxiety as a predictor of attitudes toward the Internet. *Library & Information Science Research* 26: 5-14.

Collins, Walton. 2001. Wired Walden: Distance-ed pioneer ready for global challenge. *The California Star* (November 23). http://www.californiastar.com/education/e-walden.html.

Conrad, Dianne L. 2002. Engagement, excitement, anxiety, and fear: Learners' experiences of starting an online course. (2002). *The American Journal of Distance Education* 16 (4): 205-226.

Duesterhoeft, Diane M., and Nancy A. Cunningham. 1995. The role of assessment in the development and evaluation of library instruction. In "New Ways of 'Learning the Library'–and Beyond," the Twenty-Third National LOEX Library Instruction Conference held in Denton, Texas, 5 to 6 May 1995.

Fidishun, Dolores. 1997. Can we still do business as usual? Adult students and the new paradigm of library service. *Proceedings of the Association of College and Research Libraries National Conference, Nashville, TN.* http://www.ala.org/cfapps/archive.cfm?path=acrl/paperhtm/c25.html.

Fox, Anne. 2000. The after-five syndrome: Library hours and services for the adult learner. *The Reference Librarian* 69/70: 119-126. Also published in *Reference Services for the Adult Learner: Challenging Issues for the Traditional and Technological Era*, ed. Kwasi Sarkodie-Mensah (Binghamton, NY: The Haworth Information Press, 2000): 119-126.

Garten, Edward D. 2001. Online and for-profit graduate education: A challenge of understanding and accommodation for academic librarianship. *Technical Services Quarterly* 19 (3): 1-20.

Goes, Jim, e-mail message to acadfac mailing list, April 6, 2004.

Harrell, Karen J. 2000. Reducing high anxiety: Responsive library services to off-campus nontraditional students. *Journal of Library Administration* 37 (3/4): 335-365. Also published in *Distance Learning Library Services: The Tenth Off-Campus Library Services Conference*, ed. Patrick B. Mahoney. (Binghamton, NY: The Haworth Information Press, 2002): 355-365.

Hodgkinson, Harold L. 1969/2000. Walden U: A working paper. *Soundings: An Inter-disciplinary Journal* 52: 172-185.

Mellon, C. A. 1986. Library anxiety: A grounded theory and its development. *College & Research Libraries* 47: 160-165.

Meyer, Donna K. 2003. Learner-centered library service at a distance. In *Advances in Library Administration and Organization 20*, ed. Edward D. Garten and Delmus E. Williams, 67-81. New York: Elsevier Science, JAI.

Moyo, Lesley Mutinta, and Ellysa Stern Cahoy. 2003. Meeting the needs of remote library users. *Library Management* 24 (6/7): 281-290.

Niemi, John A., and Barbara J. Ehrhard. 1998. Off-campus library support for distance adult learners. *Library Trends* 47 (1): 65-74.

Rowntree, Derek. 1992. *Exploring Open and Distance Learning*. London: Kogan Page Limited.

RUSA (Reference and User Services Association). American Library Association. 1996. Guidelines for Behavior Performance of Reference and Information Services Professionals. http://www.ala.org/ala/rusa/rusaprotools/referenceguide/guidelinesbehavioral.htm.

Sausner, Rebecca. 2003. Carving your slice of the "virtual" education pie. *University Business* 6 (7): 52-56.

Stenning, Maureen, and Marion Hemsworth. 2001. Wanting to put a name to the face. *Adults Learning* 13 (4): 21-23.

Tait, Alan. 2000. Students and attachment: The nature of electronic relationships. *Adults Learning* 11 (10): 20-22.

Veal, Robin E. 2000. Understanding the characteristics, concerns, and priorities of adult learners to enhance library services to them. *The Reference Librarian* 69/70: 113-118. Also published in *Reference Services for the Adult Learner: Challenging Issues for the Traditional and Technological Era*, ed. Kwasi Sarkodie-Mensah (Binghamton, NY: The Haworth Information Press, 2000): 113-118.

_____ 2002. The relationship between library anxiety and off-campus adult learners. *Journal of Library Administration* 37 (3/4): 407-411. Also published in *Distance Learning Library Services: The Tenth Off-Campus Library Services Conference*, ed. Patrick B. Mahoney (Binghamton, NY: The Haworth Information Press, 2002): 355-365.

Weaver, Sherrill L., and Harold A. Shaffer. 1995. Contracting to provide library service for a distance graduate education program. *The Bottom Line: Managing Library Finances* 8 (3): 20-27.

Wu, Qi (Kerry). 2003. Win-win strategy for the employment of reference graduate assistants in academic libraries. *Reference Services Review* 31 (2): 141-153.

Yob, Iris. 2000. A Guide to the Knowledge Area Modules. http://www.waldenelearning.com/kamguidebook/contents/index.shtml.

## ADDITIONAL READING

Jiao, Qun G., and Anthony J. Onwuegbuzie. (1997). Antecendents of library anxiety in college students. *The Library Quarterly* 67 (4): 372-389.

_____ (1998). Perfectionism and library anxiety among graduate students. *The Journal of Academic Librarianship* 24 (5): 365-371.

_____ (1999). Identifying library anxiety through students' learning-modality preferences. *The Library Quarterly* 69 (2): 202-216.

_____ (2001). Library anxiety and characteristic strengths and weaknesses of graduate students' study habits. *Library Review* 50 (2): 73-80.

Jiao, Qun G., Anthony J. Onwuegbuzie, and Arthur A. Lichtenstein. Library anxiety characteristics of "at-risk" college students. *Library & Information Science Research* 18 (Spring): 151-163.

Onwuegbuzie, Anthony J., and Qun G. Jiao. (1998). The relationship between library anxiety and learning styles among graduate students: Implications for library instruction. *Library & Information Science Research* 20 (3): 235-249.

_____ (2004). Information search performance and research achievement: An empirical test of the Anxiety Expectation Mediation Model of Library Anxiety. *Journal of the American Society for Information Science and Technology* 55 (1): 41-54.

# Providing Reference in a Joint-Use Library

Nora J. Quinlan

Johanna Tuñón

**SUMMARY.** As a one of a kind joint-use facility between a private university and a county government, the Alvin Sherman Library, Research, and Information Technology Center at Nova Southeastern University (NSU) provides reference services to both NSU students on and off campus and public users. Reference librarians have had to adjust to the variety of users and demands for new services and at the same time find new and creative methods of offering, promoting, and providing instruction about their services to public users as well as NSU's local and distance students. Tracking statistics can assist in identifying user needs. *[Article copies available for a fee from The Haworth Document Delivery Service: 1-800-HAWORTH. E-mail address: <docdelivery@haworthpress.com> Website: <http://www.HaworthPress.com> © 2004 by The Haworth Press, Inc. All rights reserved.]*

Nora J. Quinlan (nora@nsu.nova.edu) is Head of Reference, and Johanna Tuñón (tunon@ nsu.nova.edu) is Head of Distance and Instructional Library Services, both at Alvin Sherman Library, Research, and Information Technology Center, Nova Southeastern University, 3100 Ray Ferraro, Jr. Boulevard, Ft. Lauderdale, FL 33314. Ms. Tuñón also is an Adjunct Faculty Member at the University of Maryland University College and at NSU.

[Haworth co-indexing entry note]: "Providing Reference in a Joint-Use Library." Quinlan, Nora J., and Johanna Tuñón. Co-published simultaneously in *Internet Reference Services Quarterly* (The Haworth Information Press, an imprint of The Haworth Press, Inc.) Vol. 9, No. 1/2, 2004, pp. 111-128; and: *Improving Internet Reference Services to Distance Learners* (ed: William Miller, and Rita M. Pellen) The Haworth Information Press, an imprint of The Haworth Press, Inc., 2004, pp. 111-128. Single or multiple copies of this article are available for a fee from The Haworth Document Delivery Service [1-800-HAWORTH, 9:00 a.m. - 5:00 p.m. (EST). E-mail address: docdelivery@haworthpress.com].

http://www.haworthpress.com/web/IRSQ

© 2004 by The Haworth Press, Inc. All rights reserved.

Digital Object Identifier: 10.1300/J136v09n01_09

**KEYWORDS.** Broward County, Nova Southeastern University, joint-use library, reference services, bibliographic instruction, statistics

## BACKGROUND

Nova Southeastern University (NSU) best known for its entrepreneurial spirit and willingness to think "outside the box." Located in Fort Lauderdale, in Broward County, Florida, it is the largest independent institution of higher education in the southeast United States and the eighth largest independent institution in the United States. As of fall 2003, the university had over 23,522 students, with 18,299 in graduate or professional programs and 5,233 as undergraduate students (NSU 2004a). The university, founded in 1964, has a long history of providing alternative educational opportunities to working adults and distance students at a time when other institutions were still focused on traditional, campus-based academic programs and students.

Almost every NSU academic program or center now offers both field-based and/or online classes as well as traditional campus based classes. While some students are nationally or even internationally based, in reality 82% of all NSU students attend classes in Florida, and 73% (NSU 2004b) actually live within a sixty-mile radius of the main campus. A majority of the professional students in the Health Professions Division and the Shepard Broad Law Center, for example, attend classes on the main campus. Other students that do attend classes on campus may actually be enrolled in distance programs that meet on the main campus. These students come from throughout the United States and from abroad to attend classes on a regular or semi-regular basis during the year. This variety of modalities available to students for attending classes on and off campus accounts for the fact that only 62.6% of NSU students who take class on campus are actually residents in Florida (NSU 2003).

## A JOINT-USE LIBRARY

The development of joint-use or partnership libraries is a growing phenomenon in the United States (Crawford 2003; Hunt & Tuñón 2002; Kinsey & Honing-Bear 1994; Reno 1999) and worldwide (Bundy 2003; McNicol 2003). Just as convergence of technologies is a growing trend in the business world, library services for different types of users are beginning to converge as well. Public schools, local governments, and institutions of higher education are all looking for synergistic methods for stretching budget dollars. Having libraries share expenses and space appeals to these groups as it is a cost-effective method for offering today's increasingly expensive array of library services to a wider variety of users. The collaborative sharing of facilities, services, and resources can help eliminate duplication of services as well as the costs associated with construction, equipment, materials, and staffing. The question, however, is whether such joint-use facilities can provide an equal or better level of service than would be available to each constituent if the same services were offered in separate facilities.

Unlike many joint-use facilities that are collaborations between public libraries and public educational institutions ranging from grade schools to state universities (McNicol 2003), Nova Southeastern University and the Broward County Board of County Commissioners' collaboration is unusual. It is one of the first private academic/public library collaborative efforts in the United States and probably the first such private academic/public joint-use facility to offer truly integrated library services to both groups of users. This collaboration makes an academic-level research facility available to the public and at the same time makes NSU and its programs and services known to the local community as part of NSU's theme of "communiversity."

Collaboration between NSU and Broward County's government is an example of the right idea at the right time and place. The Broward County Library system had a history of collaborative efforts with community colleges (Lynch 1997; Reno 1999) and schools (Beach 1989) and a willingness to try new ideas (Berry, 1996). Similarly, Don Riggs, NSU's Vice President for Information Services and University Librarian, had also worked as the first director of the Auraria Library which is shared by the Community College of Denver, Metropolitan State College of Denver, and the University of Colorado at Denver.

The decision for Nova Southeastern University and the Broward County Board of County Commissioners to enter into a joint-use agreement in the late 1990s offered a "win/win" situation for both the university and the county. At the time, NSU needed to build a new library, and Broward County wanted to provide its growing population with access to an extensive research collection strategically located in the center of the tri-county region, near a major interstate and the Florida Turnpike. The fact that NSU's library would provide county residents with access to a centrally located "high-tech research facility" (Hunt & Tuñón 2002 p. 316) and the fact that the joint-use facility would be open 28 more evening and weekend hours than the Broward County Library hours of operation were also strong selling points for county residents. The two institutions wanted a cost-effective library with enhanced services that (1) maximized resources and (2) was seamless for both user groups. Moreover, Broward taxpayers liked this creative solution for stretching tax dollars to provide a research-caliber collection for the county inexpensively. Broward students in both public and private schools as well as higher education institutions in the area benefited by having access to a variety of new databases, a spacious building that was open 100 hours a week with computer labs and study rooms, and a print and online collection of research materials. NSU students benefited as well, because Broward County's contribution of funds made it possible to build the building, hire additional library staff, broaden the academic collection, and expand the media collections. The library was also able to add a children's and young adults' book collection and programs for youth and families.

The joint-use agreement made it clear the joint-use library and its contents were the property of NSU, and the staff was NSU employees. To all intents and purposes, the Broward County Board of County Commissioners had outsourced to NSU the providing of certain library services and resources to Broward county residents. This distinction was important when it came to developing library policies concerning difficult patrons, latchkey children, accessing pornography and filtering, etc., because the library was part of a private academic institution and not a government agency. It therefore only had to follow university policies, and these policies could differ from those of Broward County Public Library. This gave the Alvin Sherman Library, Research, and Information Technology Center more leeway in developing and enforcing policies that might not have been possible in the public library system.

## *PROVIDING REFERENCE SERVICES*

Like reference librarians elsewhere, the reference librarians at the Alvin Sherman Library provided all users with assistance in everything from giving building directions to helping people locate and find research information and materials. They provided ready reference as well as more in-depth research help, and offered library training for both individuals and groups. The mission of the Reference Department was to anticipate and meet the information needs of all its users in a timely, accurate, and professional manner. Librarians strove to communicate the library's services, resources, and policies to users effectively, and provide accurate and thorough assistance and information to all users. In NSU's joint-use library, this meant offering a full range of reference services to both NSU-affiliated users and the public. Every effort was made not to fall into what Crawford (2003) termed "lip-service cooperation " (p. 83) for a joint-use facility. As he noted, this would have been a "recipe for mediocrity at best" (p. 83).

## STAFFING CHALLENGES

Because the Alvin Sherman Library serves both Broward County residents and NSU students, staff, and faculty, staffing presented challenges for offering reference services to joint-use patrons. There are three departments: Reference, Public Library Services (PLS), and Distance and Instructional Library Services (DILS) providing reference-type services. Learning from past problems in joint-use facilities with supervision and chain of command (Kinsey & Honing-Bear 1994), all Library staff are NSU employees.

The Library is open 100 hours a week. It is one of only a dozen academic libraries in Florida that offer such extensive hours (NCES 2003). In addition, it is open 28 hours more a week than had been offered at that time in the Broward County system (Hunt & Tuñón 2002). The main reference desk is open seven days a week and is staffed 86 hours. Two librarians are assigned for almost all shifts, providing a total of 141 assigned staff hours of coverage. The Public Library Services (PLS) desk is open 81 hours a week and provides 81 staff hours of coverage a week. In all, the Library provides 222 assigned staff hours of reference service. NSU students and Broward County residents particularly appreciate the expanded evening and Sunday hours.

The size of the new library affected staffing significantly. The library had grown from 17,000 square feet to 325,000 square feet, making it the largest library building in Florida. Because of the planned new services, extended hours, and expanded print collection in the new joint-use facility, the joint-use agreement called for a dramatic increase in reference staff. The reference staff was increased from 2.5 to 15.5 professional librarians, resulting in 13 additional reference positions being added. The change was particularly striking in light of the fact that there had been no separate reference department in NSU's previous library.

Since the opening of the Library, public users have taken advantage of reference services, in person, by phone, and e-mail. Statistics show that on average, 40% of all reference transactions came from public library patrons. In 2001-2002 (which included three months of service at the previous library) 32,875 reference questions were answered. In 2003-2004, the total number of questions answered reached 52,610. Between January and June of 2004, 58.6% of all reference transactions were initiated by NSU-affiliated users while 41.3% were from public users. The ratio of types of users has remained consistent over the last three years of operation even as the overall usage numbers increased. The types of questions asked varied between different types of users. Public users were more likely to ask directional questions (39% vs. 33%) while, not surprisingly, NSU users asked more research/instructional questions (20.5% compared to 11.9% by public users).

Despite initial concerns about whether the public would come to an academic campus, library use by the public has skyrocketed. Ten thousand cards were issued to the public in the first year, and the total number of cards issued doubled by the end of the second year of operation. By July of 2004, the total number of registered public users had actually surpassed NSU's student enrollment when the total number of public cards issued reached 25,000.

Usage by NSU students also increased due in part to the fact that on-campus undergraduate programs at NSU had been growing dramatically. More NSU students began to use the library, drawn to its open spaces, comfortable study areas, and group study rooms as well as technological and social amenities. At the same time, students from other academic institutions in the surrounding community including Broward County Community College, the University of Phoenix, and Florida Atlantic University also began using the library's computer labs, research collections, databases, individual study carrels, and group study rooms.

## PROVIDING QUALITY REFERENCE SERVICES
## FOR DIVERGENT USER GROUPS

When the joint-use library first opened, the librarians had to learn how best to serve both public and academic walk-in users (Hunt & Tuñón 2002) as well as patrons expecting service by e-mail, phone, and more recently, digital chat. The librarians had to be able to shift gears to meet various user groups' widely divergent expectations for what they considered appropriate levels of library service. For library staff, the ultimate goal was to provide the highest level of service possible to all users, whomever they might be. The library administration encouraged all of the library staff to keep this as their first priority. With each user transaction, staff had to learn to quickly evaluate a patron, identify the user's needs and wants, and then provide the best possible service required or needed.

In a joint-use library, reference librarians had to learn to be able to adapt their service style quickly to the needs of each patron type. During a normal two-hour reference desk shift, reference librarians might use e-mail to help a NSU doctoral business student from Georgia, guide a walk-in distance student from a proximal academic institution to a full-text database, and provide digital chat reference to an unaffiliated college student in Gainesville with a ready reference question for a class assignment. During that same two-hour shift, they might also have to help a young mother locate a popular video for her child, provide phone reference for a Broward teenager looking for a music CD, and help a walk-in senior citizen find closing prices for specific stocks on December 31, 1978.

From the beginning, the recruitment of reference librarians for the joint-use facility was a challenge (MacDougall & Quinlan, 2001). Not all librarians thought the missions of public and academic libraries were compatible (Reno 1999) and some opposed joint-use libraries (McNicol 2003). NSU found that some academic librarians do not like the idea of working with the public and would have preferred to let the public libraries deal with "problem" patrons. As Crawford (2003) reported, this response was not all that uncommon. The end result was that the library administration had to work especially hard to promote a positive "can do" attitude in the staff as well as hire new people interested in and able to work in an integrated joint-use environment.

To cast the "widest net," job descriptions for the positions in reference were kept quite general. Search committees found that there were very few librarians who have had the training or the experience of multitasking with so many different responsibilities. Nor were there many librarians trained to work with such varied user groups. It quickly became obvious that library schools train their students to work in a specific environment such as public libraries, academic libraries, or special libraries and that very little (if any) crossover is promoted or accepted in the profession. As a result, NSU's search committees found it challenging to find candidates with the vision to see the potential opportunities offered by converging library services in this new hybrid library.

Retention of staff also proved to be a problem for the same reason. Some of the newly hired reference librarians found it difficult to adjust to NSU's nontraditional, entrepreneurial environment. Some did not really understand the special needs of NSU's distance students while others did not like the challenges of working in a joint-use facility that served both public and academic users. As a result, more recent recruitment efforts have placed greater emphasis on better explaining the non-traditional nature of the university and the goals of the joint-use library when interviewing possible job candidates.

## THE ROLE OF TECHNOLOGY IN THE EVOLUTION OF LIBRARY SERVICES AT NSU

Library services have changed dramatically over the last 25 years at NSU, and technology has played a strong role in this transformation. The Nova University Libraries started with two small reading rooms on campus and one off campus at the Oceanography Center. The precursor to the main library, known later as the Einstein Library, was established in 1967. Since that time, the library staff has always seen technology as a solution to problems rather than the cause of the problem. This became particularly true in the 1990s when the Einstein Library started providing networked computers with CD-ROM databases and then added online databases in 1994. As new technology-based resources became available, the Einstein Library kept pace, always looking for ways to better serve the special needs of distance students and on-campus students alike.

The Einstein Library's willingness to use the technology and then the Internet and the Web to provide library services had one unanticipated outcome. When considering a joint-use partner for a research library facility for the county, the Broward County Board of County Commissioners were interested in providing the county with access to technology (Berry 1996; Commings 1998). The Einstein Library's demonstrated track record in being highly capable in maneuvering through a technology environment and being both innovative and quick to adapt to technological change (Hunt & Tuñón 2002) caught their interest. The commissioners also found the library's academic research book and journal collections, extended hours of operation, and reputation for a high level of service attractive. All of these factors proved instrumental in the Broward County Commissioners' decision to sign the joint-use agreement with NSU in December 1999.

Even after the opening of the Alvin Sherman Library as a joint-use facility in the fall of 2001, the library continued to emphasize technology. Walk-in users were able to access many of the same online resources that NSU students were already using. Wireless laptops were available for checkout and could be used anywhere in the building. The reference librarians began offering the public training on how to use these databases for research, both in one-on-one consultations and in a variety of classes. In addition, the Library implemented the Ask-A-Librarian chat services in December of 2003 using software funded through a Library Services and Technology Act (LSTA) grant in conjunction with The College Center for Library Automation (CCLA) and the Tampa Bay Library Consortium (TBLC).

## THE INSTRUCTIONAL ROLE OF REFERENCE LIBRARIANS

When the joint-use facility first opened, defining the instructional role of the various public service librarians proved to be one of the more difficult challenges. Instruction had always played an important role for reference librarians in the Einstein Library, and the librarians wanted to continue this focus in the joint-use library because of the research focus of the facility. However, the Alvin Sherman librarians struggled with how to best accomplish this when serving both academic and public users as well as how to divide teaching responsibilities between the three public service departments. The Public Library Services librarians began offering basic computer literacy courses to children, young adult, and adult public users. It was assumed that reference librarians would teach on-campus library training sessions while the Distance and Instructional Library Services librarians were to handle the off-campus and online instruction.

This plan looked good on paper, but there were some unanticipated problems. It had been anticipated that some reference staff would have difficulty working with public users. Instead, some of the librarians had problems working with the library's other nontraditional constituent: NSU's distance students. The problem stemmed, in part, from overly idealized expectations of the "scholarly" nature of reference questions expected from graduate students. Some librarians did not understand or empathize with the challenges facing a working adult student returning to school after 15 years learning to work in an online environment for the first time. Other librarians found the distance students too demanding or too ignorant of library services. These librarians did not really understand that many distance students had had little or no training and did not always have walk-in access to an academic library in their area.

In addition, many of the newly hired reference librarians had not traveled to any of NSU's distance sites where they would have met distance students and would have better understood their needs. Librarians had to learn and understand that many returning adult students were not very "tech-savvy" or comfortable with complex online databases and were often feeling overwhelmed by the multitude of resources they could access. In addition, these students were usually juggling the stress of work and family responsibilities in addition to classes and had little time to grasp the intricacies of database searching. They simply wanted their articles now.

Another problem that had to be nipped in the bud was an "us" versus "them" attitude by reference librarians about serving local and distance students. One situation illustrates this problem. When the idea of digital chat reference was first being explored, a few reference librarians suggested that the Reference Department should offer chat for local users while the Distance and Instructional Library Services Department should provide a separate chat service for NSU's distance students. Only the library administration's firm vision of integrated, user-centered library services and its emphasis on teamwork ensured that the public service departments continued to actively collaborate in the provision of services.

Providing instruction for the public presented other types of challenges. Instruction has always played a critical role promoting the use of online resources at NSU, but when the Alvin Sherman Library opened, there were many questions about what kind of instructional role reference librarians would have when working with the public. NSU librarians had always firmly believed in the old adage: Give a man a fish and he will eat for a day; teach a man to fish and he will be able to eat for life. As a result, reference librarians grappled with the question of when to give public patrons information and when to teach them how to find information. They understood that not all people want to take the time to learn a database that they will never need or use again.

The importance of the research role of the Library was the critical factor in resolving the instructional role for NSU's reference staff with the public. The librarians wanted to *teach* people how to use the library's resources whenever possible, but they were also determined not to be pedantic or inflexible with users, particularly when working with non-university users. As a result, they decided to simply provide the desired answers or materials when deemed appropriate. This pragmatic approach proved quite workable. NSU's librarians quickly became comfortable in gauging different users' expectations and providing the appropriate level of library service on a case-by-case basis (Hunt & Tuñón 2002).

The following example illustrates how the topic of aphasia might be handled with various types of patrons. NSU's on-campus Speech Language Pathology students would be taught as part of their program how to locate articles on aphasia in the *Linguistics and Language Behavior Abstracts* database as well as *ERIC, PsycINFO,* and *MEDLINE.* They would be directed to the library's Web page and shown how to log into the databases by subject, develop a search strategy, and evaluate the results based on their research needs. Over the phone, a distance student in the same program would be guided systematically through the same process. E-mail requests from students would be directed to an instruction page to read through and then to follow the process described.

The reference help offered to public users varied depending on each user's information needs. Public users who were students from other schools such as a local high school, community college, or university would be taught how to do their own research. (Surprisingly, many of these non-NSU students have told NSU librarians that they have never received bibliographic instruction at their own institutions.) On the other hand, a member of the general public looking for general information on the communication disorder would be provided with selected resources. The librarian at the Reference Desk would access a general medical database such as *Health Reference Center* and locate some good overview full-text articles for the patron. Of course, if the user expressed an interest in knowing more about how to conduct a search, he or she would also be provided with more in-depth instruction.

Dividing the instructional class responsibilities between the three public services departments in the Library also proved problematic. The joint-use agreement never addressed the nitty-gritty details of these types of day-to-day operational details. It took cooperation to divide the training responsibilities between the departments. The department heads decided that the Public Library Services librarians would provide programming and training for children up through eighth grade as well as computer literacy classes for public adult users. Distance and Instructional Library Services librarians would continue to coordinate the overall efforts for library training for distance students, develop Web-based training for the online students, and provide training at the distance sites. In addition, the DILS librarians would pitch in with on-campus training when needed.

The role of the reference librarians was the least clearly defined because, unlike PLS and DILS librarians, reference librarians were supposed to serve both Broward County users and NSU training needs. The two positions in the Reference Department funded with Broward County monies to handle increased bibliographic instruction for public users and on-campus students were more problematic. These positions were supposed to be responsible for coordinating the increasing amount of in-house groups and individual library instruction as well as tours for students, faculty, and Broward County residents. As for the NSU students, it was assumed at first that the Reference/Instructional Librarian would coordinate efforts to serve the on-campus students while the DILS librarians would serve the distance students.

This plan sounded good in principle, but defining who were "distance" students presented problems. Distance education was integrated too tightly into the fabric of all NSU programs for training to be easily divided based on where students attended classes. For example, training for freshman English classes was offered on campus, online, and at a number of sites in Florida, the Bahamas, Jamaica, and Las Vegas, Nevada. In addition, many of the training sessions offered on campus were actually being provided to distance students. Doctoral students in the Instructional Technology and Distance Education program, for example, attended classes on campus three times a year and took the rest of their class time online. Still other hybrid classes had half of the students located on campus in a classroom while others linked into the class using compressed video from distance sites.

The problem was finally resolved by having the Head of Distance and Instructional Library Services coordinate the overall efforts for all NSU students. However, various librarians in the Reference and DILS Departments liaisoned with various NSU programs. For example, the Reference/Instructional Librarian worked with the undergraduate classes in Education and English composition while one of the subject bibliographers scheduled the training for the graduate computer science programs.

The librarians in the Reference Department became increasingly involved in providing library-training sessions as well. At first, they only provided bibliographic instruction for the required English classes for undergraduate students and an occasional class for local high schools. By 2003, however, the reference staff began providing more graduate training sessions. For example, reference librarians began to be included in the training rotation for the monthly three-hour training sessions when NSU's new distance doctoral education students came to campus for their Doctoral Student Orientation (DSO).

The question about whether reference librarians would travel to NSU's distance sites was still another topic that had to be resolved. The library administration had originally felt that reference librarians should not travel to teach at off-campus sites because their positions had been funded through Broward County funds. At the time, it was felt that they needed to be available to assist Broward county users. The reference librarians therefore concentrated on services offered to Broward patrons as well as local NSU students and distance students who came to south Florida for classes.

Later, the administration reconsidered and concluded that all library positions were actually partially funded by the county and that librarians could teach NSU's students on or off campus. This freed reference librarians to begin traveling to NSU's distance sites. The problem was that by the time the travel policy was changed, job descriptions of newly hired reference librarians did not include travel outside the tri-county area. However, because the Head of Reference thought that going to sites provided librarians with a better understanding of NSU distance students and programs, she did actively encourage reference librarians to take advantage of distance travel opportunities if they were interested and willing to travel. She did not, however, require it of them. Several have taken the opportunity to do sessions at sites throughout Florida as well as Jamaica and Nevada.

The Reference Department has also devoted efforts to provide Broward County public users with instruction. For example, librarians have taught classes for both public and private high schools in Broward County, a local hospital, and community service organizations. However, efforts have been hampered by difficulties filling the Instructional/Outreach position, which would focus on promoting this service. Few candidates have had the needed experience working with both academic and public users, and even fewer have shown an interest in relocating to south Florida.

## OTHER JOB RESPONSIBILITIES

In 2001, reference staff began working more closely with the library's Collection Development Department and NSU faculty to select materials in a wide range of disciplines for the Library's collection. The department staffing was structured so that three subject specialists worked respectively in the areas of humanities, social sciences, and science/technology. These librarians worked with the Head of Collection

Development to coordinate collection development activities with the selectors, passing on information, analyzing resources, making selection assignments, and helping to make decisions about purchases of databases. Almost all librarians served as subject selectors, but the reference librarians have taken on the bulk of collection development. The object was to build the collection from 200,000 volumes on hand when the Library opened to its goal of 1,400,000 volumes. In the three years since the joint-use library opened, a total of 130,000 additional volumes have been added so the library is well on the way to reaching this goal!

## STATISTICS AND THE NETWORKED ENVIRONMENT

In an increasingly networked environment, technology continues to affect the way that librarians interface with patrons in the 21st Century. Increasingly, librarians are helping patrons asynchronously. Although phone reference and e-mail have been used for years, chat reference is rapidly becoming more accepted and used. As mentioned already, NSU has always been innovative in using technology for training sessions. Librarians have tried everything from compressed video (Chakraborty & Victor 2004) and NetMeeting (Pival & Tuñón 1998) to current initiatives such as Elluminate and Viewlets.

With the changing nature of librarian interactions with users in a networked environment, librarians now need to find ways of capturing data that document the library's role in these new dynamics (Shim, McClure, & Bertot 2000). Like most academic libraries, the Alvin Sherman librarians developed a variety of Web-based subject guides and help pages that NSU students and public users could access asynchronously. The library surveyed NSU's site-based students in Jamaica and learned that distance students are using electronic resources asynchronously to get help. Only 4% of the Jamaican students surveyed reported calling the Reference Desk using the toll-free number and only 8% used e-mail to get answers to reference questions. Meanwhile almost one fifth or 18% of these same international students reported making use of the library's asynchronous help pages (MacFarland, 2004). This was the first concrete documentation that NSU's users were getting library help in more indirect ways than had been realized. However, quantifying changes in ways to access reference services is also more difficult.

The Internet and its networked environment are changing how reference services are offered and what statistics should be counted. As in the past, reference librarians need to continue counting synchronous transactions whether completed in person, on the phone, or via digital reference. However, in an increasingly online environment, reference librarians also need to expand their mindsets beyond only focusing on transactions when the user took the initiative and physically contacted them. In an increasingly networked environment, reference transactions by those students in Jamaica who look for library help provided on Web-based help pages and subject guides should be captured just as surely as the face-to-face transactions at the Reference Desk. After all, both asynchronous resources and traditional transactions help students, and it is important for the library to document all forms of library services.

NSU's statistical reporting on library Web page use is still in its infancy and not without some problems. In May 2004, the library introduced seven portal pages providing gateways for alumni, Broward adult users, children, teens, and NSU local and distance students as well as faculty and staff. These pages were accessed 8,767 times in just the month of June. The heaviest use was by NSU distance students (50.7%) and the lowest use was by Broward teens (2%). However, because these portal pages were not password protected, there may be some problems with the numbers because the actual type of user cannot be documented.

Database use provided statistics that are more reliable because each person had to use his or her user name and password in the Web Access Management authentication process. Between January and May of 2004, there were more that 9 million transactions in the NSU databases. Two numbers were particularly striking. A total of 53.4% of all users were distance graduate students excluding students in the professional schools (Health Professions and Law School). Meanwhile, only .018% of database users were logging in as Broward children (ages 0-12). In spite of the greater reliability of these statistics because of the authentication process, some questions about these numbers still arose. For example, there was no way to verify whether the low numbers for Broward County children were due to parents using their own card numbers to log their children into the databases. Not withstanding the low use of databases by the public, approximately 57% of all items checked out of the joint-use library are being checked out by the public.

Capturing usage statistics of Web and networked resources will continue to become increasingly important. ARL's E-metrics project (Shim, McClure, & Bertot 2000) has suggested a number of new statistics that libraries should start tracking as documenting usage becomes increasingly important. A joint-use library would also like to track internal and external access numbers by academic and public users alike.

Unfortunately, capturing these kinds of statistics presents some challenges. Currently, the Alvin Sherman Library is not yet able to document when people are accessing these types of resources from within the building or from outside the library's network, but collecting this type of data is becoming a library priority.

## CONCLUSION

The winds of change are impacting not only how reference librarians access information but also whom they serve and how they serve those patrons. Academic institutions, public schools, and local governments are all collaborating to connect people and resources in new ways, and new technologies mean that libraries can and are providing people with access to information and quality services whether the users are physically in the library or accessing these resources remotely. As other institutions consider joint-use collaborations in an effort to take advantage of economies of scale, the lessons learned at the Alvin Sherman Library offer some new and creative solutions to public and academic librarians alike: Joint-use libraries can do a good job of integrating services to a variety of types of users when the librarians truly share a commitment to serving both groups.

## REFERENCES

Beach, C. P. 1989. The public library as provider of library services to educational institutions. *Journal of Library Administration* 11 (1-2): 173-187.

Berry, John. 1996, June 15. Library of the year 1996: Broward County Library. *Library Journal* 30: 28-31.

Broward County bond referendum. 1999, March 7. *Sun Sentinel*, Broward Metro, 2G. Retrieved June 21, 2004, from Newsbank Sun Sentinel database.

Broward County Public Schools. 2003, September. *District overview*. Retrieved May 30, 2004, from http://www.browardschools.com/about/overview.htm.

Bundy, Alan. 2003. Places of connection: New public and academic library buildings in Australia and New Zealand. *Australasian Public Libraries and Information Services* 17 (1): 32-47. Retrieved August 28, 2004, from Wilson Library Literature and Information Science Full Text database.

Chakraborty, Mou, & Victor, Shelley. 2004. Do's and don'ts of simultaneous instruction to on-campus and distance students via videoconferencing. *Eleventh Off-Campus Library Services Conference proceedings*. Mount Pleasant, MI: Central Michigan University.

Commings, Karen. 1996. High tech learning centers. *Computers in Libraries* 16 (6): 16, 18.

Crawford, Walt. 2003. The philosophy of joint-use libraries. *American Libraries* 34 (11): 83. Retrieved August 28, 2004, from Wilson Library Literature and Information Science Full Text database.

Eberhardt, George M. 1999. Three plans for shared-use libraries are in the works. *American Libraries* 30 (1): 21.

Goldberg, Beverly. 2000. Broward County Library sued over cybersmut. *American Libraries* 31 (3): 14-15.

Goodes, P. A. 2001. Privacy versus security: What's at stake. *American Libraries* 32 (11): 52-56. Retrieved August 29, 2004, from Wilson Library Literature and Information Science Full Text database.

Hunt, Carey, & Tuñón, Johanna. 2002. Partnerships: The wave of today. *Public Libraries* 41 (6): 315-316. Retrieved August 28, 2004, from Wilson Library Literature and Information Science Full Text database.

Kinsey, Sally, & Honig-Bear, Sharon. 1994. Joint-use libraries: More bang for your bucks. *Wilson Library Bulletin* 69: 37-39.

Lynch, Sherry. 1997. Partnerships produce results. *Public Libraries* 36: 340-341.

MacFarland, T. 2004. *Students in Jamaica evaluate resources and services of the Nova Southeastern University Library, Research, and Information Technology Center: Summer term 2003* (Report No. 03-18). Fort Lauderdale, FL: Research and Planning, Nova Southeastern University. Retrieved March 20, 2004, from http://www.nova.edu/cwis/urp/pdfs/03-18EntireReport.pdf.

MacDougall, Harriett D., & Quinlan, Nora J. 2001. Staffing Challenges for a Joint-Use Library: The Nova Southeastern University and Broward County Experience. *Resource Sharing & Information Networks* 15: 131-150.

McNicol, Sarah. 2003. Joint use libraries in the UK. *Australasian Public Libraries and Information Services* 16(2): 81-90. Retrieved August 28, 2004, from Wilson Library Literature and Information Full Text database.

National Center for Education Statistics. 2003, November. *Academic Libraries: 2000 E.D. Tabs.* Washington, DC: Department of Education. Retrieved May 30, 2004, from http://nces.ed.gov/pubs2004/2004317.pdf.

Nova Southeastern University. 2003b. Table 5: Permanent residence of students: Calendar year 2003. *NSU fact book.* Retrieved May 30, 2004, from http://www.nova.edu/cwis/urp/factbook/tables/table2.pdf.

Nova Southeastern University. 2004a. Table 1: Growth in fall enrollment. *NSU fact book.* Retrieved June 21, 2004, from http://www.nova.edu/cwis/urp/factbook/tables/table1.pdf.

Nova Southeastern University. 2004b. Table 6: Proportion of students that attended classes in Florida and the tri-county area during the calendar year 2003. *NSU fact book.* Retrieved June 21, 2004, from http://www.nova.edu/cwis/urp/factbook/tables/table6.pdf.

Oder, N. 1998. Tampa PL to filter; Broward to "limit." *Library Journal* 123 (7): 22.

Pival, P., & Tuñón, J. 1998. NetMeeting: A new and inexpensive alternative for delivering library instruction to distance students. *College & Research Libraries News* 59 (10): 758-760.

Reno, Eric E. 1999. Joint-use libraries: A college president's perspective. *Colorado Libraries* 25 (2): 10-11. Retrieved August 28, 2004, from Wilson Library Literature and Information Full Text database.

Shim, W., McClure, C. R., & Bertot, J. C. 2000, December. Data gathering practices in the networked environment. *ARL: A Bimonthly Report on Research Library Issues and Actions from ARL, CNI, and SPARC* (213), 6-8. Retrieved March 20, 2004, from http://www.arl.org/nwsltr/213/data.html.

U.S. Census Bureau. 2004, May 26. *State and County QuickFacts*. Retrieved May 20, 2004, from http://quickfacts.census.gov/qfd/states/12/12011.html.

# Centralizing Information
# About Library Services and Resources:
# Delivering the Library to Users
# at Any Distance

## Mary Feeney

**SUMMARY.** The School of Information Resources and Library Science at the University of Arizona (UA) has a mix of local and distance students in its program. The librarian at the UA Library who works with this program developed a Web site that centralizes information about several library services and resources that benefit distance learners: online orientation and research guides, chat reference, document delivery, and more. Bringing together this information with a focus on distance learners provides a platform for delivering the library to all users, whatever their distance from the library. *[Article copies available for a fee from The Haworth Document Delivery Service: 1-800-HAWORTH. E-mail address: <docdelivery@haworthpress.com> Website: <http://www.HaworthPress.com> © 2004 by The Haworth Press, Inc. All rights reserved.]*

**KEYWORDS.** Distance students, library services

Mary Feeney (feeneym@u.library.arizona.edu) is Librarian for Library and Information Science, Business and Journalism, University of Arizona Library, 1510 East University Boulevard, Room A204, Tucson, AZ 85721.

[Haworth co-indexing entry note]: "Centralizing Information About Library Services and Resources: Delivering the Library to Users at Any Distance." Feeney, Mary. Co-published simultaneously in *Internet Reference Services Quarterly* (The Haworth Information Press, an imprint of The Haworth Press, Inc.) Vol. 9, No. 1/2, 2004, pp. 129-146; and: *Improving Internet Reference Services to Distance Learners* (ed: William Miller, and Rita M. Pellen) The Haworth Information Press, an imprint of The Haworth Press, Inc., 2004, pp. 129-146. Single or multiple copies of this article are available for a fee from The Haworth Document Delivery Service [1-800-HAWORTH, 9:00 a.m. - 5:00 p.m. (EST). E-mail address: docdelivery@haworthpress.com].

http://www.haworthpress.com/web/IRSQ
Digital Object Identifier: 10.1300/J136v09n01_10

## INTRODUCTION

The School of Information Resources and Library Science (SIRLS), an ALA-accredited Master's program in library and information studies at the University of Arizona (UA), has had a distance learning program for many years. In fact, it was the first Library and Information Science (LIS) program to deliver courses nationally with a cable provider[1] and the first department at the UA to start teaching on the Web.[2] Off-campus courses are offered at sites in Phoenix, about two hours driving time from the UA campus, and online through WebCT, an online course management system, to users in places as varied as Alaska, Georgia, and Arizona. Hybrid online classes, which combine a large portion of the course online with a few weekends of in-person or on-site class meetings, are also offered. Distance students and local students alike may enroll in any of the "virtual" or "distance" classes regardless of how they are offered. This sometimes makes it difficult to distinguish between on- and off-campus students, as acknowledged by Goodson.[3]

Graham and Grodzinski explain that remote users may be categorized in three groups: on-campus, off-campus, and distance education users. On-campus remote users include customers using library resources from a dorm, office, or other on-campus location outside the library. Off-campus remote users are primarily traditional users who use the library from locations away from campus. Distance learner remote users are beyond "off-campus"; they access library resources from greater distances than the other groups, and remote access may be the only way they can use the library.[4] SIRLS students fit into all three categories of remote users: on-campus, off-campus, and distance.

According to the ALISE Library and Information Science Education Statistical Reports, the percentage of full-time equivalent (FTE) students at SIRLS who are off-campus has declined over the years (see Figure 1).[5]

At the same time, the number of courses offered away from the home campus has almost tripled from 1999 to 2003, from four courses to eleven courses.

Despite the declining proportion of distance students to resident students at SIRLS, the impact that serving distance students has had on the UA Libraries is significant. We are realizing that *all* users are "distant" in some sense. As Anderson stated, "There are degrees of remoteness."[6] Small found in her 1995 study of resident and distance graduate students at the School of Information Studies at Syracuse University that

FIGURE 1. Percentage of Off-Campus FTE–SIRLS

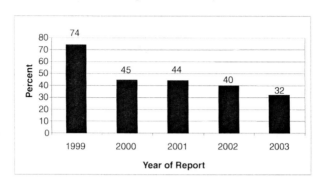

sixty percent of distance students, compared to only thirty-six percent of resident students, used the Internet at least four hours per week to complete coursework.[7]

In her follow-up 1999 study, Small found that the number of students in each group spending at least four hours per week using the Internet to complete coursework had increased: seventy-one percent of distance students and forty-eight percent of resident students.[8] Small acknowledges that these increases may be due to the growth in using the Internet to deliver course content. It would be interesting to know how much of the students' time using the Internet was spent doing "library" research, such as accessing online databases licensed by the library, as opposed to reading lectures and other course-specific work. Whatever the reason, it is clear that both distance and resident students in library studies are relying more heavily on the Internet.

While SIRLS is less than half a mile from the library, many of the students who are local/on-campus students have schedules that make it difficult for them to get to the library. As "non-traditional" students, some of these graduate students work full-time during the day and take classes in the evening. Even "traditional" library users have "become modern remote users."[9] At the same time, the typical or traditional student has expectations of accessing information and doing research online. The Pew Internet and American Life Project found that almost three quarters (seventy-three percent) of college students say they use the Internet more than the library for information searching, and that "students have come to expect . . . near-ubiquitous Internet access."[10]

## IMPROVING LIBRARY SERVICES AND RESOURCES

As the librarian for Library and Information Science (LIS) and the liaison to SIRLS, the author was keenly aware of the challenges distance students faced and interested in enhancing the services and resources provided to students who could not physically use the UA library. SIRLS students are not only doing their own research and working on assignments as graduate students; they are also preparing and developing for their careers as information professionals. As Latham and Smith point out, "The library services available to distance education students in LIS programs is a particularly intriguing area of study because of the obvious connection between provision of library services and the education of future information providers. It would be especially ironic and vexing if students enrolled in LIS distance education programs were receiving limited and/or inferior services."[11] Burnett and Painter also reinforce this important point in their paper studying the School of Information Studies at Florida State University. Providing support is "crucial to the success of the School of Information Studies distance learning initiatives, especially since our students need to study the format and delivery of such resources as well as making use of their contents."[12]

The LIS librarian first focused on improving the amount of information that library science students could access online, including moving from print to electronic indexes and adding additional online full-text availability. The UA Library already subscribed to the *Library Literature* database online through FirstSearch. The LIS librarian investigated the full text available online from H.W. Wilson, the publisher of *Library Literature*, and the library added a subscription to *WilsonSelectPlus* in July 2001. This resource, which the UA Library accesses through FirstSearch, provides more than one hundred titles in full text for periodicals indexed in *Library Literature*, or about one-third of the titles indexed.

At the same time, the LIS librarian also began a trial of the online version of *Library and Information Science Abstracts (LISA)*, which the library previously had only in print, making it completely inaccessible to distance students who could not come to campus. The UA online subscription started in October 2001. Ironically, comments received after announcing the new database on the school's electronic mailing list were all from local faculty and students, who were as thrilled about having online access as any distance students would be. The UA Library also recently added access to the online counterpart of the second edition of *The Encyclopedia of Library and Information Science.*

To ensure that distance students would indeed be able to access these new online resources, the LIS librarian arranged with the UA's CatCard office (the UA faculty and student identification card) and the SIRLS program manager for distance students to get their CatCard numbers without having to come to campus to get their student IDs. They would need their CatCard number to access licensed library resources remotely, as well as to make online interlibrary loan (ILL) requests and to use some other library services.

## SURVEY OF DISTANCE STUDENTS

Adding additional online access was the first step in enhancing library resources for distance students. Next, we wanted to hear from them what they needed. In late Fall 2001 and early Spring 2002, the LIS librarian and a colleague conducted two needs assessment surveys of SIRLS distance learners. In the first survey, distance students were asked what types of assignments they were working on, what types of materials and resources they used to complete these assignments, and whether they encountered any barriers to obtaining the materials. They were also asked if there were any materials or services that the library provided that helped them complete their assignments, and if there were anything else the library could have done to help.

In the second survey, their satisfaction with various library services and resources was addressed: ILL of journal articles, ILL of books, electronic reserves, library science indexes, online library orientation, research consultations, Askref (the library's e-mail reference service at that time), and research aids such as subject pathfinders. The distance students were asked to rate their satisfaction with each from 1 to 6 (low to high); one of the choices for each question was also "didn't know about the resource." The UA Library's Document Delivery Team (DDT) also included a few questions in the survey about what students would be willing to pay for articles and books owned by the library to be delivered to them. This was a service that DDT was beginning to explore at that time.

While the surveys conducted are not the focus of this article, and the response rate was low, we did find that several of the respondents did not know about the services listed in the survey, including interlibrary loan and e-mail reference. One respondent indicated confusion about whether distance students were even allowed to use ILL. Other comments made it clear that there was a lack of common understanding or knowledge among distance students regarding exactly what the library provided.

In addition to the survey results, the LIS librarian had also received e-mails over the years from distance students who emphasized the need for as much information online as possible. Some of these students live in areas that have little or no access to physical library resources, or the resources available to them locally do not support a graduate-level program.

Thus, what was learned from distance students is that they need access to information online as much as possible and that some of them were not aware of the resources and services provided by the library. This lack of awareness persists, in spite of sending regular announcements several times each semester to the school's electronic mailing list, to which all SIRLS students are required to be registered. Cooper and Dempsey also found lack of awareness of some library services to be an issue with distance students they surveyed at DePaul University, but point out that "if nothing else, a survey can be a useful tool for making users aware of services and resources."[13] Likewise, it also makes the library aware that not everyone knows about what we provide, and we need to continually market our services.

## OTHER DEVELOPMENTS

In April 2002, the LIS librarian attended the Tenth Off-Campus Library Services Conference in Cincinnati, Ohio. One theme that seemed to recur is that many libraries have a person designated as a distance learning librarian, a distributed learning librarian, or some equivalent title. In Latham and Smith's evaluation of Web sites of academic libraries with ALA-accredited LIS programs, "57% of the libraries responding indicated that they have staff designated specifically to work with distance students."[14] The UA Library does not have such a position. Public services librarians at the UA are largely organized by subject specialty, with responsibilities including collection management, reference and research assistance, and instruction of faculty and students in their designated subject areas. If there were distance students in their programs, interaction with them would be integrated in their job. Most of these subject specialists do not have distance students enrolled in their given departments, but because from 1/3 to 3/4 of the full-time equivalent students at SIRLS over the past five years are off-campus students, the LIS librarian has become a contact in the library for issues concerning distance students.

Several projects were developing concurrently in the library that would improve library services for all our users, but would particularly benefit distance students: online library orientation, chat reference, and alternative ways to deliver materials to users. Every semester, the LIS librarian conducts a library orientation for SIRLS students, primarily using a PowerPoint presentation. Some distance students who live in Phoenix, Arizona, would travel to the orientation, but most distance students could not attend.

While the orientation does have some focus on physically using the library, it also provides information about accessing resources remotely, whom to contact for help, and other information pertinent to both on- and off-campus students. Since the SIRLS master's degree program requires a minimum of six credit hours in residency, all students, including distance students, must take six units of coursework on the UA campus. So even the physical aspects of the library presented in the orientation would be important to distance students at some point. With the benefit of technology, the LIS librarian started loading the PowerPoint presentation to the Web in Summer 2000, and notified all students of its location via the school's electronic mailing list.

During this same time period, a project team in the library investigated implementing virtual, or chat, reference, and after a pilot program in Fall 2001, "Ask a Librarian" was implemented in Spring 2002. This service expands upon the e-mail (asynchronous) reference service the library already provided, allowing real-time interaction with customers, as well as the ability to "push" pages to them and show them how to conduct searches. One challenge that remains for distance students is the time zone difference some of them face when using this service. Ask-a-Librarian is currently available from 10 a.m. to 4 p.m. and 6 p.m. to 8 p.m., Mountain Standard Time (MST), during the regular Fall and Spring semesters and from 10 a.m. to 4 p.m., MST, during Summer Sessions.

In 2002, the Document Delivery Team was formed, bringing Interlibrary Loan, Electronic Reserves, the Photocopy Center, and Document Delivery together under one team. Distance students were already benefiting from ILL and e-reserves. They could receive materials like articles and book chapters that the library did not own through ILL, and they could access course reserves, primarily articles and book chapters, that were made available electronically. They still could not easily access materials the library did own that were not put on reserve by their professors. One option was "copies by mail," through which one could call the library and request that copies of articles or sections from books be copied, for a fee, and mailed to the user. But the library's millions of print volumes were still largely out of distance students' reach.

In Spring 2003, DDT ran a pilot project for delivering library-owned materials to distance students; SIRLS distance students were part of the pilot. This service has now been expanded to campus users who do not want to come in to the library. For a fee, articles and book chapters are delivered electronically to the user, distant or local. Currently, only distance students may have complete books from the UA Library's collection mailed to them.[15]

## *NEW WEB SITE FOR DISTANCE STUDENTS*

Between the distance students' lack of awareness of library services and resources available to them, and the development of even more new services and resources that would benefit them, there clearly was a need for a centralized place with information for distance students. While Latham and Smith found in their Web site evaluation and survey that libraries where there are ALA-accredited programs in LIS "appear to be providing adequate services to distance learning students,"[16] there was certainly room for improvement on the UA Library site. As Linden points out, "for distance students who seldom or never visit your library physically, the library's Web site *is* the library"[17] and "putting all this information in one place, on a distance learners page, is efficient."[18]

The LIS librarian began working on a Web site that would bring all of this information together. In June 2003, the site was previewed to some of the SIRLS faculty and staff, as well as to members of DDT, and it was made public in August 2003. An announcement was sent to the SIRLS distribution list with details about the new Web site, including a note that while the site is geared toward students who are not located in Tucson, it should be of use to all SIRLS students who want to access library services and resources from outside the library. The creation of this Web site highlighted the need to provide this kind of centralized information for all students.

The site was also presented to students during the Fall 2003 and Spring 2004 orientations, and reminders about it are sent out periodically to the SIRLS distribution list. Reminders about the site are also sent to library staff who should be aware of challenges faced by distance students and who may get questions from them.

The Web site, Library Services and Resources for Distance Students, is available at http://www.library.arizona.edu/users/mfeeney/distance/ (see Figure 2). It is linked from the UA Library's Subject Guide for Library and Information Science, since that is the user group the site currently targets. The Web site is divided into five sections: orientation to the library, reference/research assistance, locating information on LIS topics, getting materials, and research guides.

The section "Getting Started: An Orientation to the University of Arizona Libraries" links to the Web version of the PowerPoint presentation and includes the LIS librarian's speaker's notes to provide context and more explanation for the students who cannot attend orientation in person.

The section "Reference/Research Assistance" is a page that explains the ways a user can get help with reference questions or research (see Figure 3). This includes getting reference assistance in person, by phone, through chat reference, or by contacting the subject specialist li-

FIGURE 2. Screen Capture of Web Site, Library Services and Resources for Distance Learners

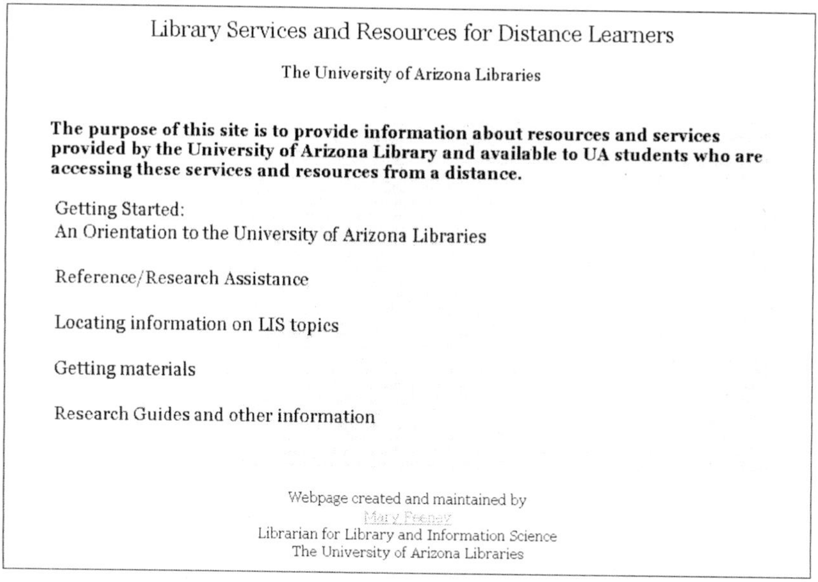

Library Services and Resources for Distance Learners

The University of Arizona Libraries

**The purpose of this site is to provide information about resources and services provided by the University of Arizona Library and available to UA students who are accessing these services and resources from a distance.**

Getting Started:
An Orientation to the University of Arizona Libraries

Reference/Research Assistance

Locating information on LIS topics

Getting materials

Research Guides and other information

Webpage created and maintained by
Mary Feeney
Librarian for Library and Information Science
The University of Arizona Libraries

FIGURE 3. Screen Capture of Web Page, Reference/Research Assistance

---

Library Services and Resources for Distance Learners

The University of Arizona Libraries

### Reference/Research Assistance

**I have a reference question and/or need help with my research. Who should I contact?**

You may:

a) Come to the Information Commons Reference Desk (if you're in Tucson!)

b) Call the Main Library Information Desk at (520) 621-6441.

c) Use our virtual reference service "Ask a Librarian" at
http://www.library.arizona.edu/askalibrarian.

**OR**

d) For more in-depth research assistance, contact the subject specialist for Library and Information Science, Mary Feeney.

Return to Library Services and Resources for Distance Learners main page.

Webpage created and maintained by
Mary Feeney
Librarian for Library and Information Science
The University of Arizona Libraries

---

brarian for library science. The link on the subject specialist's name leads to a Web form that the user may complete with his/her name, contact information, and question(s), which is then submitted to the LIS librarian's e-mail address.

Students interviewed by Kazmer said that "having one person in an office as a contact point to answer all questions from distance students was helpful."[19] While the UA Library is not organized with one central person serving distance learners, as a subject specialist who deals with distance students, the LIS librarian is able to answer many of their questions. Furthermore, different parts of the site link to the Web sites and contact information of teams like document delivery and interlibrary loan, as well as the program manager of SIRLS, who can also answer specialized questions from distance students in their areas of expertise.

Because the Web site is geared toward graduate students in library science, the section "Locating information on LIS topics" focuses on how to find citations to articles and other materials in two LIS databases, *Library Literature* and *Library and Information Science Abstracts (LISA)* (see Figure 4). It explains how to access these databases

FIGURE 4. Screen Capture of Web Page, Locating Information on LIS Topics

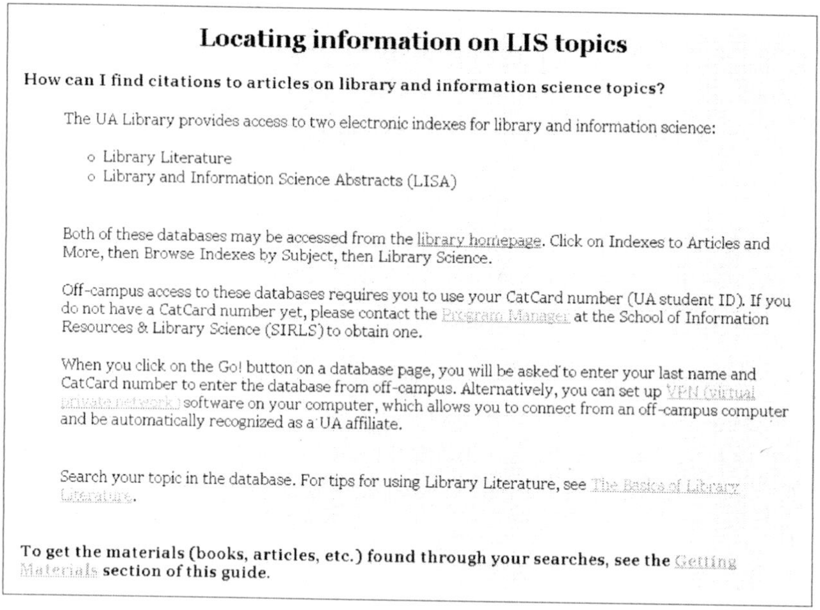

## Locating information on LIS topics

**How can I find citations to articles on library and information science topics?**

The UA Library provides access to two electronic indexes for library and information science:

- o Library Literature
- o Library and Information Science Abstracts (LISA)

Both of these databases may be accessed from the <u>library homepage</u>. Click on Indexes to Articles and More, then Browse Indexes by Subject, then Library Science.

Off-campus access to these databases requires you to use your CatCard number (UA student ID). If you do not have a CatCard number yet, please contact the <u>Program Manager</u> at the School of Information Resources & Library Science (SIRLS) to obtain one.

When you click on the Go! button on a database page, you will be asked to enter your last name and CatCard number to enter the database from off-campus. Alternatively, you can set up <u>VPN (virtual private network)</u> software on your computer, which allows you to connect from an off-campus computer and be automatically recognized as a UA affiliate.

Search your topic in the database. For tips for using Library Literature, see <u>The Basics of Library Literature</u>.

**To get the materials (books, articles, etc.) found through your searches, see the** <u>Getting Materials</u> **section of this guide.**

from off-campus using either their CatCard number (UA ID) or virtual private network (VPN) software. There is also a link to a basic guide for searching *Library Literature*.

The "Getting materials" section is probably one of the most pertinent to distance students. Several students who completed our survey indicated that they wanted more and better access to full-text materials, as well as delivery of materials. Kazmer found, when interviewing distance students at the Graduate School of Library and Information Science at the University of Illinois at Urbana-Champaign, that they "expressed strong support for one service in particular: expedited document delivery."[20] Some SIRLS distance students, as mentioned earlier, may not have access to a large college library, let alone the research holdings of the UA, so getting access to materials we own is especially important to them.

The "Getting materials" page explains that some databases, such as *Library Literature*, have some full-text articles online directly through the database. If an article is not available that way, users can search the library catalog (see Figure 5). Three scenarios of what one may find when searching a journal title in the catalog are explained:

1. There may be electronic access through one of the several aggregators and electronic sources to which the library subscribes (see Figure 6).
2. The library may own a print copy of the journal. Here, the page explains that library-owned items may be received through document delivery (see Figure 7).
3. The library may not have print or electronic access to the title. Here, the page explains that non-library owned items may be requested through ILL (see Figure 8).

At the bottom of the "Getting materials" page, document delivery and ILL services are briefly explained, and links to additional information are provided (see Figure 9).

The last section of the Web site, "Research Guides," links to the library and information science subject guide/pathfinder.

## *AWARENESS OF SERVICES AND MARKETING*

Maintaining faculty and student awareness of this Web site and what resources and services the library provides still seems to be an ongoing challenge. Viggiano states that marketing may be the "most challenging

FIGURE 5. Screen Capture of Top of Web Page, Getting Materials from Citations

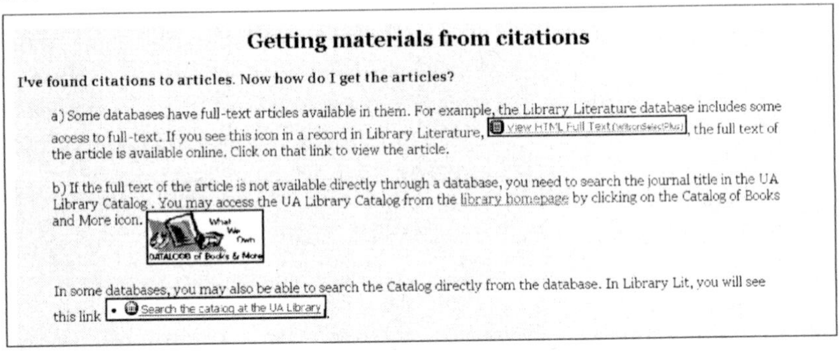

**Getting materials from citations**

I've found citations to articles. Now how do I get the articles?

a) Some databases have full-text articles available in them. For example, the Library Literature database includes some access to full-text. If you see this icon in a record in Library Literature, [View HTML Full Text (NetworkedPlus)], the full text of the article is available online. Click on that link to view the article.

b) If the full text of the article is not available directly through a database, you need to search the journal title in the UA Library Catalog. You may access the UA Library Catalog from the library homepage by clicking on the Catalog of Books and More icon. [CATALOG of Books & More]

In some databases, you may also be able to search the Catalog directly from the database. In Library Lit, you will see this link [• Search the catalog at the UA Library]

FIGURE 6. Screen Capture of Web Page, Getting Materials–Link in Catalog

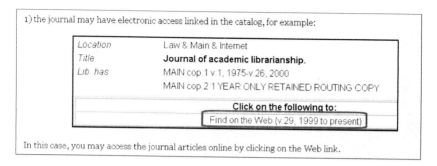

1) the journal may have electronic access linked in the catalog, for example:

| | |
|---|---|
| Location | Law & Main & Internet |
| Title | **Journal of academic librarianship.** |
| Lib. has | MAIN cop.1 v.1, 1975-v.26, 2000 |
| | MAIN cop.2 1 YEAR ONLY RETAINED ROUTING COPY |

**Click on the following to:**
Find on the Web (v.29, 1999 to present)

In this case, you may access the journal articles online by clicking on the Web link.

FIGURE 7. Screen Capture of Web Page, Getting Materials–Paper Copy

2) the library may own a paper copy of the journal, for example:

| | |
|---|---|
| Location | Main Current Journal |
| Title | School library journal. |
| | **School library journal : SLJ.** |
| Lib. has | MAIN cop.1 v.8-<21>-25, 1961-1979; 27-<34>, 1980- |
| Z675.S3 J6 | |
| Latest Received | August 2002 48:8 |

In this case, you may request that the article from this journal be delivered to you through Document Delivery. See Document Delivery below for more information about this service.

aspect of providing library services to distance learners."[21] Every semester, new students begin the graduate program and need to be educated about the site, and others forget that the services are available. As mentioned earlier, e-mail reminders are sent to the SIRLS distribution list every semester with information about the library and links to the site, as well as other resources. Based on the data of how many "hits" the main page of the "Library Services and Resources for Distance Learners" site gets, use of the site spikes whenever a reminder is sent (see Figure 10). The first announcement about the new site was sent in August 2003. Another announcement was sent in April 2004. In addition, the site was presented at library orientation in August 2003 and January 2004. Kirk and Bartelstein reinforce that librarians who work

FIGURE 8. Screen Capture of Web Page, Getting Materials–Interlibrary Loan

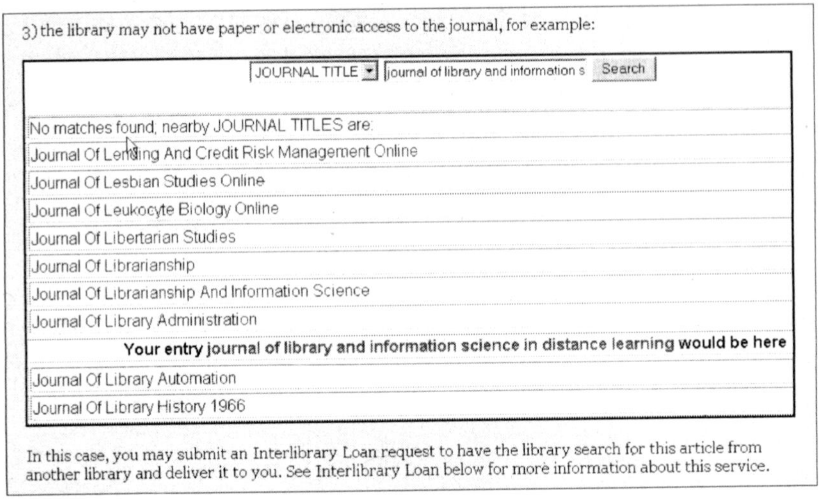

3) the library may not have paper or electronic access to the journal, for example:

| JOURNAL TITLE ▼ | journal of library and information s | Search |

No matches found; nearby JOURNAL TITLES are:

Journal Of Lending And Credit Risk Management Online

Journal Of Lesbian Studies Online

Journal Of Leukocyte Biology Online

Journal Of Libertarian Studies

Journal Of Librarianship

Journal Of Librarianship And Information Science

Journal Of Library Administration

**Your entry journal of library and information science in distance learning would be here**

Journal Of Library Automation

Journal Of Library History 1966

In this case, you may submit an Interlibrary Loan request to have the library search for this article from another library and deliver it to you. See Interlibrary Loan below for more information about this service.

FIGURE 9. Screen Capture of Web Page, Getting Materials–Document Delivery and ILL

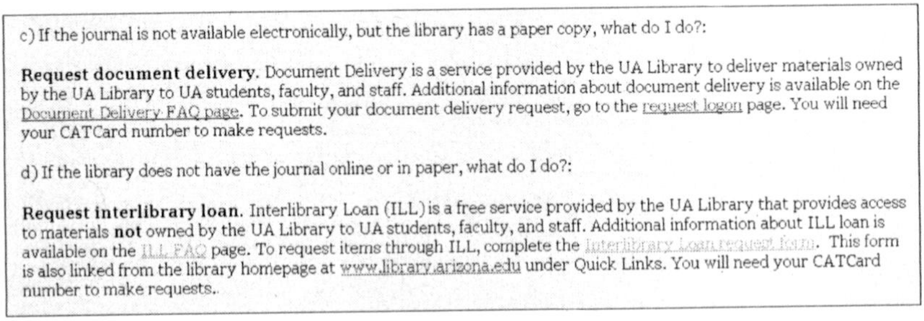

c) If the journal is not available electronically, but the library has a paper copy, what do I do?:

**Request document delivery.** Document Delivery is a service provided by the UA Library to deliver materials owned by the UA Library to UA students, faculty, and staff. Additional information about document delivery is available on the Document Delivery FAQ page. To submit your document delivery request, go to the request logon page. You will need your CATCard number to make requests.

d) If the library does not have the journal online or in paper, what do I do?:

**Request interlibrary loan.** Interlibrary Loan (ILL) is a free service provided by the UA Library that provides access to materials **not** owned by the UA Library to UA students, faculty, and staff. Additional information about ILL loan is available on the ILL FAQ page. To request items through ILL, complete the Interlibrary Loan request form. This form is also linked from the library homepage at www.library.arizona.edu under Quick Links. You will need your CATCard number to make requests.

with distance students "cannot afford to be reactive," but rather must be proactive in providing service to this customer base.[22]

## *IMPROVEMENTS AND FUTURE RESEARCH*

Like any useful Web page, this site is an ever-evolving resource. One future improvement could include adding more research guides and on-

FIGURE 10. Hits on Web Page, Library Services and Resources for Distance Learners, http://www.library.arizona.edu/users/mfeeney/distance/

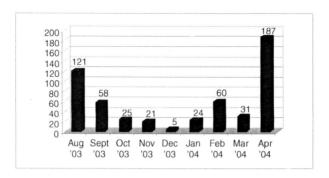

line library instruction, including a guide to using the *LISA* database. In addition, the screen captures on the site need periodic updating as our library resources change. For example, the UA Library has been implementing Serials Solutions and Innovative Interfaces' Electronic Resources Management (ERM) module, both of which change the appearance of our catalog records. The screen captures on the site showing parts of the library catalog will need to be revised.

Marketing efforts of library resources and services should be intensified, including working with faculty teaching online courses to include this information in their course pages in WebCT. A link to the site has recently been added to the School's Distance and Virtual Education Web page.

There are also possibilities for further research regarding how distance students are using these library resources and services once they know about them. Does it change the way they do research? Hoy and Hale concluded in their study that "off-campus students appear not to be at a disadvantage in gaining access to scholarly work."[23] Is this the case with SIRLS distance students? In addition, who is using the site–distance students, local students, or both?

This last question is key. The LIS librarian is considering changing the name of the site by taking out "for distance learners." While the site was originally conceived as being an aid for distance students, it has become clear that all SIRLS students would benefit from having centralized information about how to use basic library services and resources.

## CONCLUSION

Distance learners have taught libraries not only how to change the way we provide services but also how to present information about our services to users. By focusing on a specific group of users and their challenges, the LIS librarian at the UA Library was able to focus more clearly on what is best for *all* users.

Pace concludes that "improving libraries for our most removed users will improve libraries for those closest to us."[24] In other words, does it matter if they're distant? This was the very subject of a Library and Information Technology Association (LITA) panel at the American Library Association Annual Conference 2004 in Orlando, Florida: "Is 'Distance Learning' Passe?" The description of the program states, "The practice of enhancing classroom teaching with Web-based courseware is commonplace. Chat reference services can be used anywhere, even within the library. Many patrons now receive documents electronically from interlibrary loan. With numerous electronic services available to all library patrons, is the need to distinguish between 'distance' and 'on-campus' becoming less necessary? This panel will address how technologies developed with distance learning in mind now have broader use."[25] Viggiano proposes that "libraries begin to consider blending distance library services with traditional services"[26] since "distance learners aren't always very distant, and traditional on-campus learners aren't always as traditional as we think."[27]

We do need to "understand the unique needs of distance learners when providing services to them,"[28] as Cooper and Dempsey state, but while the user "a few buildings away from the library on campus encounters a situation different from the student . . . thousands of miles [away],"[29] they both want the same thing: convenient access to information. Kirk and Bartelstein conclude: "Libraries that decide that what works for distance-based patrons works for patrons across the quad, and vice versa, will be well positioned to meet the challenges of the future."[30] Goodson also emphasizes that "the kinds of library support services often supplied to off-campus students can and should be the prototype for future library services as well."[31] Keeping our eyes in the distance will help us see better what's right in front of us.

# NOTES

1. Dan Barron, "Distance Education in Library and Information Science: A Long Road Traveled," [Introduction to special issue on distance education] *Journal of Education for Library and Information Science* 43, 1 (Winter 2002): 3.

2. Charles A. Seavey, "Distance Education at the School of Information Resources and Library Science," in *Benchmarks in Distance Education: The LIS Experience*, ed. Daniel D. Barron, 5-11 (Westport, CT: Libraries Unlimited, 2003).

3. Carol Goodson. *Providing Library Services for Distance Education Students: A How-To-Do-It Manual* (New York: Neal-Schuman Publishers, Inc., 2001).

4. Krista Graham and Alison Grodzinski. "Defining the Remote Library User: An Online Survey," *portal: Libraries and the Academy*, 1, 3 (2001): 291.

5. Association for Library and Information Science Education, *Library and Information Science Education Statistical Report*, 1999-2003 editions, http://ils.unc.edu/ALISE/ (accessed June 4, 2004).

6. Rick Anderson, "Reaching Out–The Library's New Role," in *Attracting, Educating, and Serving Remote Users through the Web: A How-To-Do-It Manual for Librarians*, ed. Donnelyn Curtis (New York: Neal-Schuman Publishers, Inc., 2002).

7. Ruth V. Small, "A Comparison of the Resident and Distance Learning Experience in Library and Information Science Graduate Education," *Journal of Education for Library and Information Science*, 40, 1 (Winter 1999): 32.

8. Ruth V. Small, "The Evolution of a Distance Learning Program in Library and Information Science: A Follow-up Study," *Journal of Education for Library and Information Science*, 43, 1 (Winter 2002): 51.

9. Rachel Viggiano, "Distance Learners: Not Necessarily Distant," *The Southeastern Librarian*, 51, 3 (Fall 2003): 31.

10. Steve Jones et al., "The Internet Goes to College: How Students are Living in the Future with Today's Technology," Pew Internet and American Life Project, http://www.pewinternet.org/pdfs/PIP_College_Report.pdf (accessed July 6, 2004).

11. Dan Latham and Stephanie Maatta Smith, "Practicing What We Teach: A Descriptive Analysis of Library Services for Distance Learning Students in ALA-accredited LIS Schools," *Journal of Education for Library and Information Science*, 44, 2 (spring 2003): p. 122.

12. Kathleen Burnett and Marilia Painter, "Learning From Experience: Strategies for Assuring Effective Library and Information Services to Web-based Distance Learners" in *Crossing the Divide: Proceedings of the Tenth National Conference of the Association of College and Research Libraries, March 15-18, 2001, Denver, Colorado*, ed. Hugh A Thompson, 131-136 (Chicago: Association of College and Research Libraries, 2001).

13. Rosemarie Cooper, Paula R. Dempsey, Vanaja Menon, and Christopher Millson-Martula, "Remote Library Users–Needs and Expectations," *Library Trends*, 47, 1 (Summer 1998): 60.

14. Latham and Smith, p. 127-128.

15. For more information about fees and the library's document delivery service, see http://www.library.arizona.edu/library/teams/ill/ddfaq.html.

16. Latham and Smith, 130.

17. Julie Linden, "The Library's Web Site is the Library: Designing for Distance Learners," *College & Research Libraries News*, 61, 2 (February 2000), 99.

18. Linden, 101.

19. Michelle M. Kazmer, "Distance Education Students Speak to the Library: Here's How You Can Help Even More," *The Electronic Library*, 20, 5 (2002): 396.

20. Ibid.

21. Viggiano, 34.

22. Elizabeth E. Kirk and Andrea M. Bartelstein, "Libraries Close in on Distance Education," *Library Journal*, 124, 6 (April 1, 1999): 42.

23. Catherine Hoy and Martha L. Hale, "A Comparison of References Cited by On-campus and Off-campus Graduate Library Science Students," in *The Fifth Off-campus Library Services Conference Proceedings, Albuquerque, New Mexico, October 30 to November 1, 1991*, compiled by Carol J. Jacob, http://ocls.cmich.edu/5thOCLSCP. pdf (accessed June 4, 2004).

24. Andrew K. Pace, "Distance Learning Service: It's Closer Than You Think," *Computers in Libraries*, 21, 4 (April 2001): 51.

25. "ALA Annual Conference 2004 Preliminary Program," *American Libraries*, 35, 3 (March 2004): 156.

26. Viggiano, p. 31.

27. Viggiano, p. 34.

28. Cooper et al., 53.

29. Cooper et al., 43.

30. Kirk and Bartelstein, p. 42.

31. Carol Goodson, "I Have Seen the Future, and It Is Us!" *The Journal of Library Services for Distance Education*, 1, 1 (August 1997), http://www.westga.edu/~library/jlsde/vol1/1/CGoodson.html (accessed June 22, 2004).

# Designing and Developing Internet Reference Services to Support Firefighter Distance Learners in Illinois

Lian Ruan

**SUMMARY.** This article discusses issues surrounding the development of a small special library's Internet reference services to support firefighter distance learners for the University of Illinois Fire Service Institute's (IFSI) online Firefighter II Certification Program, the first of its kind in the nation. Planning for the Internet reference services involves consideration of user needs, funding, staff management, and collection development. In addition, this article explores how the IFSI Library has established a collaboration and partnership with the online course and Information Technology teams, and local public and community college libraries. *[Article copies available for a fee from The Haworth Document Delivery Service: 1-800-HAWORTH. E-mail address: <docdelivery@haworthpress.com> Website: <http://www.HaworthPress.com> © 2004 by The Haworth Press, Inc. All rights reserved.]*

Lian Ruan (lruan@fsi.uiuc.edu) is Director/Head Librarian, Illinois Fire Service Institute, University of Illinois at Urbana-Champaign, 11 Gerty Drive, Champaign, IL 61820.

[Haworth co-indexing entry note]: "Designing and Developing Internet Reference Services to Support Firefighter Distance Learners in Illinois." Ruan, Lian. Co-published simultaneously in *Internet Reference Services Quarterly* (The Haworth Information Press, an imprint of The Haworth Press, Inc.) Vol. 9, No. 1/2, 2004, pp. 147-172; and: *Improving Internet Reference Services to Distance Learners* (ed: William Miller, and Rita M. Pellen) The Haworth Information Press, an imprint of The Haworth Press, Inc., 2004, pp. 147-172. Single or multiple copies of this article are available for a fee from The Haworth Document Delivery Service [1-800-HAWORTH, 9:00 a.m. - 5:00 p.m. (EST). E-mail address: docdelivery@haworthpress.com].

http://www.haworthpress.com/web/IRSQ
© 2004 by The Haworth Press, Inc. All rights reserved.
Digital Object Identifier: 10.1300/J136v09n01_11

**KEYWORDS.** Firefighters, special library, fire service library, distance education, distance learning, virtual library, fire information service, management of distance learning service

## INTRODUCTION

Illinois Fire Service Institute (IFSI), University of Illinois at Urbana-Champaign, is the statutory State Fire Academy with 80 years experience in firefighter emergency training. The Institute has developed a unique and effective curriculum, maintained the highest level of instructional expertise, and built a statewide network of 350 adjunct instructors. The Institute's central objective is to prepare and help Illinois firefighters, and other emergency services providers, develop the core skills required to effectively meet the emergency fire service needs of their communities. The major programs include Fire Fighting, Hazardous Materials and Counter-Terrorism, Rescue, Investigation and Fire Prevention, Industry and EMS (Emergency Medical Services). Since 1997, under the new Vision 2000 and Vision 2010 for the Future, the Institute's goal is to find the best ways to reach every Illinois firefighter with the training, education, and *information* he/she requires each year.

The IFSI Library was established in 1990 as an in-house library to support the training and teaching of the Institute's instructors and students. It also serves the local fire departments throughout the State from time to time via phone, fax, or mail requests. Subject strengths of the Library are arson investigation, fire fighting, hazardous materials, counter-terrorism, rescue, fire education, fire safety, fire services management, emergency management, Emergency Medical Services, and general training. With a series of grant awards from the Illinois State Library, a division of the Office of the Illinois Secretary of State, in-house support from the Institute, and other external support from funding organizations, and the Illinois fire service and library communities, the Library's Outreach Program, which provides no cost library and information services to Illinois firefighters, has been a great success since its inception in 1999. The IFSI Library is the only fire-dedicated library in Illinois (eliillinois.org) and one of the three fire academy libraries in the nation (www.inFIRE.org). The Outreach Program also designed and developed new Internet reference services to support firefighter distance learners for the Institute's online Firefighter II course, and later for the Online Hazardous Materials Awareness course and the Online Emergency Response to Terrorism: Basic Concepts course.

## FIREFIGHTER DISTANCE LEARNERS

Understanding the Illinois firefighter distance learners and the Institute's online Firefighter II Certification Program was the first crucial step for the IFSI Library to design a usable Internet reference service for distance learning program. Although distance learning has been an approach to delivering educational programs for many decades, in the world of fire service training, it is a relatively new concept. For fire service in Illinois, there are 1,293 fire departments and 42,675 firefighters. Of these firefighters, 70% are volunteers. There are 6,000 to 8,000 entry-level firefighters that enter the system each year in Illinois. The Illinois Office of the State Fire Marshal, Division of Personnel Standards and Education, establishes the guidelines for the Illinois firefighter certification procedures and curriculum. Firefighter II certification is the minimum professional qualification, whether paid or volunteer. This minimum training level is designed to assure a firefighter who can safely function at a fire emergency, and the Institute's training experience suggests it requires a minimum of 250 hours of instruction, in addition to other requirements.

Illinois firefighters have the following avenues available to them to complete the required cognitive and psychomotor objectives: (a) attend a 6-10 week residential academy; (b) belong to a department that conducts the approved training; (c) attend a local community college that delivers the needed classes; and (d) attend classes provided by the Illinois Fire Service Institute. According to separate statewide surveys done by the Institute, the Illinois Fire Chief's Association, and the Illinois Office of the State Fire Marshal, shortage of discretionary time was the number one reason firefighters are unable to receive Firefighter II certification training. For volunteer firefighters, full-time employment, family, and other major commitments are the primary reasons for their inability to attend training courses. Throughout Illinois, the fire service experiences an annual turnover rate of 20%. If Illinois is to maintain a well-trained firefighting force for the 21st Century, it is necessary to implement a new training delivery system to reach potential firefighters.

The Institute designed and developed the new Online Firefighter II Certification Program, which was made available in September 2000. This was America's first online Firefighter II Certification Program.

The unique online approach has provided access to the critical initial certification level for firefighters who did not have access to traditional firefighter academy courses. The student population is estimated at 6,000 to 8,000 annually. The Office of the State Fire Marshal (OSFM) applauded "this effort as it supports the OSFM mandate to 'reduce death, injury, and property loss of Illinois citizens from fire,' and the Division of Personnel Standards and Education's mandate to 'improve the levels of education and training for firefighters.'" Figure 1 shows numbers of firefighters enrolled in the Institute Online Firefighter II Certification course in the past four years.

An integrated library information service is essential to help remote Firefighter II students complete the course successfully. Students at remote sites may have no facilities comparable to those easily accessed by on-campus students. Additionally, many remote site students face difficulties in obtaining information because of a variety of reasons, which differ from site to site. Telecommunication facilities, equipment, site conditions, local libraries, educational background, and previous library experience are all factors in the accessibility of library services and materials to the offsite student.

Making appropriate learning resources and services available for online Firefighter II distance learning students is one of the most important components for the IFSI Library Outreach Program since the library resources and services are an essential part of a strong academic distance education program. When the Institute embarked on a new distance-learning program in 2000, the IFSI Library emphasized its essential role in contributing to the quality of such programs. Students at remote sites should have consistent access to library informa-

FIGURE 1. Online Firefighter II Certification Students

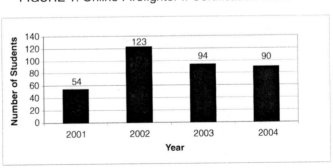

tional and research materials in order to develop and broaden their understanding of the ideas and research in their disciplines, to bring new ideas to their off-site classrooms, and to acquire and develop their skills in research. These resources are as essential to the remote student as to those on campus. The IFSI Library needed to ensure the provision of, and access to, adequate learning resources and services required to support the Firefighter II course. The IFSI Library needed to provide guaranteed access, sufficient collections, and services for off-campus Firefighter II students wherever they are. It also became apparent that providing access to digital resources is a critical factor in the long-term success or failure of libraries, which holds true for the IFSI Library.

## SOLUTIONS

As defined by the ACRL (Association of College & Research Libraries) Guidelines for Distance Learning Library Services in July 1998 (see 2000 revision at http://www.ala.org/ala/acrl/acrlstandards/guidelinesdistancelearning.htm), distance learning library services refers to those library services in support of college, university, or other *post-secondary* courses and programs offered away from a main campus, or in the absence of a traditional campus, and regardless of where credit is given. The 1998 Guidelines recognized that "special funding arrangements, proactive planning, and promotion are necessary to deliver equivalent library services and to maintain quality in distance learning programs."

Innovative approaches in developing and implementing distance learning library services were needed to provide online Firefighter II students with electronic access to the fire information they required to complete their study more effectively and successfully. With the emergence of the Internet, information access capabilities have proliferated enormously. Implementation of Internet reference services for firefighter distance learners shows a very promising future to fulfill the IFSI Library's vision and objectives because it facilitates resource sharing by providing access to databases, electronic newsletters and bulletin boards, data archives, library catalogs, and electronic discussion groups.

In addition to the benefit of resource sharing, the Internet can be used for document delivery, and rapid dissemination of information all over the state. The ability to reach the widely dispersed off-campus Firefighter II students was made possible with electronic access to the library services. The Internet provided the IFSI Library with efficient ways of locating information and eliminated many physical barriers (e.g., distance, time, limitation of collections and subscriptions) for rapid dissemination of information. The Library used the Internet resources to cater to the information needs of firefighter distance learners.

Although there was a high level of commitment, additional staff and other needed support for the new service were not possible from the Institute due to budget obligations and constraints. It was also difficult to obtain substantial local start-up funding for distance learning library services initiatives because the benefits seemed indirect and as yet largely unproved and because few volunteer/paid-on-call fire departments had any substantial funds of their own for a library project like this one. Grant support was needed for this initiative because the partners had the expertise and experience, but not the start-up resources. The IFSI Library had very limited e-resources and no systematic distance education services in place. The IFSI Head Librarian actively sought new funding resources and applied successfully for the 2001 LSTA (Library Services and Technology Act) grant program, sponsored by the Illinois State Library.

### Grant Support

The 2001 LSTA grant, entitled "Developing the Distance Learning Library Services for Illinois Firefighters: An Integrated Information Service with Online Firefighter II Certification," was awarded $49,570 for the IFSI Library to create integrated distance learning services (Ruan 2001). It was built on the foundation already developed by the previous year's LSTA Full Year Grant project efforts and arrangements (Ruan 2001). Four areas were considered appropriate for funding. They were: (1) Collection development to support the online Firefighter II Certification Program by developing electronic and digital resources; (2) Document delivery to enhance and improve the cost-effective information retrieval and delivery system by determining the most feasible means of technology access for Firefighter II course assignments, and developing a new service- and problem-centered retrieval and delivery structure for offsite Firefighter II students and instructors; (3) User instruction training program to provide a virtual user instruction training program to offsite Firefighter II students and instructors, and to teach them how to use the distance learning library services, in addition to the Library OPAC, Web Home Page, e-mail and listserv system; and (4) Partnership with local libraries in the State's regional libraries systems to continue enhancing the Library's partnership with local public and community college libraries to provide a better quality of library distance learning services to remote and off-campus Firefighter II students and instructors.

The grant award provided the much-needed one-time, start-up money for human resources, library materials, and equipment to complete the project and launch the new service in a more timely and effective manner. Much of the grant was used for service development. The new service linked students in remote and different locations and allowed them to communicate, access the library services and resources, and participate effectively in the existing statewide interlibrary loan delivery system. The grant project also provided the organization, expertise, and encouragement for partnership among the IFSI Library with public and community college libraries to help improve information sharing in fire safety throughout Illinois. While continuing to provide quality and timely library services, this project fit right in the mix of other services the IFSI Library offered.

The major project tasks and milestones with an implementation schedule within the contract time frame were divided into three phases within eight months. The first phase lasted three months for preparation and development of services by identifying the distance learning library services for the Online Firefighter II Certification Program. The IFSI Head Librarian, serving as Project Director, hired and trained the actual project staff. The project staff developed the basic service model and pattern for e-collection development, e-reserves, copyright compliance, document delivery, and user instruction training. The project staff also had a training videotape made, provided reference services, online help, various research and evaluation forms, tested the new service and access mechanisms at the Firefighter II site, as well as the Library Web Home Page, OPAC, FireTalk-IFSI thesaurus (using MultiCGI Internet license), e-mail, and listserv system.

The second phase lasted another three months, focusing on implementation of services and collection of research data. Training workshops were held at local libraries, and virtual training sessions were conducted as Chat Sessions and on the Web Board for online Firefighter II students and instructors. The contents of services and training materials were revised based on feedback from students and instructors. The project staff continued to improve the Firefighter II site, the Library Web Home Page, OPAC, e-mail, listserv system, and FireTalk-IFSI thesaurus. Phase three, the final phase, lasted two more months. Main tasks were to upgrade document delivery services and instructional products, conduct research and evaluation, assess outcomes, and continue to improve the Firefighter II site, the Library Web Home Page, OPAC, FireTalk-IFSI thesaurus, e-mail, and listserv system.

## Partnership and Collaboration

The IFSI Library has expanded and enhanced alliances and partnerships with local libraries and the State's library systems. Through cooperation and collaboration the IFSI Library has shown that great things can be accomplished this way.

Based on the 1998 Outreach Program survey, which showed that a majority of fire departments have access to the statewide online system, ILLINET, and to broaden the Library's capability to serve the public interest in every community in Illinois, the Library obtained Full Membership as a special library in the Lincoln Trail Libraries System (LTLS) in November 1998 (see Figure 2). The Library's systematic interlibrary loan services started in March 1999 with all twelve of the State's regional library systems and received positive feedback from librarians and users.

To insure that offsite Firefighter II students obtain library materials and assistance at local libraries convenient to them, the most efficient and effective way is to cooperate with other local libraries in closer proximity to those online Firefighter II students and their instructors. The local public and community college libraries have provided library reserves and other services as needed to nearby online Firefighter II students.

The IFSI Library has worked hard to create an integrated library architecture linking firefighters wherever they train with the local and online library support they require to assist them in their studies. The 2000 LSTA grant for Internet outreach training helped launch a statewide effort to provide Internet outreach to and training of Illinois fire service personnel, public librarians, and community college librarians for electronic access to online fire safety information. It built the Library's partnership with fire departments, and local public and community college libraries. The 2001 LSTA grant for firefighter distance learners continued and strengthened the Library's partnership with local library communities. Both projects have reinforced the synergistic effect this has on the sharing of information and training materials.

Working with online course instructors is another partnership and alliance to form. Students need to access resources that support the curriculum via electronic means. The instructor's awareness of library

FIGURE 2. Library Systems in Illinois

services and resources is crucial to student success. Instructors who use the Library encourage students by assigning papers necessitating the use of library resources. Instructors direct students to appropriate resources if they are aware of them (Buehler et al., 2001). The IFSI Library works with instructors in various ways. The IFSI Head Librarian scheduled a meeting with instructors. E-mail and phone continue to be an effective medium to consult with instructors or help work out questions or problems they encounter in using the Library. The instructor provides the IFSI Library with new student roster lists. A goal of the Head Librarian is to be included in the online learning course process from the beginning. The Head Librarian also regularly attends staff meetings to remain abreast of changes that may influence what and how the Library provides information to off campus students. Instructors coordinate with the library's virtual training workshops, help promote the library services to students, and ensure smooth evaluation data collection for the services.

The University Web Technology Group (WTG) provided technical support both to the Institute's online Firefighter II course in its early years and the library grant project staff, who enhanced the Library Web Home Page to develop the specific Firefighter II site. WTG was the University of Illinois at Urbana-Champaign campus entity that supported instructors and academic departments in their efforts to develop and offer online courses and degree programs. The Library now works closely and directly with the Institute IT Office.

In addition, the Graduate School of Library and Information Science (GSLIS), the Library and Information Science Library, University of Illinois at Urbana-Champaign, and the University Academic Outreach Office have served as a consulting source of expertise, and help contribute an organizational environment rich in expertise related to citizens' information needs, community information services, system design and information retrieval applications. The electronic reserves services offered by the University's Library and Information Science Library were studied, and used as a successful model program to address needs similar to the IFSI Library's in serving distance learning students.

## CORE INTERNET REFERENCE SERVICES

The IFSI Library surveys in 1998 and 2003, and library training workshop evaluations reveal that accessibility determines the frequency of use of information channels by firefighter end users. Firefighting and emergency response are technical activities. Firefighter end users just want a specific answer in terms and format that is intelligible to them, not a collection of documents that they must sift, evaluate, and translate before they can apply them. In other words, firefighter end users just want the answer. It became clear that if the IFSI Library's Internet reference services to support firefighter distance learners were going to succeed, the Library had to make sure that services were easily accessible and allowed users to find the answers quickly. The IFSI Library's resources and services have evolved to support distance learners in their quest for information and research assistance. As the Institute's online course programs grow, the IFSI Library has undergone a major transformation in how it is perceived and how it provides services for fire emergency responder distance learners.

Online Firefighter II students are required to secure Internet access and an electronic mail account to participate in the course and library distance learning services. Students for each of three modules have not exceeded 25 members in each class. Modules are delivered so students have four months to complete both the cognitive and psychomotor skills before advancing to the next module. The next group of 25 students is concurrently enrolled. The Online Firefighter II Certification Program follows a different schedule and does not conform to the calendar for on-campus courses. Students in the courses work independently at their own pace, not following a common schedule. The program is a part of the Institute's multi-faceted Firefighter II training program, which is conducted through hands-on training workshops available to every Firefighter II student statewide and through CD-ROM- and Internet-based training programs. The multi-faceted program now reaches 5,000 students annually.

The IFSI Library uses the World Wide Web as the delivery mechanism with a Web-based search engine for accessing the Library distance learning services (see Figure 3). Online Firefighter II students with a three-shift working schedule, using a wide range of computer operating systems and browsers, access Web-based information 24 hours a day, seven days a week, i.e., any time they desire. The Online Resource side bar offers students a list of online library resources and services to assist in their quick access to and retrieval of information for their research. Contact information for library assistance is also included (see Figure 3).

Enrolled students are provided a password to the site. The Library continues to respond to interlibrary loan requests for library materials that are submitted during regular business hours. The Library also provides direct delivery service in response to an emergency request to accommodate the remote user's immediate need.

Based on the parameters of the Online Firefighter II Certification Program, the following areas of library services have helped accommodate the needs of the firefighter as a distance learner during the grant

FIGURE 3. Online Firefighter II Distance Learning Library Services

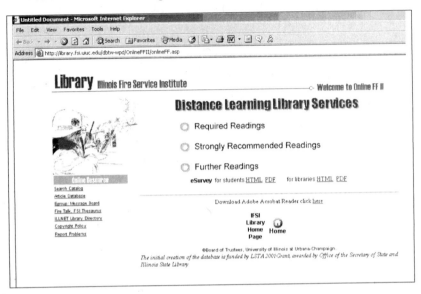

Used with permission.

project period. The services continued, after the grant project ended, with strong in-house support.

The IFSI Library follows the model of academic libraries, which often maintain reserve collections for use by students taking on-campus courses. Firefighter distance learners need access to the same types of materials typically included in physical reserve collections. Support for electronic reserves involves scanning of documents, maintenance of a server on which electronic documents can be stored, creation of indexes for documents (i.e., inMagic database) available on electronic reserve, and provision for controlled access to these documents that adheres to fair use provisions of copyright. Students (with a password) can read, download, and print online reserves materials consistent with copyright law. The IFSI Library makes it easy for students to access e-reserves. Acrobat's PDF (portable document format) is predominantly used.

All of the Firefighter II Certification requirements are contained within the online materials. The Library contacts instructors requesting a list of assignments or materials used for the course in advance. Instructors compile resources for specific online courses. Distance learning instructors typically have far more materials that need to be scanned than the average on-campus instructor for the same or similar courses. The online Firefighter II program has chosen to supplement the learning objectives by adding *Essentials of Firefighting* (published by International Fire Service Training Association) as a reference to reinforce the learning. The Library assumes responsibility for scanning and posting materials online requested by instructors. It also assumes responsibility for information dissemination regarding access to these materials. The IFSI Library scans several chapters of *Essentials of Firefighting*. Because of the sheer size of many of these materials, student use started slowly and is often limited to students who have high-speed Internet access either through work, the library, or another location. The IFSI Library carefully scrutinizes materials being offered electronically and examines ways to cut file size down and increase student use. The IFSI Library posts each chapter as a separate link to reduce file size to result in faster download times. The IFSI Library works closely with instructors to develop assignments that can be completed using those library resources accessible to students working at a distance.

For copyright issues, the IFSI Library follows Guidelines for University of Illinois at Urbana-Champaign Library Electronic Reserves and posts the policy on the Web, with the University Library Administrative Council's permission. The University Library's copyright policy for e-reserves is linked from the IFSI Library Web site and is directly accessible at (http://www.library.uiuc.edu/administration/services/policies/electro_reserve.htm). The IFSI Library uses the University Copyright Clearance Center to obtain permissions for any use that exceeds the policy. The IFSI Library policy also requires obtaining permission for the use of the same article in subsequent Firefighter II sessions if requested by instructors. The IFSI Library assumes responsibility for helping instructors contact publishers for copyright permission.

For electronic and digital collection development, the IFSI Library holds unique materials of interest to online Firefighter II students and instructors by building up satellite multi-media collections tailored to the Firefighter II program offered at remote sites. For site-independent programs serving students in many different locations like this one, purchase or licensing of electronic resources, e.g., *Online National Fire Codes* with multi-user access, becomes necessary so that these resources can be accessed easily from remote locations. Licenses for such electronic resources include Firefighter II distance learners as valid users and do not restrict use to those who happen to be on-site at the Library.

Because certain technical concepts are not visible to the naked eye or are dangerous to perform, the online Firefighter II program has added videos and animations to enhance the learning objectives. The IFSI Library provides additional videotapes and printed materials at the library site and local public and community college libraries sites, which are close to registered students, as reserve materials.

The online Firefighter II program content is presented in an asynchronous manner. Learning activities in the modules are objective-based and require each student to complete the unit successfully before moving on to the next. The student has the ability to select the unit, complete the required learning objectives, perform a learning exercise or activity, and take the end-of-unit evaluation. For the reading assignments of each unit in the three modules, the IFSI Library scans full text articles and makes them available on the Web. The Library also uses inMagic interactive WebPublisher with a full-text feature, which means a direct hot link from an inMagic database record to the full-text file, and search capabilities for easy and convenient access. To aid more end users to perform better subject searches by using the FireTalk-IFSI thesaurus on the Web, the Library purchased and uses a MultiCGI Internet license.

The instructors and library staff are available to answer questions from the students through e-mail, the class Web Board, weekly chat sessions, or the daily synchronous office hours. Students interact with the assigned Institute's instructors and library staff initially as well as with other students, by e-mail and by using the features of the delivery system. The Web Technology Group (WTG) and later the Institute's Information Technology teams designed the online template with a link to the IFSI Library's Firefighter II course specific Web Site, developed by the library grant project staff and maintained by the Institute IT office after the grant project ended. The Institute's Information Technology team administers and manages the class specific Web Board and Chat Area. Students click a module to see the underlying units and library services. They have easy access to the primary features for the course (Web Board, Chat area, videos, animations, and photographs) and the library services through appropriate icons and text tags, which are visible to them whenever they are logged into the site.

Each unit has homework assignments designed to acquaint the student with library services, local operations, and equipment. The tracking system developed by the Institute's Information Technology team gave the instructor and library staff the information needed to track each student and how they have used the library services. Students have available online technical support through the Library Online Help.

Planning and development of the library services have little impact unless these services are effectively promoted to online Firefighter II instructors and students. The Library provides several options for communicating with Firefighter II students and instructors at a distance: synchronous (supporting communication by two individuals at the same time) and/or asynchronous (allowing individuals to communicate at times convenient for them). The IFSI Library works closely with instructors for orientation training for firefighter distance learners in the beginning of the course, explaining how to use the library and how to access the IFSI Library and local libraries. The IFSI Library contacts each student directly for his local library preference. To promote the distance learning library services, the IFSI Library includes a brochure and "OPAC Training Manual" both in print and Web versions in the Firefighter II Orientation package.

The IFSI Library also promotes the services through the Library listserv, Institute and local library newsletters, and individual contacts. All avenues are used to make instructors and students aware of the resources and services available to support teaching, learning, and research connected with the online Firefighter II Certification Program. The IFSI Library has a toll-free telephone number reducing the expense for individuals at a distance, library fax number, postal service, electronic mail, and text chat. Statistics reveal that e-mail is the most popular mode used to ask the librarian questions about library navigation. One student even contacted the IFSI Library from Spain by e-mail to forge a personal connection in gathering library information.

Online Firefighter II students and instructors have access to library staff that can respond to ready reference questions as well as requests for more in-depth consultation about search strategies. The most common method of providing Internet reference services and the most commonly used channel for communication for firefighter distance learners is through e-mail. Electronic mail is used to submit reference questions or requests for assistance. E-mail allows distance learners and the librarian greater flexibility and convenience in transactions in that each party does not need to be simultaneously present. The IFSI Library embraces new technologies and formulates policies that ensure that the Web-based reference services provided are of as high a quality as those provided within the library. Chat technologies (MyLibrarian, i.e., ask a librarian live) as another means for providing reference services are being set up by collaborative efforts among several special libraries within Lincoln Trail Libraries System. The online Firefighter II students can call the reference desk toll-free for general search assistance, advice on search strategies or database selection, or for information on available services.

The IFSI Library collaborates with the National Fire Academy Library's Web site (http://www.lrc.fema.gov) and other fire emergency resources to better meet informational needs of online Firefighter II and other online course students and instructors. While electronic reserves can satisfy some student needs for documents, some online Firefighter II students require access to copies of additional library materials, including books, videotapes, and journal articles, as part of their studies. These materials are sometimes placed as reserves at the local libraries near them or delivered to them through Interlibrary loan (ILL) services. Students working at a distance sometimes need rapid delivery of documents in order to complete their assignments by stated deadlines. In addition to electronic reserves, the Library provides both ILL services to the local library near the Firefighter II student (minimum 5-10 days delivery time), U.S. mail, fax, or FedEx services upon an emergency request (1-2 days delivery time). Articles can be scanned and delivered electronically via Ariel (http://www.infotrieve.com/ariel/index.html, a document transmission software from Research Libraries Group), if a distance learner chooses. The IFSI Library processes requests for all materials and handles all shipping.

For users at a distance, navigational tools created by the library must compensate for the lack of opportunity to explore the physical library. Such tools include online pathfinders or gateways and the course-specific Firefighter II Web site that allow the user to focus attention on resources likely to be helpful, rather than randomly searching the Web.

One important aspect of instruction is training in the use of the technology required to access library resources available in electronic form. The IFSI Library teaches students virtually and trains local librarians in person to effectively use the online catalog, bibliographic databases, and reference sources, which require mastery of several different interfaces and methods of searching. The IFSI Library is aware that many of the materials and services in the library are not truly accessible without some kind of training or instructional assistance. This is especially true in two areas: assistance in the use of some electronic products, and assistance with the selection process.

Where should the student start his/her research? What electronic product or service should be the starting point? What search terms will be effective in the search? These and similar questions can be answered through a library instruction program. A variety of library services and products need to be explained to students (Figure 4). The IFSI Library

## FIGURE 4. Online Course Database

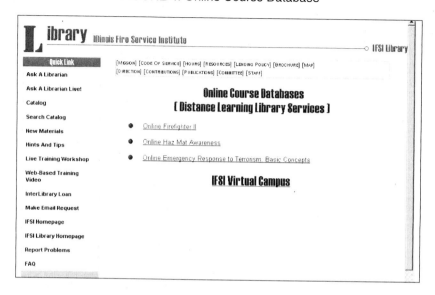

teaches search concepts and transferable methods for using any library. Students working at a distance need various forms of instruction to take full advantage of library resources in support of their coursework and research. This takes the form of orientation to available resources and staff, point-of-use instruction for a particular resource, and course-related instruction coordinated with an instructor. As there are few opportunities for face-to-face instruction with students working at a distance, the IFSI Library placed emphasis on developing Web-based hypertext tools and videotape as a guide to various library materials for the course. These are self-paced products for any individual in the program to use.

The University of Illinois WILL TV Station was hired to develop a 15-minute video/audio streamed instruction during the project focusing on an overview of using databases, with individual instruction modules on using specific databases and techniques (Ruan et al., 2002). It is also available in CD-ROM format and can be mailed to students upon request. In developing streamed instruction, learning becomes more meaningful. It is less abstract learning when students are able to participate in their own education by interacting with an online tutorial. Virtual instruction is invaluable for students at a distance as firefighter distance learners do not have the localized convenience of asking friends, a librarian, or a professor when questions arise about how to navigate the Library. A print Reference Guide has also been developed to assist students who need access to library materials that support their study.

In partnership with local public and/or community college libraries, the IFSI Library made sure the personal touch was retained while providing the library distance learning services to the online Firefighter II students and instructors. The 1998 ACRL Guidelines indicated, "Because students and faculty in distance learning programs frequently do not have direct access to a full range of library services and materials, equitable distance learning library services are more personalized than might be expected on campus." This personalization required a commitment of library staff and resources to meet the special needs of Firefighter II users at a distance.

There was a concern in some local libraries that too many participants would make it difficult for the local librarian to answer questions fast enough. Implementation showed that it has been manageable. Students visited the local libraries at regular hours. For example, there were fourteen libraries participating in the grant project. They were: Alpha Park Public Library, Belleville Public Library, Cairo Public Library, Gail Borden Public Library, Homewood Public Library, Lake Bluff Public Library, Moraine Valley Community College Library, Peoria Public Library, Rock Island Public Library, St. Joseph Township Public Library, St. Joseph Township Swearington Memorial Library, Tri Township Public Library, and Warren Newport Public Library.

Because of its success, the IFSI Library's integrated Internet reference services to the Firefighter II Certification Program has served as a model for other online courses, which are Online Hazardous Materials Awareness (37 enrolled students in 2003, 11 in 2004), Online Emergency Response to Terrorism: Basic Concepts (42 enrolled students in 2004), and Online Technical Rescue courses (upcoming). These services will continue to grow as the Institute's online programs grow.

## EVALUATION AND NEEDS ASSESSMENT

As the online Firefighter II Certification Program evolves, it is important for the IFSI Library to monitor the needs for resources and services on an ongoing basis. This requires close collaboration with the teaching instructors and communication with students and local librarians to identify problems they face in gaining access to materials needed to complete their coursework. The IFSI Library refines new library services and access schemes, based on the Firefighter II student testing and their feedback.

The following areas have been identified as key areas for evaluation; other areas may be added as needed:

- Has the IFSI Library made provision to ensure timely access to appropriate learning resources?
- Are a majority of online Firefighter II students in each module using those access methods?
- Do the Library and partner libraries adequately support access methods?
- Are online Firefighter II students informed about available learning resources in an effective way?
- Which training strategy about information resources is most effective?
- How important a role does the partner library play?
- What speed of Internet connection is used?
- How often do the distance learning students use the IFSI Library Internet reference services?
- What are their overall experiences using the Internet reference services?
- Who do the students contact if they have problems?
- Have the students used interlibrary loan? Were they satisfied? In what alternative formats would they like to receive articles?
- Where do students obtain their information (Web, library, other libraries, and fellow firefighters)?

A series of open-ended questions asking users to make comments (positive or negative), and give suggestions about using the IFSI Library from a distance are also asked. Questions are formatted to provide information about using the library while at the same time garnering information about the user's library experience. As a result of student survey responses, library staff have made changes by improving and providing new services to distance firefighter learners.

## OUTCOMES

There are major outcomes resulting from the grant project and continuing after the project ended.

The new Internet reference services have enhanced the quality of the Online Firefighter II Certification Program and other online courses. With access to the library resources and services, online Firefighter II and other online course students bring new ideas and reports of supporting or conflicting research to the classroom. Further, providing access to library services and materials enhances the opportunity for an interested student to develop an understanding of how to navigate among the myriad resources of the library, how to identify and locate needed material, and how to begin the journey to independent evaluation of resources and research conducted in their fields.

This has helped enhance the educational value of students' academic experience. It is imperative that students in the online Firefighter II program and other online courses become competent Internet/technology users not only for a particular certification program, but also for their local training programs and activities. The Internet reference services have strengthened cost-saving partnerships with local libraries, deepened interagency cooperation, and improved public safety for Illinois citizens.

The electronic collection has been developed and use of the IFSI Library by offsite firefighters has increased. All materials purchased as part of the grant project were cataloged and entered into the Library Online Public Access Catalog (OPAC) and are available for resource sharing through the Internet (http://library.fsi.uiuc.edu/) with no password required when they are not on reserve status, except full-text articles and online subscriptions. Thousands of Illinois firefighters, forty-six community colleges with fire science programs, and the general public have benefited from the enhanced library services and collections.

Currently, 70% of fire departments are volunteer/paid-on-call fire service. The IFSI Library has reached about 15% of Illinois fire departments with materials and services. The IFSI Library would like to increase greatly the number of volunteer firefighters who use the Library, since they could benefit the most from access to information concerning basic firefighting, career advancement (e.g., career move from volunteer to a paid firefighter, or to become Fire Chief for a volunteer or paid fire department), and training opportunities.

Partnerships with local libraries have been strengthened to provide timely library services to Illinois firefighter distance learners. This innovative approach for distance learning library services has encouraged and strengthened partnerships between the IFSI Library and local libraries to provide better library services to Illinois firefighter distance learners and help protect public communities from danger of fire and other hazards.

The development and the implementation of Internet reference services for firefighter distance learners represent an essential partnership and community involvement. Throughout the planning and implementation process, the draft of the grant proposal was shared with community representatives, including the Library Committee, Lincoln Trail Libraries System (LTLS), University librarians who have distance learning services experiences, the Office of the State Fire Marshal (OSFM), and key Illinois fire service organizations, to seek their understanding and solicit their input and support. Participants from the community provided input to the grant project and continue to assist in the development of the new services after the project ended.

Like many libraries and organizations that have recognized the benefits of providing digital reference service through collaborative services (Sloan 2001), in 2004, the IFSI Library began participating in a virtual reference service, called MyLibrarian, provided through the cooperative work of East Central Illinois librarians, organized by Lincoln Trail Libraries System in Illinois (http://www.mylibrarian.info/). The MyLibrarian service is made possible by the Illinois State Library's AskUs!Illinois virtual reference project, a U.S. Department of Health and Human Services' Centers for Disease Control and Prevention grant, and through the cooperative efforts of Lincoln Trail Libraries System, participating LTLS member libraries, and the Illinois Department of Public Health. Existing library consortia, like Lincoln Trail Libraries System, are adding digital reference to current shared services, and networks of libraries and "Ask A" services in different locations are banding together to share question loads and expertise (Kasowitz 2001). Through the exposure to telecomputing library services, the IFSI Library has improved information and resource sharing among local libraries devoted to serving fire emergency service and public safety.

The evaluation plan created during the grant project has guided both the grant project and expansion of the distance learning services beyond the project year initiatives. The evaluation has integrated qualitative and quantitative methodologies. Formative (ongoing) assessment has helped identify problems in keeping the project on the right track and opportunities to better meet participant needs. Summative (final) assessment has offered data on the extent to which the IFSI Library has achieved intended outcomes and allowed a fuller understanding as a model of what worked, what didn't, and why. This evaluation is used to measure, as a whole, the impact of developing and implementing the distance learning library services to fire/emergency training programs in Illinois, and how the IFSI Library could expand these services to other online academic training programs.

The IFSI Library incorporates changes, upgrades, etc. into the ongoing process. The IFSI Library considers enrollment projections. Enrollments of students studying at a distance are likely to grow dramatically with the potential of thousands of firefighters annually. The IFSI Library considers how the approaches planned for delivery of library services will scale up to meet the likely increase in demand. The IFSI Library was able to demonstrate success of the grant project and marshal funds for continuation. The IFSI Library plays an important role and has great responsibilities for the success of the online Firefighter II Certification Program. Many facets of library service are planned to be adapted to meet the needs of distance learning students. Professor Linda Smith points out that, as campuses become more networked, development of services to support distance learners and instructors may also benefit on-campus students and instructors (Smith 1999).

Due to the increasing Internet access from improved technology infrastructure, the IFSI Library has benefited by enhancing its ability to meet the needs of the wide variety of fire service personnel through these new Internet reference services to firefighter distance learners. The IFSI Library has also benefited by filling current gaps in content relevant to fire service needs, and perhaps most importantly, developing the expertise, better knowledge, and programs needed to sustain and extend these improvements in the future. The IFSI Library has also benefited from the improvement of its interface and retrieval mechanisms. The services have surely improved the IFSI Library system's ability to support information seeking and sharing across the fire service community, and ultimately, its value as an important information resource center for fire service and public problem-solving.

## MANAGEMENT CHALLENGES

As discussed in previous sections, there are many issues that surround the management of Internet reference services for the IFSI Library's firefighter distance learners, such as user needs, funding support, staff management, and collection development, information delivery and copyright, and maintenance of the infrastructure. The most pressing issues of these, however, are staff and budget. Internet reference services has evolved quickly over the last decade, moving from a place of last resort to a mainstream application. The IFSI Library has responded in innovative ways to connect its users with information available on the Internet. However, superior Internet reference services requires substantial investments that administrators have to consider.

Many institutions have appointed or hired distance education librarians to help provide services to distance learners (Backhus and Summey 2003). However, at the IFSI Library, there is no distance learning librarian position that focuses on the needs of firefighter distance learners and their instructors. At the beginning of the Internet reference services for distance learners, a solo librarian (Head Librarian) and a graduate assistant team of two handled the new services. From 2002 to 2003 after the grant project ended, the staff budget has not grown to keep pace with the demands placed on it. The tuitions paid by online students have not necessarily been allocated to support the integrated library services. Due to heavy demands for library programs from non-distance learners, and shortage of staff, the IFSI Library had to assist firefighter distance learners for online courses on a "by need" basis. Recent decisions to hire a part time reference librarian, add a permanent full-time librarian, and maintain an active graduate student team of several students from the University of Illinois Graduate School of Library and Information Science will address challenges in this area and keep consistent quality services and meet new demands from new online courses.

The IFSI Library has also provided increased access to a wide variety of materials, most of which the IFSI Library does not own locally. Thus, document delivery and copyright have become an increasing area of concern. As a result, interlibrary loans have increased, and instructors and students are demanding faster turnaround times. The IFSI Library must maintain its own copyright files for articles that it receives.

Budgetary decisions in Internet reference services for the distance learning program have become more complicated at the IFSI Library. Costs can be assigned to either operating or collection budgets (or both) depending on how the costs are perceived. Costs associated with the network have also increased. Remote users require that Internet accessibility to the library's resources increase. The Institute's Information Technology Office has expanded the network requiring wiring, network boards, additional CD-ROM drives, etc. Such costs mount up quickly. These costs come from the Institute's operating or Information Technology budget.

In addition to the subscription and equipment costs associated with Internet reference services, the IFSI Library has to also consider the very real costs associated with supporting and maintaining the infrastructure needed by the databases, such as telecommunications charges and printing costs as tangential costs, which are drawn from the operating budget. The determination of the true cost of an information source in the digital library should always include consideration of both of these additional factors. The costs of acquiring and maintaining the hardware necessary to provide these services should also count. These costs have been borne primarily by the operations budget with additional supplements being given by the Institute's administration.

As online course registrations grow at the Institute, there will be an increased need for diverse online resources and services that support varied firefighters' learning styles. The ability to "push" information out to online library users is critical, as is updating software systems that effectively serve the firefighter end users at a distance. Firefighter end users also need to take responsibility for becoming familiar with the IFSI Library's services and resources.

The Internet reference services for firefighter distance learners cannot be developed in a vacuum. Money must be found to pay for the systems, user needs must be understood and met, and the collections must be developed. The decisions that must be made when approaching Internet reference services must be grappled with in order to provide quality service to firefighter distance learners.

## CONCLUSION

The continuing revolution in information technology represented by the Internet and its rapid acceptance by the general public have made it very clear that librarians must do their best to embrace the new technology. The Internet expedites reference services. The Internet facilitates resource sharing as well as improved access to information. Because of the Internet, libraries have been undergoing a major transformation and are rapidly changing. Librarians must reexamine their priorities in light of the current changes and work together to maintain and strengthen the quality of library services that people in communities expect and deserve. Librarians must expand ways to share knowledge, ideas, resources, and expertise.

Recognizing that the Internet dramatically changes how libraries provide services, the IFSI Library's goal has been to provide a thoughtful analysis of where it has been and where it is going. It does seem as if today's special librarian is more than simply a librarian, and must be able to play several roles: manager, researcher, tester, project leader, designer, information architect, and Web manager. The LSTA grant project discussed in previous sections helped pilot new ways of developing and implementing Internet reference services oriented to practical fire and emergency online training programs in Illinois, serving as a model. The IFSI Library became more responsive to the needs of fire emergency service personnel.

The scheme for the online Firefighter II and other online courses to organize and retrieve information on the online course site, Web Home Page, OPAC, e-mail, and listserv system in a problem- and user-centered manner, goes beyond typical Internet access mechanisms and distance learning services models. The IFSI Library has created a model in partnership with local libraries to bring information tools and resources directly to off-campus Firefighter II and other online students through a mechanism that provides technology training and critical knowledge and information, empowering fire service personnel not only as computer users and library participants, but also as more qualified firefighters better able to provide protection to the communities of Illinois.

## REFERENCES

Backhus, Sherry Hawkins and Terri Pedersen Summey. "Collaboration: The Key to Unlocking the Dilemma of Distance Reference Services." *The Reference Librarian*, 83/84 (2003): 193-202.

Buehler, Marianne, Elizabeth Dopp, Kerry A. Hughes, and Jen Thompson. "It Takes a Library to Support Distance Learners." *Internet Reference Services Quarterly*, Vol. 5, no. 3 (2001): 5-24.

Kasowitz, Abby S. 2001. "Trends and Issues in Digital Reference Services, ERIC Digest." ERIC Clearinghouse on Information and Technology, Syracuse, NY, ED457869.

Ruan, Lian. "Libraries in the 21st Century: Developing the Distance Learning Library Services for Illinois Firefighters: An Integrated Information Service with Online Firefighter 2 Certification Program, Final Narrative Report." *Illinois Libraries* 83, no. 4 (Fall 2001): 19-63.

Ruan, Lian. "Final Narrative Report, Internet Outreach to and Training of Illinois Fire Service Personnel, Public and Community College Librarians for Electronic Access to Fire Safety Information, Final Narrative Report." *Illinois Libraries* 83, no. 1 (Winter 2001): 18-33.

Ruan, Lian, John Paul, Jeff Cunningham, and Sarah Windau. "Virtual User Instruction at the University of Illinois Fire Service Institute Library: Producing a Web-Based Training Video for Illinois Firefighters." *Illinois Libraries* 84, no. 2 (Spring 2002): 48-62.

Sloan, B. 2001. "Ready for reference: Academic libraries offer live Web-based reference." [Online] Available: http://www.lis.uiuc.edu/~b~sloan/r4r.final.htm [Sept. 25, 2001].

Smith, Linda C. "The Academic Library's Role in Distance Education." *Summary of Proceedings of the 53rd Annual Conference of the American Theological Library Association.* Evanston, IL: ATLA, 1999, pp.125-132.

# Distance Library Services
# for Doctor of Pharmacy Students:
# A Case Study

Ulrike Dieterle

Gerri Wanserski

**SUMMARY.** Doctor of Pharmacy students at the University of Wisconsin-Madison spend their final year of study working side-by-side with pharmacists throughout Wisconsin. Clerkship rotations often take place outside of Madison, away from familiar and dependable library resources and services. To make the transition from campus to community as smooth as possible, librarians have developed a focused orientation and a detailed field guide to provide students with the tools for a productive and successful year working and studying at a distance.

This article will outline the library's orientation program, describe the elements included in the distance services field guide, and highlight the pre- and post-clerkship assessment tools to be used in measuring satisfaction with the program in the future. *[Article copies available for a fee from The Haworth Document Delivery Service: 1-800-HAWORTH. E-mail address: <docdelivery@haworthpress.com> Website: <http://www.HaworthPress.com> © 2004 by The Haworth Press, Inc. All rights reserved.]*

Ulrike Dieterle (udieterle@wisc.edu) is Distance Services and Outreach Coordinator, and Gerri Wanserski (grwanser@facstaff.wisc.edu) is Health Sciences Librarian, both at Ebling Library, University of Wisconsin-Madison, 750 Highland Avenue, Room 2340, Madison, WI 53705-2221.

[Haworth co-indexing entry note]: "Distance Library Services for Doctor of Pharmacy Students: A Case Study." Dieterle, Ulrike, and Gerri Wanserski. Co-published simultaneously in *Internet Reference Services Quarterly* (The Haworth Information Press, an imprint of The Haworth Press, Inc.) Vol. 9, No. 1/2, 2004, pp. 173-188; and: *Improving Internet Reference Services to Distance Learners* (ed: William Miller, and Rita M. Pellen) The Haworth Information Press, an imprint of The Haworth Press, Inc., 2004, pp. 173-188. Single or multiple copies of this article are available for a fee from The Haworth Document Delivery Service [1-800-HAWORTH, 9:00 a.m. - 5:00 p.m. (EST). E-mail address: docdelivery@haworthpress.com].

http://www.haworthpress.com/web/IRSQ
© 2004 by The Haworth Press, Inc. All rights reserved.
Digital Object Identifier: 10.1300/J136v09n01_12

**KEYWORDS.** Distance education, pharmacy education, bibliographic instruction, remote access, University of Wisconsin-Madison Ebling Library, health sciences libraries

## *INTRODUCTION*

At the University of Wisconsin-Madison, Doctor of Pharmacy (Pharm.D.) students spend their final year doing a series of clerkship rotations away from campus. For many, the clerkship means a year in cities or rural areas of Wisconsin far removed from many of the convenient information resources they became accustomed to during prior years of study.

Before students disperse, they are provided with a series of orientations to prepare them for a year in the field working with practicing pharmacists, administrators, or researchers. Among the tools presented to future clerkship students are *Library Resources for Clerkship Students*,[1] a library field guide, and optional hands-on sessions based on the guide to assist them in a smooth transition from theory to practice, from local to distant access. The hands-on sessions are scheduled to coincide with the students discovering where they will be located for clerkship rotations and take place in March and April of the spring semester. The guide is incorporated into the School of Pharmacy Clerkship Manual which is given to students during an all-day orientation session at the end of the semester.

The Ebling Library Pharmacy Liaison works closely with School of Pharmacy faculty and coordinates with other library staff to ensure that students are prepared to deal with issues related to access, retrieval, and anticipated levels of support services. Whether it is availability of databases, digital delivery of articles to the desktop, physical delivery of books, reference support, or access to their home campus through familiar Web pages, the goal is to equip fourth-year Pharm.D. students with guidelines so they are able to work more effectively in their new surroundings without losing touch or access to necessary information resources or support services.

The University of Wisconsin-Madison campus is a large and complex environment with numerous academic and professional programs, schools, and institutes spread over 933 square acres. While the campus itself poses daunting "distance" education issues, being off campus for long periods of time can result in feelings of isolation from familiar research resources and dependable services. In keeping with the spirit of the Association of College and Research Libraries' (ACRL) Guidelines for Distance Learning Library Services, librarians provide not only information about relevant resources and services, but also guidance in how to prepare for remote use well in advance of students' departures.[2] This approach also provides support to professional programs that adhere to distance education standards. The Accreditation Council for Pharmacy Education Standard for Library and Educational Resources specifies, among other things, that students should be provided instruction in the use of library and educational resources, and that they should have access to technologies and programs that make it possible for them to use library information from locations remote from campus.[3]

In addition to the School of Pharmacy, Ebling Library supports faculty, staff, and students in the professional programs of the Medical School and the School of Nursing. Prior to June 2004, the library consisted of three separate facilities: Middleton Health Sciences Library, the main health sciences library adjacent to the Medical School; Weston Clinical Sciences Center Library, a satellite library in the UW Hospital and Clinics; and the F. B. Power Pharmaceutical Library which was located within the School of Pharmacy building for over 30 years. In serving these dispersed and mobile user groups throughout the years, our librarians have addressed many obstacles associated with remote use,[4] achieving varying degrees of success along the way. One of the library's greatest success stories in supporting distance initiatives to date has been working with the Pharm.D. students who are venturing out to complete a series of clerkship rotations in pharmacies, clinics, hospitals, and healthcare centers throughout Wisconsin.

## BACKGROUND

The UW-Madison School of Pharmacy, founded in 1883, includes 60 full-time faculty, slightly over 500 full-time Pharm.D. students, 25 students in the baccalaureate Pharmacology/Toxicology program, 60 graduate-level students, and more than 500 clinical instructors working in diverse pharmacy practice settings throughout Wisconsin. The School of Pharmacy is the only institution of higher learning in the state to award a professional pharmacy degree and draws students from all corners of Wisconsin and beyond.

The pharmacy curriculum is rigorous and resource dependent. Students complete two years of pre-pharmacy coursework prior to entering the Pharm.D. program, then complete an additional four years in the program. Approximately 115-130 students are enrolled in each class. To qualify for original licensure to practice as a pharmacist in Wisconsin, individuals must graduate from an accredited institution, complete required internships, and pass both national pharmacy board exams and state licensure testing.[5] Currently, the state of Wisconsin requires 1,500 hours of internships.[6]

Throughout most of the 1990s, completion of a baccalaureate degree was sufficient to obtain professional licensure to practice as a pharmacist in the state of Wisconsin. A post-baccalaureate Pharm.D. program was available to students desiring clinical pharmacy experience beyond the baccalaureate degree. These programs were phased out until, beginning in 1997, the only professional pharmacy program available was the six-year Pharm.D. This is in accord with national standards set by The Accreditation Council for Pharmacy Education (ACPE) which established that, effective July 1, 2000, the Doctor of Pharmacy program is the only professional pharmacy program.[7]

This transition led to the establishment, in 1997, of a special Nontraditional Doctor of Pharmacy (NTDP) program allowing pharmacists already licensed and holding a baccalaureate pharmacy degree to earn a Pharm.D. degree. The NTDP program granted these students up to six years to complete requirements for a Pharm.D. degree on a part-time basis as distance education students through the University of Wisconsin-Madison.[8]

Another outcome of the transition to an all-Pharm.D. program was the need for additional clerkship sites, as some 115-130 students each year were now required to fulfill internship requirements in order to graduate. In contrast, the baccalaureate program required completion of one eight-week clerkship at an inpatient site and one four-week clerkship at a community pharmacy site. When the Pharm.D. degree was optional, there were only 25-35 students in the program each year who needed placement at clerkship sites.[9] This meant that until the curriculum change in 1997, most students in the baccalaureate and optional Pharm.D. programs were able to complete their clerkship rotations in and around Madison. While this had some disruptive effects on students, their clinical instructors, School of Pharmacy faculty, and the Pharmacy Library were all within a convenient walk or commute for students.

When students request their desired clerkship regions for the final year, most students request to stay in the Madison area. However, there simply are not enough local clerkship sites available to accommodate all requests and approximately half (55-65) of the students are assigned to sites scattered throughout the state in the Fox Valley (Appleton/ Green Bay/Oshkosh), Eau Claire, LaCrosse, Milwaukee, and Wausau/ Stevens Point regions. In addition, a few students elect to complete clerkships elsewhere in the U.S. One student completed rotations in her native state of Hawaii, to which she planned to return upon graduation. Other students elect to complete a rotation at the Food and Drug Administration offices in Washington, D.C.

The number of volunteer clinical instructors participating in experiential courses or lectures is now over 500, and the number of practice sites has grown to more than 250, according to Mara A. Kieser (oral communication, July, 2004), clinical instructor and coordinator of experiential education for the UW-Madison School of Pharmacy. These sites include hospital pharmacies, HMO or community pharmacies, and specialty sites such as long-term care, research, pediatrics, or nutrition sites.[10]

As the number of students completing the Pharm.D. program has increased, so has the distance between student and information resources and services. Fortunately, as licensing and curricular changes have resulted in clerkship students being dispersed around the state for a year, information technologies have become more robust with increasing numbers of journals and electronic services coming online. Library staff has responded by developing written and Web-based guides and implementing special sessions in the months before students depart to give them an adequate send-off with a distance survival toolkit at their disposal.

## PREPARING STUDENTS FOR CLERKSHIP ROTATIONS AT A DISTANCE

### Library Participation

Over the years, the School of Pharmacy and Pharmacy Library have developed a close working relationship and interdependence, which has resulted in provision of access to quality resources, responsive services, and solid curriculum support. Before the emergence of electronic services and resources such as digital delivery of documents or access to e-journals, most students completed clerkships in Madison and were able to visit campus libraries to locate the required information for course assignments. For those students outside of the Madison area, the School of Pharmacy made special arrangements with the hospital libraries of clerkship sites for students to use resources at those facilities. In addition, Pharmacy Library staff faxed or mailed documents to off-campus faculty and students.

As the availability of online resources and services has increased, so has the library's participation in preparing students for rotations. In 2000, the first version of a field guide was developed that provides a point-by-point reminder of access to resources and services important to students working at a distance and serves as a research refresher, survival tool, and a helpful reference that anticipates potential problems, provides answers and, above all, identifies sources of help. Instead of severing relationships through distance, we strengthen ties by building students' skills and awareness. Librarians have also recognized that an extension of preparing students is to provide training to clinical instructors, the licensed pharmacists who supervise clerkship students at their sites. In the past, librarians have provided training in the use of MEDLINE and other health-related electronic resources at introductory and thank-you sessions for the clinical instructors. More recently, a separate guide has been developed for distribution to clinical instructors since they are also authorized to use UW-Madison library resources.

Each year since the guide was developed, additional library services and resources of interest to distance students have been included. The streamlining of remote access to e-journals and databases, implementation of book delivery services, and development of efficient document delivery services are available to all faculty, students, and staff of the University, but are of special interest to distance students and detailed in the guide.

Although students will have access to information they need in the printed and Web-based guides, hands-on sessions were scheduled to alleviate concern many students express about losing physical access to the library. During these sessions, students are encouraged to plan ahead, introduced to known or anticipated changes in service or support, presented with a to-do list of items to take care of before they leave campus, and provided an opportunity to ask questions before they embark upon their clerkship experiences.

The most recent version of the clerkship field guide has 13 sections which are listed and described below:

- Plan ahead
- What to do before you leave town
- How to connect to the campus network to access databases, e-journals, e-books

- Best Web sites to start with
- E-books for pharmacy
- PubMed (free MEDLINE access)
- Linking to full-text journal articles
- How to order journal articles or book chapters that aren't available electronically (Library Express service)
- Free book delivery services
- Help is available!!! (e-mail; online Live Reference; phone)
- University and public libraries in your clerkship region
- Handouts (this year's included: bibliographies on PDA products for drug information; selected Internet resources; and Citation Style Guides on the Web)
- When your clerkship is over . . .

*Plan Ahead*

The 2004 field guide included a section notifying students of a major change which would take place during their year away, the physical merger of the Pharmacy Library with two other libraries into a new facility. The merger affected students directly due to the need to close the health sciences libraries for three weeks during the move. Students' first clerkship rotation began during the closure and students were encouraged to do research early for their first drug information assignment. Students were also provided with information about the new facility since this will be their main library from this point forward.

*What to Do Before You Leave Town*

This section of the field guide highlights a few important items that students need to take care of or become familiar with before they leave the campus. For example, students are encouraged to think about how they will connect to the campus network, and to put money on their campus debit card before leaving campus so they can order journal articles and other documents from the campus electronic document delivery service.

*How to Connect to the Campus Network to Access Databases, E-Journals, E-Books*

This section reassures students that they will have easy access to databases, full-text books, and journals while they are away. Students are reminded that they will need to connect to the campus network to use most library resources due to licensing restrictions and presented with various methods of connecting from off-campus. The School of Pharmacy provides free dial-in Internet access for students residing in their assigned clerkship region. Additionally, while connectivity has traditionally been a major impediment for students working and studying at a distance, technological improvements at institutions of higher education and business environments have minimized the negative impact. At UW-Madison, authentication and access to licensed-restricted or copyright-restricted electronic resources have been streamlined for remote users by installation of EZProxy software. This software allows students to use the resources of their home campus from any computer with Internet access, whether at their clerkship site, public library, or other location. Access from near and far is virtually seamless since students simply enter their unique campus identification number and last name for authentication.

The connectivity portion of the guide also lists common problems related to remote access along with suggested resolutions posted by the campus Library Technology Help Group, along with contact information for computer support from the library and the School of Pharmacy. Students are urged to experiment with their remote connections early so they can seek help with any problems that arise before assignments are due.

## Best Web Sites to Start With

The next part of the orientation reinforces and refreshes content covered in course-related instruction. Although students have heard the information before, they exhibit great interest because they realize they will be much more dependent upon electronic access to information than they were in the past. A *Best Web Sites to Start With* section identifies Ebling Library Web pages and a pharmacy-specific portion of the site as excellent starting points since they include links to health-related databases, full-text resources, online request forms, and subject-specific resources that students are likely to need. The general UW-Madison library Web page is also identified as a site to visit for non-subject specific resources such as dictionaries, encyclopedias, or e-journals outside of the health sciences subject area.

## E-Books for Pharmacy

Ebling Library subscribes to hundreds of electronic books and provides access to a list of hundreds more that are freely available on the

Internet. Licensed collections of e-books of interest to pharmacy students include *STAT!Ref, MD Consult,* and *MICROMEDEX.* All of these books are available through the proxy server and accessible to students from multiple sites. Librarians also point out sources of free online books, such as those at the National Library of Medicine (NLM) Web site, which may be of continued use to students after graduation.

## PubMed

Twenty minutes of each hands-on session and a substantial portion of the print guide are devoted to introducing search capabilities and special features of PubMed, NLM's free, high-quality MEDLINE database. The orientation to PubMed is considered crucial by both librarians and faculty since, at the request of faculty, librarians teach pharmacy students how to use Ovid MEDLINE throughout their curriculum. PubMed includes special features that will be of use to students during their year away from campus such as Link-Out access to over 2,000 e-journals that campus libraries subscribe to, a citation matcher for completing citations, and a journal browser which will help students locate journal abbreviations for references in their papers. The print guide includes detailed examples complete with screen shots. The primary goal is to introduce students to PubMed so they can use it in their professional practice after they graduate. Ovid MEDLINE is only available to faculty, students, or staff with a valid campus ID, and many students no longer affiliated with UW-Madison after graduation will rely solely on PubMed to locate citations to primary literature, as well as the free e-journals and online books that NLM makes available at the Web site.

## Linking to Full-Text Journal Articles

Although most students have used e-journals during their tenure at UW-Madison, this part of the session inevitably draws much interest from students who realize they won't be able to physically come to the library to look at journal articles during their rotations. The orientation walks students through the most efficient ways to access known journal articles, including linking to e-journals through lists arranged alphabetically; through MadCat, the campus library computer catalog, and a reminder that many databases provide links to online library resources.

*How to Order Journal Articles or Book Chapters That*
*Aren't Available Electronically (Library Express Service)*

Another major focus of the orientation is explaining the campus document delivery service, Library Express, which offers delivery of digital documents in one to three days for a fee of $2.00 per article. This topic triggers many questions from students who are concerned about how they will get journal articles that are not available electronically. Although librarians have described this service in previous library instruction sessions, informal surveys indicate that most students have not taken advantage of the service at this point in their academic career, opting instead to go to a library for articles. Students are encouraged to logon to the Library Express system prior to leaving campus to make sure their ID number is recognized, put money on their WisCard account so they can purchase articles through Library Express, and request an article so they know what to expect in the coming year.

Since this popular service plays an important part of delivering distance services to the students, a more detailed explanation and history of the service is detailed in Box 1.

*Free Book Delivery Services*

To accommodate the fact that UW-Madison faculty, students, and staff use more than forty separate campus libraries scattered over 933 acres, libraries have developed a Book Retrieval service which allows faculty, students, and staff to have books delivered to them from another campus library. In recent years, this service has been expanded, as a result of collaborative efforts of UW-System librarians, making it possible for books, videos, and other "returnables" to be borrowed from one campus, delivered to another campus of choice within days, and returned to any campus within the UW Library System. This provides maximum access at maximum convenience for people on the move and far away.

Many students are assigned to regions outside of Dane County and are not proximate to any other UW-System library. These students, along with any faculty, staff, or other student of UW-Madison residing outside of the county are eligible for a campus service which provides free mailing of books to them. Books, other than reserve or reference books, are shipped free of charge to students within three business days and can be requested using an online form.

## BOX 1

**Library Express as Example of Meeting an Identified Need**

One of the most valued services UW-Madison libraries offer is Library Express. It provides digital delivery to the desktop of any UW-Madison student, faculty, or staff willing to pay a $2.00 fee per article.

Pharmacy clerkship students were among the early participants in the Library Express service. In spring of 2000, as the first class of Pharm.D. students was preparing for a clerkship year "abroad," the library was in the early stages of testing this new and innovative document delivery service which had a goal to provide speedy, convenient, and dependable delivery of articles to the desktop.

Clerkship students were identified as ideal testers for the initial phases of the pilot because they had a continued and substantial need for journal articles while performing their clerkship responsibilities at a distance. The librarians and School of Pharmacy faculty members knew that these students would benefit from the seamless, convenient access to familiar resources that would otherwise prove difficult to retrieve in a timely manner. Faculty, staff, and students in the School were invited to participate in the pilot of this revolutionary service, which promised delivery of digital documents in one to three days. The Pharm.D. students posed a variety of "real-world" challenges throughout the pilot phase, since they often worked in rural areas or pharmacies with only basic computer services and little back-up support. The diverse work environments represented across the State offered a new dimension to the pilot project and posed challenges not yet measured, namely, how to deliver large PDF files via e-mail to users with minimal hardware configurations, through firewalls, and over slow modem connections.

A brief evaluation conducted in May 2000 revealed Pharm.D. students truly appreciated the opportunity to join the project and were eager to help "build a better mousetrap." The survey also indicated that students anticipated requesting 0-10 articles per week, needing the materials for school assignments more than for patient care and that they would be able to navigate the service without assistance. This evaluation also confirmed earlier suspicions that older computers were not uncommon in the workplace and that occasional technical problems would continue. To help bridge the distance even more, Library Express staff formulated helpful online components which could serve as a trouble-shooting aid for distance as well as campus users.

In exchange for their input throughout the pilot phase, Pharm.D. students received, at no cost to them, an unlimited supply of digitized articles. Needless to say, they embraced this offer and, through their input of the next two years, helped the library build a stronger, more responsive document delivery system with peripheral services such as FAQs, a user tutorial, online assistance, and quick response.[1]

Today, access to library resources through Library Express is also extended to School of Pharmacy clinical instructors. Over the years, Library Express has become a dependable information lifeline, and a principle information service for students and instructors at a distance.

1. Dieterle, U. Digital document delivery to the desktop: distance is no longer an issue. *J Libr Adm* 2002; 37(1/2): 243-50.

## *Help Is Available*

A primary reason for the field guide and optional face-to-face sessions is to make sure clerkship students know that library staff will continue to be available to provide reference assistance and support even from a distance. The pharmacy liaison and other instructors emphasize to students that although the students will be going away, library staff will not be and will remain available for help. Ebling Library staff responds to questions through an e-mail reference service and phone assistance is available. Additionally, since the pharmacy librarian has had personal contact with many of the students, her personal e-mail and phone number are provided to students. Students are also given information about the campus virtual reference service *Live Help* through which librarians respond, in real time, to questions using a Web interface. With the technology used by *Live Help*, staff can also lead a caller to a useful database or Web site. This service, supported by fifty campus librarians, can be used from home or work with the use of a free browser plug-in.

## University and Public Libraries in Your Clerkship Region

University and public libraries are located within each clerkship region of the state. The field guide includes a list of these along with a link to the Web page of the library. Students can walk in to use public university libraries in Wisconsin and most provide access to public computers, printers, and copy machines. The pharmacy liaison contacts the collaborating libraries each year to ensure that recent policies and current information are included. In addition to this, reciprocal borrowing agreements make it possible for Pharm.D. students to borrow materials from public universities or two-year college libraries upon showing their valid UW-Madison ID, and students are eligible to receive a public library card in their region.

## Handouts

A brief updated bibliography of print and Web-based resources on relevant topics is provided in the field guide each year. The most recent guide featured a bibliography of articles evaluating PDA products for drug information, selected Web sites for career information, and a list of recommended citation style guides available on the Web.

## When Your Clerkship Is Over . . .

Students are asked to provide feedback and make recommendations once their clerkship rotations are completed. Questions librarians are interested in include: Were you able to locate and use the databases, online books, and e-journals you needed? Were there any other library resources or services that you needed to make your clerkship a success? What else can the library do to make your clerkship successful?

In 2004, the pharmacy liaison and the Ebling Library Outreach Coordinator collaborated with a faculty member to develop and administer a formal survey which was given to students in mid-May before they left for their clerkships.[11] A mid-year survey will be issued to all Pharm.D. students in late December when they return to campus to take an objective structured clinical examination (OSCE). Although students will still have one semester of rotations remaining, administering the evaluation at this time assures that all students will respond. Librarians will then have the opportunity to use evaluation data to adjust and realign services, if necessary.

## PROBLEMS AND IMPLICATIONS

One of the most vexing recurring problems for distance students in years past has been the issue of easy and complete access to online information databases. While dial-in access through a modem pool has long provided a fair equivalent of campus access, distance students were continually frustrated by connectivity issues, difficulty of browser configuration, and general unevenness of database availability. In the past two years, since the implementation of the campus EZ Proxy server, distance students have informally reported virtually seamless access to hundreds of online library resources.

Another problem for many students is the $2.00 fee attached to each Library Express article delivered. While the access the service provided was much appreciated, the growing cost for students with large research needs often poses a financial burden. While there are no immediate remedies, the pharmacy librarian and distance coordinator hope to find acceptable solutions for the clerkship students to have their research needs covered at no cost while working and studying at a distance.

Continued collaboration between librarians and the School of Pharmacy has also resulted in improvements for the Nontraditional Pharm.D. (NTPD) students, who may never set foot on the UW-Madison campus, as well as the clinical instructors around the state. Under a previous system, each NTPD student was required to come to Madison to have a photograph taken and a physical ID card prepared before they were eligible to use library resources. This posed considerable problems for this group of students who worked during the week, were distant from Madison, and unable to come to town when university offices were open. Clinical instructors, until recently, did not have the same level of access to library resources as the Pharm.D. students they supervised. Fortunately, a new system was put in place which provides both groups with UW-Madison campus identification codes without the need to physically come to campus. This provides access equivalent to students coming directly from the UW-Madison campus.

Librarians have found that distance students need reference assistance in many areas, some not related to the specialty area of study. For example, in past years distance students repeatedly requested information on citation styles and formats needed to complete assignment papers. When recurring questions are identified, they are addressed and added to the next version of the field guide to assist the next group of students venturing out on clerkship rotations the following year.

## PROGRAM EVALUATION

In 2004, the Ebling Library staff asked fourth-year clerkship students to evaluate their awareness and use of library resources and services. Working with the School of Pharmacy to develop and administer a formal assessment process is an entirely new endeavor for library staff. It will provide not only important data leading to better understanding and improved services, but also to many collaborative opportunities for librarians and School of Pharmacy faculty and staff to work toward common goals.

The master assessment plan includes three self-assessment instruments–a pre-clerkship assessment, a mid-year or formative assessment, and a summative assessment at the end of the clerkship year before graduation. The pre-clerkship self-assessment completed in May 2000 will provide a baseline of information from which to evaluate future changes. The mid-year self-assessment will allow librarians to evaluate the adequacy of library support, services, and resources. With this input, librarians will also be able to more completely assess the effectiveness of the field guide and the face-to-face orientation provided to new clerkship students in May. Both qualitative and quantitative data will be gathered to improve subsequent library programming.

## FUTURE ENHANCEMENTS

The popularity of the field-guide approach has spread and has recently been adapted for use by the library liaison working with Physical Therapy students leaving for rotations. The pharmacy model is being replicated by other librarians for other departments and professional schools. The Ebling Library staff will continually assess and improve the resources and services available to our remote users using feedback from the clerkship students. By having students provide input at various stages of their distance experiences, librarians hope to learn how the library can best assist in their preparation and provide continued support while they are working and studying at a distance. Librarians will investigate the feasibility of having the hands-on sessions required for all students, perhaps as part of the full day orientation session that the School of Pharmacy provides to students. Finally, as students have gained streamlined access to a wide variety of library educational and informational resources at their clerkship sites, clinical instructors have shown a growing interest in gaining access to the resources. An expanded outreach program at the library will allow librarians to provide training to clinical instructors, perhaps at an annual state continuing education conference for pharmacists.

## REFERENCES

1. Wanserski, G. R. *Library Resources for Clerkship Students.* Available at: http://www.hsl.wisc.edu/pharmacy/clerkship.cfm. Accessed July 2, 2004.

2. ACRL Guidelines for Distance Learning Library Services. Draft revision of 2000. Available at: http://www.ala.org/ala/acrl/acrlstandards/guidelinesdistancelearning.htm. Accessed June 9, 2004.

3. Standard for library and education resources. In: *Standards 2000 Self-Study. Amended May 2000: A Self-Study Guide for Accreditation Standards and Guidelines for the Professional Program in Pharmacy Leading to the Doctor of Pharmacy Degree. Adopted June 14, 1997 and Effective July 1, 2000.* Available at: http://www.acpe-accredit.org/deans/standards.asp#6. Accessed June 3, 2004.

4. Wanserski, G. R. Advanced technology, shared resources: A look at Wisconsin library services for pharmacists and other health care professionals. *J Pharm Soc Wis.* Jan-Feb 2004: 20-22.

5. Pharmacist–Credentialing. State of Wisconsin Department of Regulation and Licensing. Available at: http://drl.wi.gov/prof/phar/cred.htm. Accessed June 30, 2004.

6. Pharmacy Examining Board. Chapter Phar 17: Pharmacy Internship. http://www.legis.state.wi.us/rsb/code/phar/phar.html. Accessed June 30, 2004.

7. Accreditation Council for Pharmacy Education. Scope of Accreditation. Available at: http://www.acpe-accredit.org/deans/policies.asp. Accessed June 30, 2004.

8. Nontraditional Doctor of Pharmacy in University of Wisconsin. In: *1997-98 Student Handbook and Resource Manual.* Madison, WI: University of Wisconsin School of Pharmacy; 1997: 38-39.

9. School of Pharmacy. The University of Wisconsin School of Pharmacy in brief. In: *1997-98 Student Handbook and Resource Manual.* Madison, WI: University of Wisconsin School of Pharmacy; 1997:1.

10. Affiliated Sites. In: *2003-2004 Student Handbook and Resource Manual. School of Pharmacy University of Wisconsin Madison.* Available at: http://www.pharmacy. wisc.edu/Student_Services/pharmd/sectionc_hb.pdf. Accessed June 4, 2004.

11. Wanserski, G. R., Dieterle, U., Kieser, M. Spring 2004 Survey of University of Wisconsin Madison Pharmacy Students Leaving for Clerkship Rotations. Available at: http://www.hsl.wisc.edu/pharmacy/clerkshipsurvey2004. Accessed July 2, 2004.

# The Buck Stops *Where*?
# Establishing a University
# Information and Referral Service

Doris R. Brown

Kara Malenfant

**SUMMARY.** University students–whether adult, distance learner, or traditional age–need access to university services and quick accurate answers to their questions beyond traditional "business" hours. Students' busy schedules and changing life patterns dictate that university services meet their needs. At DePaul University in Chicago, student focus groups repeatedly pointed to the need for one central place to get an answer or solve a problem. *DePaul Central* was created as an information and referral service to satisfy that student need, at the same capitalizing on the value of the librarian skill set. *[Article copies available for a fee from The Haworth Document Delivery Service: 1-800-HAWORTH. E-mail address: <docdelivery@haworthpress.com> Website: <http://www.HaworthPress.com> © 2004 by The Haworth Press, Inc. All rights reserved.]*

**KEYWORDS.** Academic libraries, distance education, adult students, college and university students, library services, information and referral, collaboration, DePaul University

---

Doris R. Brown (dbrown@depaul.edu) is Associate Vice-President for Teaching & Learning Resources, DePaul University, DePaul Center, 1 East Jackson Boulevard, Chicago, IL 60604. Kara Malenfant (kmalenfa@depaul.edu) is Coordinator for *DePaul Central*, DePaul University Libraries, 2350 North Kenmore, Chicago, IL 60614.

[Haworth co-indexing entry note]: "The Buck Stops *Where*? Establishing a University Information and Referral Service." Brown, Doris R., and Kara Malenfant. Co-published simultaneously in *Internet Reference Services Quarterly* (The Haworth Information Press, an imprint of The Haworth Press, Inc.) Vol. 9, No. 1/2, 2004, pp. 189-208; and: *Improving Internet Reference Services to Distance Learners* (ed: William Miller, and Rita M. Pellen) The Haworth Information Press, an imprint of The Haworth Press, Inc., 2004, pp. 189-208. Single or multiple copies of this article are available for a fee from The Haworth Document Delivery Service [1-800-HAWORTH, 9:00 a.m. - 5:00 p.m. (EST). E-mail address: docdelivery@haworthpress.com].

http://www.haworthpress.com/web/IRSQ
© 2004 by The Haworth Press, Inc. All rights reserved.
Digital Object Identifier: 10.1300/J136v09n01_13

## INTRODUCTION

During the past decade, the life of the adult student has been studied and discussed in higher education circles as often as the life of the fruit fly is in high school Biology classes. The competing time demands of work duties or family responsibilities and class schedules or assigned course work is bemoaned constantly, whether by the faculty or the students themselves. Adult students' issues are often the same as those of the distance education student, and in many cases, they are embodied in the same person since many distance education students are adult students.[1]

Today's student may follow any one of the multiple paths described by Alexander McCormick, with "swirling" from one institution to another as well as one discipline to another and other multi-institution attendance patterns.[2] The distance learner–whether "traditional" age or adult–fits within McCormick's attendance patterns and also is included in the population requiring accommodation for their academic support needs. For this study, the authors use the following definitions: (1) the "traditional student" is the 18-23-year-old, recognizing that the definition of "traditional" as the 18-year-old high school graduate starting college in the fall is no longer the only pattern that the new high school graduate follows; (2) the "adult student" is any person age 24 and over; and (3) the "distance education student" takes a class online without the physical presence of the instructor.

DePaul University in Chicago has a long tradition of developing programs and reaching out to adult students and distance learners. As of 2004, DePaul offers full online degrees and certificates in five areas:

- Bachelor of Arts Degree offered by the School for New Learning (SNL);
- Master of Science Degrees offered by the School of Computer Science, Telecommunications and Information Systems (CTI); DePaul CTI developed a software program called "Course Online" in which all parts of the in-person faculty lecture to a live class are captured and then Webcast three hours after the live class is over. The CTI student can therefore choose the method of attending the class which best fits his or her work and personal schedule-all online, some sessions live and some online, or all sessions live.
- Professional Certification Programs offered by the Office of Continuing and Professional Education (OCPE);

- MBA through the College of Commerce; The College of Commerce MBA is a blend of online and in-person, using *Blackboard* as the delivery method, with CTI's "Course Online" providing the video component.
- Illinois Teaching Certificate in Secondary Math or Science in the School of Education (SOE); The School of Education's program also uses *Blackboard* as the software structure for the online certificate.

DePaul is the largest Catholic university in the United States, with over 23,000 students on seven campuses in the Chicago land area and with international programs in Bahrain, Hong Kong, and the Czech Republic. DePaul is dedicated to teaching, research, and public service, but it views itself primarily as a teaching institution rather than a research university, placing its highest priority on programs of instruction and learning. The Vincentian mission of DePaul is based on the life of St. Vincent de Paul, the founder of the Congregation of the Mission, a Roman Catholic male religious community whose members, known as Vincentians, established and continue to sponsor DePaul University. The University mission is embodied in a focus on the dignity of each person, with emphasis on religious personalism through a sensitivity to the needs of each other and of those served, and with the university curriculum and programs designed to be a means to engage cultural, social, religious, and ethical values in service to others.

Given the nature of the University,

> there's no such thing as a typical DePaul student, and with the wide variety of individuals, academic programs, class schedules and campuses comes an even broader range of student needs. Services already exist to meet the vast majority of those needs, but finding the right office or resource sometimes can prove to be a challenge for even the most seasoned senior, let alone part-time, evening or suburban campus students.[3]

DePaul's students—whether adult, distance learner, or traditional—need access to university services and quick accurate answers to their questions beyond traditional working hours. The *DePaul Central* information and referral service, described below, uses the slogan "Get Answers" to brand its function of meeting student information needs on a schedule which fits students' lives.

## UNIVERSITY STRATEGIC PLAN AND LIBRARY SERVICES

Entitled *Vision 2006*, DePaul University's strategic plan sets three main academic goals for the University which guide the development of programs and services for multiple types of students and their varying needs. The *Vision 2006* goals are:

- Goal I: To provide all full-time students with a holistic education that will foster extraordinary learning opportunities through a highly diverse faculty, staff, and student body.
- Goal II: To be a nationally and internationally recognized provider of the highest quality professional education for adult, part-time students.
- Goal III: To research, develop, deliver, and transfer innovative, educationally-related programs and services that will have significant social impact and will give concrete expression to the University's Vincentian mission.

The strategic planning process also focused on changing the university infrastructure and examined Enterprise Resource Planning (ERP) software to provide state of the art technology with concomitant rethinking of internal processes. *PeopleSoft* was selected as the ERP software and replaced DePaul's legacy systems in June 1999. ERP implementation was aimed to improve students' access to their own information, with online availability any time, any place.

All of these university-wide strategic planning ventures meshed perfectly with the operations of the DePaul University Libraries, which have a long history of developing specialized services for distance learning and adult students. DePaul has had campuses in Chicago's suburbs for over 30 years, and international programs and cohorts of students at non-DePaul locations since the 1980s, so the DePaul University Libraries had already developed comprehensive services for distance students. The Libraries' service plan included means to provide essential library services any time and any place, with digital collections, e-reserves, and overnight book shipment all designed to satisfy student needs within a "reasonable" time. According to the Libraries' philosophy of service for distance students, "The basic metric . . . is that services provided to distance learning students must be equivalent to those that are provided to students on campus."[4]

The Libraries offer a variety of services to distance education students including document delivery, research assistance and instruction, library database access, and assistance for instructors teaching off-campus or in online courses. The use of the Libraries by students at a distance is directly related to their awareness of and convenient access to these services. The vision for remote services at the DePaul Libraries is to improve and expand library services for distance learning students to meet their needs in the e-learning environment, to make them aware of the full range of services through aggressive marketing, and to make service delivery seamless regardless of location or time zone.

The Libraries' existing programs for supporting distance students proved themselves effective as DePaul's colleges and schools moved courses online and as faculty implemented the *Blackboard* course management system into their classrooms. The *Blackboard* course management system was introduced to DePaul in 1999, and a collaborative effort between the Libraries and the Instructional Technology Development group promoted linking library-sponsored electronic resources to the *Blackboard* course site to allow students to complete course work without entering the physical library building.

The Libraries' commitment to serving distance education students is evidenced in its most recent strategic plan, focusing on three areas: collection development and management, marketing resources and services, and distance education support services. The vision of the distance education focus area states that DePaul University Libraries are committed to providing library services that are equivalent to those available on the Chicago campuses. Goals for supporting the distance education program address:

- Document Delivery: To provide students at a distance with books, journal articles, and online resources that support the curriculum in a convenient, clearly specified procedure.
- Reference Services: To provide students at a distance with reference services in both asynchronous and synchronous delivery, balancing research guidance with delivery of information as appropriate to the student's needs.
- Instruction Services: To provide students at a distance with instructional support for course-related research needs.
- Connecting Remotely: To advocate for a system by which students at a distance may connect to library resources conveniently and reliably and to support their ability to connect with telephone, e-mail, and chat technical support.

## EARLY HISTORY OF DEPAUL CENTRAL

The Libraries' history of providing services to satisfy the needs of distance students and its flexibility in adapting services and introducing programs to satisfy their needs led to a prominent role for the Libraries when the University organized a special study of the adult student in 2002. This special study formed part of the University's review of its progress toward accomplishing the goals set forth in its *Vision 2006* strategic plan. Goal II (to be a nationally and internationally recognized provider of the highest quality professional education for adult, part-time students) took on special importance after the dot.com bust and the September 11, 2001 fallout, when enrollments in the College of Commerce and CTI began to decline at DePaul, as they did elsewhere in the U.S. Both these schools had very heavy enrollment of adult students in their graduate programs, whether in-person or online.

In the best academic tradition, a committee, the Goal II Student Services Group (SSG), was formed to review all areas of the University that provide support for adult, part-time students outside the curricular programs, which are under the purview of the faculty. SSG reviewed support services for all Goal II students (e.g., Financial Aid, ID Card Services, Libraries) whether students were located at a physical campus or taking courses through a complete or partial distance-learning medium. The SSG included representatives from all pertinent areas of the University and was chaired by Doris Brown, Associate Vice-President for Teaching and Learning Resources, and Jim Doyle, Vice-President for Student Services.

SSG's review of services for Goal II students demonstrated that there was no university standard or uniformity and no overall pattern of availability of services; the individual units determined their hours of services, and the overwhelming pattern was still the 9-5 work day for DePaul employees, rather than accommodation to the Goal II student's need for physical or telephone access outside his/her work schedule. The University overall still operated within a "bricks and mortar" mindset, rather than a combination of "bricks and mortar" and "Web." Some units had made progress to a combined bricks and mortar/Web approach for their services, but the University was still far from a 24x7 approach to services.[5]

SSG reviewed services from four aspects: (1) physical presence, (2) Web presence, (3) phone presence (voice and fax), and (4) delivery presence, recognizing from the outset that not every service would necessarily have all "presences." This analysis of the University's presences also unearthed a recurring student complaint about getting quick and accurate answers to their questions, with voice mail roadblocks and cyberspace e-mails listed as frustrating examples of not finding out what they needed to know. Student focus groups repeatedly pointed to the need for one place to contact to get an answer–and so *DePaul Central* was born.

The idea of *DePaul Central* had been germinating in the Student Services division during earlier University-wide strategic planning discussions. The focus on Goal II students through SSG's review brought the *DePaul Central* idea into wider discussion and gave it a university-wide perspective. Initial thinking had centered on basic premises:

* Students want *personalized* services delivered when they need it.
* Students want quick resolution to issues that affect their education.
* Students expect university business to be conducted beyond traditional office hours.
* Technology is an integral part of today's students' lives and should be aggressively leveraged to improve their educational experience and facilitate their transactions with the university.

Those premises fit together with all the strategic planning, technology upgrades, and review of services which had been occurring as described above. The Student Services divisions had continually branded *DePaul Central* as "one-stop shopping" for students, but they wanted the concept to be much more by:

* Becoming a key destination point for students to quickly and easily access information and conduct transactions essential to their academic success. The mission of *DePaul Central* was designed to minimize the university's "red tape" (perceptual or real) so students could focus on learning. *DePaul Central* would empower students to become their own problem solvers. Through high-tech and high-touch options they would have the necessary tools to successfully navigate around the university whether their needs were informational or transactional.
* Providing "roadside assistance" for those individuals experiencing difficulties with navigation. Students don't necessarily think of the university the way staff and faculty have organized it. Complicated organizational structures can create impediments to learning and cause frustration for students. *DePaul Central* could pro-

vide another opportunity for early intervention so small problems wouldn't grow into larger ones.

- Putting control of information and transactions into students' hands so they could self-navigate early on in their college careers, allowing them to conduct business when convenient for them. Navigation and access tools would reflect student intuition, acknowledging that the majority of DePaul students are not 18- to 23-years old. Access would be convenient and comfortable, which means services must be available on an extended basis.

Routing or shuffling students to various offices (what Student Services called "throwing the problem over the wall") would not be allowed. Students would be directed elsewhere only after being armed by *DePaul Central* with concrete, accurate information that would lead to successful resolution of their issue. In effect, the buck had to stop somewhere, and *DePaul Central* was seen as the service which could stop any buck passing.

## WHY THE LIBRARY?

With the concept of *DePaul Central* fixed in their minds, Student Services looked for a way to implement the new service, and the Goal II SSG committee chairs determined that the Libraries were the natural locus for the service because of their student-centered focus, adaptability to change, and creativity in providing services to students. Librarians were viewed as having unique abilities to interpret questions, such as understanding information-seeking behavior and finding information quickly and efficiently. DePaul's Libraries had already responded to the needs of distance and adult students, with well-established services. Additionally, the Libraries already had extended hours and could better support evening and weekend calls from a diverse student body needing answers beyond "standard" 9-5 office hours.

Many academic libraries have been responsive to changing patterns of teaching and learning by moving services to the Web and e-mail; altering physical space to include computer labs, coffee bars, and other 21st century services; and collaborating with IT staff to reduce duplication and cut costs. The value of the librarian skill set, however, has been overlooked at many universities. At DePaul, librarians play key roles in implementing new services that meet new needs of faculty and students regardless of University fiscal constraints. Librarians to be involved with *DePaul Central* were perceived as having skills in knowledge management, marketing, outreach, reference, and information organization and access which they would use to build bridges with other departments and provide improved service to students.

DePaul Libraries' reference staff had always answered questions about university programs, events, and services, but with *DePaul Central*, staff took on a more active role in providing answers about all things DePaul and ensuring sound referrals, following the model of public libraries providing community information through information and referral services (I&R). With the advent of I&R in public libraries, librarians' roles expanded beyond their historical role and they demonstrated new service attributes, becoming:

- Information providers regardless of format (sometimes it's a person, not a book or database)
- Information brokers/intermediaries (switching center for information)
- Negotiators (clarifying specific information need)
- Facilitators/analysts (provide access to broad range of information)
- Advocates (assisting users to obtain information to improve quality of lives)[6]

*DePaul Central* gave DePaul's librarians the opportunity to move beyond the usual academic library model and assume the public or special library model for I&R.

## PLANNING DEPAUL CENTRAL

To provide the right answers and the best referrals, *DePaul Central* staff had to understand all the facets of DePaul. An Advisory Board, consisting of key staff from a variety of areas providing services to students, was formed to provide direction and advice to get *DePaul Central* off the ground. Many board members were part of the SSG that had fleshed out the *DePaul Central* concept, and others were brought in to represent their specific areas. The Board members help create intra-university links, provide overviews of their functional areas, and market the new service. The Advisory Board members have been fundamental to the success of *DePaul Central* by promoting interdepartmental cooperation and encouraging a shift in the service mindset of their departments to focus on *student* need rather than *staff* need.

During the early planning stages, *DePaul Central* staff looked at similar services offered in the corporate and academic worlds.[7] Staff also examined call center operations,[8] attended the Help Desk Institute Annual Conference and Expo in Las Vegas in March 2003, and worked closely with DePaul's Technology Assistance Center (Help Desk) to explore use of ticketing software to log calls and track resolution. DePaul is upgrading to *PeopleSoft* version 8.0 during FY05 and will probably implement the *PeopleSoft* Help Desk software with ticketing and knowledge base components. In light of this probable change, *DePaul Central* staff held off adopting the *HEAT* software currently used by DePaul's Technology Assistance Center for ticketing.[9] *DePaul Central* staff also shadowed the University telephone operators to identify telephone information patterns and copied their cheat sheets to use for quick reference in answering routine questions.

Because there were only two new staff positions assigned to the new service, it was critical to the success of *DePaul Central* to build ownership with the library staff who were to be scheduled for the *DePaul Central* service. Staff needed to believe in the value of the new service and not view it as just one more task on their already full plates. Months prior to launch, *DePaul Central* staff held a discussion forum with the Libraries' reference staff allowing them the opportunity to voice concerns about *DePaul Central* and its impact on existing library services. *DePaul Central* staff held training in mid-August just prior to the September launch, trained new student workers in the fall, and developed one-on-one training for new staff members. In spring they formed a Libraries' *DePaul Central* Working Group, composed of library staff who provide *DePaul Central* service along with the manager of the University's "DePaul Information Directory," to communicate regularly with ideas, comments, and suggestions for the new service. *DePaul Central* has made immediate changes based on the Working Group's feedback to increase the ease of providing the service from the Libraries' staff perspective.

To support the variety of staff members providing the service, *DePaul Central* staff created an online procedure manual listing what to do when, what to say when, the pattern of response times for University offices, frequently requested phone numbers, a DePaul thesaurus (for translating "DePaul speak" and determining which office handles a particular program or function), and a "Critical Contacts" list (names of individuals in key offices who are known to take the tough calls and sort out problems). The online manual links to critical but hard to find information on the DePaul Web site (like graduation information for each college and school), FAQs from the various student services departments, and hot questions as they come up.

## IMPLEMENTATION

DePaul Central is staffed by two full-time librarians (Kara Malenfant, Coordinator of *DePaul Central*, and Janice Dillard, University Information Librarian) and other Libraries' staff scheduled from any DePaul campus during assigned shifts. Service is delivered using:

- A toll-free number (1-800-4-DEPAUL) shared with Enrollment Management; admissions-related inquiries are routed directly to Enrollment Management by University operators during office hours and all other calls go to *DePaul Central*. During evening and weekend hours, the 800 number is programmed to route calls directly to *DePaul Central*. An additional line is designated as *DePaul Central* and is forwarded to the particular campus where the scheduled staff member fields callers' questions and requests.
- A Web site (http://depaulcentral.depaul.edu) from which students and others can submit questions via e-mail to the *DePaul Central* e-mail account monitored by the scheduled staff member during their shift.
- The *DePaul Information Directory* (*http://directory.depaul.edu*), an online guide, maintained by Administrative Services, which serves as a core resource used by *DePaul Central* to provide information and give referrals to University offices and colleges. *DePaul Central* staff work closely with Administrative Services to expand and enhance the *Directory* so that it serves as a current, central repository for University-wide information.

Statistics from the Libraries' Reference staff, the University Help Desk, and University telephone operators helped determine potential call volume peaks and plan staffing patterns for the initial year of service. Current hours are:

| | |
|---|---|
| Monday-Thursday | 8:00 a.m. to 10:00 p.m. |
| Friday | 8:00 a.m. to 5:00 p.m. |
| Saturday | 11:00 a.m. to 5:00 p.m. |
| Sunday | 12:00 p.m. to 10:00 p.m. |

After in-person service hours, the 1-800 number goes to voice mail; both voice mail and e-mail are checked and answered by the first shift the following day. Both voice mail and e-mail are monitored to help plan future hours and to decide whether to expand to 24x7 coverage.

DePaul Central staff have found that the keys to a successful environment are identical to those for public librarians first implementing I&R service in the 1970s:

- Commitment from the top
- Vigorous and ongoing publicity
- Integration of the service with other standard services
- Positive relations with other departments
- Awareness of the challenges when introducing change[10]

## *PUBLICITY AND MARKETING*

With input from Advisory Board members, *DePaul Central* staff identified marketing opportunities and are using the following methods:

- Ads in the *DePaulia* student newspaper and the print-version of the *DePaul Information Directory*
- Feature article in the faculty/staff newsletter
- Presentations at departmental meetings and the Advising Network brownbag lunch
- Information tables at the Student Center, the Resident Advisor fair, and the Student Involvement fair with a banner, postcards, and a laptop for answering on-the-spot questions
- Interview on DePaul student radio WRDP "Spotlight DePaul" program
- Listing in *Student Guide* and *Student Handbook*
- Message on University online bulletin board "Townsquare"
- Postcards in new student orientation packets, literature stands, various offices
- Posters in Residence Halls, Student Centers, suburban campuses, and departmental offices
- Slides on "Windows to DePaul" Loop street level promotional space, residence halls TV, and the Student Center Information Channel
- Table tents in dining rooms and study areas in Student Unions, Libraries, and classroom common areas

## *METHOD FOR CALL TRACKING*

As mentioned above, because DePaul may implement the *PeopleSoft* Help Desk software for ticketing, *DePaul Central* has held off on adopting the *HEAT* software used by the University's Technology Assistance Center. Instead, DePaul Central adopted *QuickData*, a locally developed data collection tool that provides the database back-end as an interim solution for recording customer interactions. *DePaul Central* staff created an online form to collect data about patron transactions (see Appendix). Once collected, data are downloaded into a spreadsheet or database application for further analysis. QuickData also provides a reporting feature which automatically updates reports as data are submitted, so staff can view activity on an internal staff site.

DePaul Central responded to a total of 3,134 inquiries from its inception in September 2003 through Spring Quarter 2004, all questions which otherwise might not have been answered or might have been "thrown over the wall." A greater impact of the introduction of *DePaul Central* though may have been the Libraries' insistent focus on the needs of adult and distance education students, a focus which then led other University offices to change their schedules and their staffing patterns.

Winter quarter showed a peak in activity, with a drop in inquiries Spring quarter, which is consistent with patterns at other service points within the Libraries. Of the 3,134 inquiries, 83 percent were telephone inquiries, with almost all of the remainder submitted using e-mail. Voice-mail messages were less than one percent of the total. With 53 percent of the inquiries submitted after 5:00 p.m. or on weekends, the expectation was met that *DePaul Central* would address a need for students to have their questions addressed outside of "regular" office hours. Monday and Tuesday were the busiest days, accounting respectively for 21 and 19 percent (see Figure 1).

The hour between 5:00 p.m.-6:00 p.m. was the busiest of the day, accounting for 19 percent of the questions received on weekdays and 14 percent of total questions. Evening hours after 6:00 p.m. showed a gradual decline in activity, with only three percent of inquiries being submitted via e-mail or voice mail during the 10:00 p.m.-8:00 a.m. slot when *DePaul Central* is not staffed (see Figure 2 for Monday-Friday hourly breakdown). Those hours are being closely monitored to determine whether in-person hours should be expanded further or whether the voice and e-mail coverage is sufficient.

FIGURE 1. Questions Submitted by Day of Week

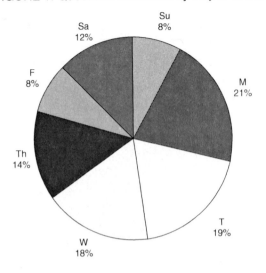

FIGURE 2. Monday-Friday Questions by Hour

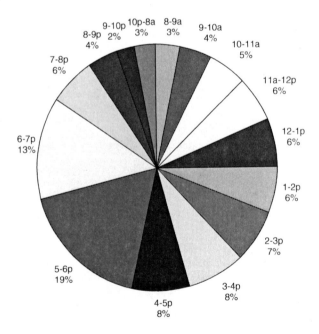

In another move to expand service for students, *DePaul Central* arranged that the Libraries and other student service offices provide extended hours starting at 8:00 a.m. on the first two Saturdays of Winter and Spring Quarters, rather than the normal 10:00 a.m. start time. On the first of these Saturdays (January 3, 2004) *DePaul Central* received 30 inquiries, making it the service's busiest Saturday to date and providing evidence of the urgent need for a University I&R service during the first days of the quarter.

## NATURE OF INQUIRIES

As had been expected when *DePaul Central* agreed to share the toll-free telephone number (1-800-4-DEPAUL) that had historically been publicized by the Office of Admission, 32 percent of the inquiries received were admissions-related. The subjects of other questions were widely distributed, with these areas most heavily represented: Academic Resource Center [i.e., registrar, student records, general advising]–9 percent; Internal Information (addresses, directions)–7 percent; General University Information (events, dates)–5 percent; Student Financial Accounts–4 percent; College of Liberal Arts & Sciences–4 percent; and Student Housing–4 percent. Apart from these four areas, no other department or college totaled more than 3 percent of all inquiries.

Even though the impetus for founding *DePaul Central* had been to satisfy the special needs of the adult or distance student, no one particular population dominated usage of the service. Indeed staff make no distinction in services offered among the type or level of student, nor do staff ask for the student's status. From what callers volunteer it's clear that the majority of callers are the students themselves, with some parents and spouses also calling on behalf of their relative.

## RESOLUTION OF INQUIRIES

Seventy-one percent of the inquiries received by *DePaul Central* were referred to specific DePaul offices for resolution. Sometimes the inquiring party knew the specific office which could resolve the issue, and *DePaul Central* either made a telephone transfer or gave the appropriate information from the office's Web site. Otherwise *DePaul Central* staff determined which office should handle the problem/issue and then put the student in direct contact with that office, thereby eliminating the "bouncing" or "buck passing" that students had complained of during the Goal II focus groups. Some examples of referrals include:

> Q1: Mother of prospective student, calling for tour times, directions to campus from Milwaukee, and other details about DePaul.

> A1: Gave her Admissions number to make appointment for the tour. Answered other questions. Very excited to reach a real person on Saturday.

> Q2: I'm a student having problems with the washing machines in my dorm. The machine deducted money but didn't start washing.

> A2: Problems with laundry machines can be reported at: www.aalaundries.com. If student has already paid, can get a refund during business hours from Housing Services.

> Q3: Do you rent conference rooms to the public? I'd like to rent a board room-type room for an all-day board meeting.

> A3: Told her yes and gave URL which describes facilities. Also gave contact names, phone numbers, and e-mails for Conference Services staff.

*DePaul Central* staff alert University offices to errors or confusion with their Web sites, and the *DePaul Information Directory* continues to be expanded and edited based on information issues raised through *DePaul Central*. From the 29 percent of questions not referred to another University office, in 2 percent of the cases DePaul Central staff intervened and worked with other University offices to create solutions for the student's unique problems. The remaining 27 percent of the inquiries were basic questions answered immediately by *DePaul Central* staff. Examples of these basic questions are:

- How can I schedule a campus tour?
- How do I make a tuition payment by phone?
- When does registration for December session start?
- I need to request transcripts, how do I do this?
- How can my son add money to his dining plan?
- Is there a machine to watch a videotape made in England?
- Which residence halls are co-ed?

- How do I access my son's grades?
- When is Mass at St. Vincent's Parish?

## *FUTURE PLANS*

From its inception, Customer Relationship Management (CRM) software has been a desired element of the *DePaul Central* model. CRM software ensures that individual departments can receive and respond quickly to requests from students. With the flexible and detailed reporting features of such software, managers will be much better prepared to evaluate service soft spots, determine accountability, consider possible program or service enhancements, and gauge overall success relative to established benchmarking standards. Equally important, CRM will allow students to follow up on the status of their original service requests.

*DePaul Central* is uniquely positioned to be a pilot for implementation of CRM as both a business strategy and set of software tools. By implementing *PeopleSoft* CRM, *DePaul Central* could be a role model and facilitate peer pressure for change in other areas of the University. As new CRM software is implemented, *DePaul Central* will facilitate a seamless student experience.

> For example, a student may make a service request via the Internet in the morning, fax back-up documentation an hour later, e-mail a correction after lunch, and call to check on the request's status later in the afternoon. If the student chooses to stop by the administrative office in person to check on the request's status, the customer service officer will have electronic access not only to those contacts the student had made earlier in the day but also to the information the student had requested.[11]

*DePaul Central* was conceptualized as a catalyst for change in the way disparate parts of the University currently operate, creating bridges between departments and improving knowledge sharing. At its best, *DePaul Central* will affect how many departments do business, and this requires cultural, not just technological, changes. Necessary changes in business practices will undoubtedly take months, perhaps years, before the benefits are realized. Change will come as students are increasingly viewed as customers who have heightened expectations that the university environment mirror the services of online business.

## CONCLUSION

Librarians in academic settings have always managed explicit knowledge, which can be captured and shared within their libraries by organizing finding aids, bibliographies, and research guides. Librarians also maintain tacit knowledge of internal processes in rolodexes, manuals, and tip sheets. Some libraries are moving explicit and tacit knowledge to knowledge bases to improve library operations.[12] Although academic libraries often do not lead their universities and colleges in managing the institutions' knowledge, librarians should seek to play a key role.[13]

DePaul's recognition of the specific skill set of librarians and use of those skills to establish and implement *DePaul Central* has proven to be a success. The I&R model has worked also since it gives one place where students can get answers to their questions or at least can get the proper referral to someone who can solve their problem. The idea of "one stop" where a student could get any question answered or problem fixed immediately is difficult if not impossible in a complex university, just as it is in a major bank or a large business, since no one university office can master all the intricacies of financial aid and course advising and visa requirements, to name a few of the issues faced by today's student. One service, though, can answer the common questions and can know who does what to put the student in direct contact with the correct office–making sure that a live person takes care of the issue, rather than leaving a voice mail message or sending an e-mail to cyberland. Student comments laud the efforts of the new service, since *DePaul Central* makes sure the buck stops where it is supposed to.

## NOTES

1. The U.S. Department of Education has released a study showing that older women with families and jobs were more drawn to undergraduate distance-education programs during the 1999-2000 academic year than were members of other groups. The report offers the most recent large-scale research into who enrolls in distance-education programs. Anna Sikora, "A Profile of Participation in Distance Education: 1999-2000" Available <http://nces.ed.gov/pubsearch/pubsinfo.asp?pubid=2003154> Accessed April 28 2004.

2. Victor M.H. Borden, "Accommodating Student Swirl," *Change* 36, no. 2 (March/April 2004): 10-17.

3. "New service provides answers for students," *DePaul University Newsline* March 15, 2004.

4. Frank Cervone and Doris Brown, "Transforming library services to support distance learning," *C&RL News* 62, no. 2 (2001): 148.

5. For more information on creating student services online see Pat Shea and Sue Armitage, "WCET LAPP Project Beyond the Administrative Core: Guidelines for Creating Student Services Online." Western Cooperative for Educational Telecommunications by the Western Interstate Commission for Higher Education. Available <http://www.wcet.info/projects/laap/guidelines/>. Accessed 3/17/2004. This three-year collaborative project was designed to address time- and location-independent access to student support services for distance education students.

6. Thomas Childers, "Trends in public library I&R services," *Library Journal*, 104 (October 1, 1979): 2037-2038, rptd. in Teresa Demo, "Information and Referral in the Academic Library: Lessons in Attitudes and Service from the Public Library," *The Reference Librarian* 21 (1988): 101.

7. University of North Carolina Greensboro, "Information Station" <http://infostation. uncg.edu>. University of Minnesota, "One Stop" <http://onestop.umn.edu>. Iowa State, "Student Answer Center" <http://www.answer.iastate.edu>.

8. Steve Coffman, "Reference as Others Do It," *American Libraries* 30, no. 5 (May 1999): 54.

9. For a discussion of CRM in higher education see Gary B. Grant and Greg Anderson. "Customer Relationship Management: A Vision for Higher Education" in *Web Portals & Higher Education: Technologies To Make IT Personal*. Jossey-Bass Higher and Adult Education Series (San Francisco: Jossey-Bass, 2002). See also *Knowledge Management: Building a Competitive Advantage in Higher Education*. New Directions for Institutional Research 113 (San Francisco: Jossey-Bass, 2002).

10. Clara S. Jones, *Public Library Information and Referral Services*. Syracuse: Gaylord, 1978: 157. rptd. in Teresa Demo, "Information and Referral in the Academic Library: Lessons in Attitudes and Service from the Public Library," *The Reference Librarian* 21 (1988): 105.

11. Michael Fayerman, "Customer Relationship Management," in *Knowledge Management: Building a Competitive Advantage in Higher Education*. New Directions for Institutional Research 113. (San Francisco: Jossey-Bass, 2002): 59-60.

12. Ron Jantx, "Knowledge management in academic libraries: Special tools and processes to support information professionals," *Reference Services Review*, 29 no. 1 (2001): 33-39.

13. Charles Thomas Townley. "Knowledge management and academic libraries," *College & Research Libraries*, 62 no. 1 (January 2001): 44-55.

## APPENDIX. Online Form to Collect Data About Patron Transactions

| | |
|---|---|
| **Staff member answering** | Select Library Staff ▾ |
| **Time/Date** (OPTIONAL - if not time entered) | January ▾  1 ▾  2004 ▾ OPTIONAL<br>9 ▾ 00 ▾ am ▾ OPTIONAL |
| **Client status** | ○ Prospective<br>○ Student<br>○ Staff<br>○ Faculty<br>○ Alumnus<br>○ Other (vendor, employer)<br>○ Unknown |
| **Interaction via** | ○ E-mail<br>○ Telephone<br>○ In Person |
| **Question** | |
| **Subject** | Select Subject ▾<br>if "Other" state: |
| **Resolution** | ○ Answered fully<br>○ Referred (gave some info, suggested other office)<br>○ Transferred (simply switchboard, no info given)<br>○ Intervened (worked with other office to resolve) |
| **Other info** | |

Submit    Clear Form

View Results Here

Back to DPCL Internal Staff Home Page

# Index

# BOOK ORDER FORM!

Order a copy of this book with this form or online at:
http://www.haworthpress.com/store/product.asp?sku=5614

## Improving Internet Reference Services to Distance Learners

_____ in softbound at $29.95 ISBN: 0-7890-2718-6.
_____ in hardbound at $49.95 ISBN: 0-7890-2717-8.

| | |
|---|---|
| **COST OF BOOKS** _____ | ❑BILL ME LATER: |
| | Bill-me option is good on US/Canada/ |
| **POSTAGE & HANDLING** _____ | Mexico orders only; not good to jobbers, |
| US: $4.00 for first book & $1.50 | wholesalers, or subscription agencies. |
| for each additional book | ❑ **Signature** _____ |
| Outside US: $5.00 for first book | |
| & $2.00 for each additional book. | ❑ **Payment Enclosed: $** _____ |
| **SUBTOTAL** _____ | ❑ **PLEASE CHARGE TO MY CREDIT CARD:** |
| In Canada: add 7% GST. _____ | ❑ Visa ❑ MasterCard ❑ AmEx ❑ Discover |
| **STATE TAX** _____ | ❑ Diner's Club ❑ Eurocard ❑ JCB |
| CA, IL, IN, MN, NJ, NY, OH, PA & SD residents | **Account #** _____ |
| please add appropriate local sales tax. | |
| **FINAL TOTAL** _____ | **Exp Date** _____ |
| If paying in Canadian funds, convert | |
| using the current exchange rate, | **Signature** _____ |
| UNESCO coupons welcome. | _(Prices in US dollars and subject to change without notice.)_ |

| PLEASE PRINT ALL INFORMATION OR ATTACH YOUR BUSINESS CARD |
|---|
| Name |
| Address |
| City          State/Province          Zip/Postal Code |
| Country |
| Tel          Fax |
| E-Mail |

May we use your e-mail address for confirmations and other types of information? ❑Yes ❑No We appreciate receiving your e-mail address. Haworth would like to e-mail special discount offers to you, as a preferred customer.
**We will never share, rent, or exchange your e-mail address. We regard such actions as an invasion of your privacy.**

Order from your **local bookstore** or directly from
**The Haworth Press, Inc.** 10 Alice Street, Binghamton, New York 13904-1580 • USA
Call our toll-free number (1-800-429-6784) / Outside US/Canada: (607) 722-5857
Fax: 1-800-895-0582 / Outside US/Canada: (607) 771-0012
E-mail your order to us: orders@haworthpress.com

**For orders outside US and Canada,** you may wish to order
through your local
sales representative, distributor, or bookseller.
For information, see http://haworthpress.com/distributors

_(Discounts are available for individual orders in US and Canada only, not booksellers/distributors.)_
**Please photocopy this form for your personal use.**
www.HaworthPress.com                                    BOF05